The Indomitable Investor

For Suzy,

Thank you for your readership.

My best,

Steve

21 May 2012.

The Indomitable Investor

Why a Few Succeed in the Stock Market When Everyone Else Fails

Steven M. Sears

WILEY

John Wiley & Sons, Inc.

Published by John Wiley & Sons, Inc., Hoboken, New Jersey.
Published simultaneously in Canada.

For general information on our other products and services or for technical support, please contact our Customer Care Department within the United States at (800) 762-2974, outside the United States at (317) 572-3993 or fax (317) 572-4002.

Wiley also publishes its books in a variety of electronic formats. Some content that appears in print may not be available in electronic books. For more information about Wiley products, visit our web site at www.wiley.com.

Library of Congress Cataloging-in-Publication Data:

Sears, Steven M.
    The Indomitable investor : why a few succeed in the stock market when everyone else fails/Steven M. Sears.
        p. cm.
    Includes bibliographical references and index.
    ISBN 978-1-118-11034-8 (cloth); ISBN 978-1-118-22433-5 (ebk);
    ISBN 978-1-118-23739-7 (ebk); ISBN 978-1-118-26239-9 (ebk)
        1. Stocks. 2. Risk management. 3. Speculation. 4. Portfolio management. I. Title.
    HG4661.S36 2012
    332.63'22—dc23

2012004096

10 9 8 7 6 5 4 3 2 1

For Kitya,
Onward, to Ithaca

Contents

I must create a system, or be enslaved by another man's.

—*William Blake*

The Indomitable Investor

Chapter 1

Risk

I t is a dirty fact, but everyone on Wall Street knows the stock market could not function without Dumb Money. Dumb Money— and that is how Wall Street classifies outsiders—always does what most benefits Wall Street. Dumb Money buys stocks when it should sell, and panics and sells when buying makes more sense. This is a primary reason why Wall Street makes so much money when most everyone else fails, or inches forward, in the stock market. If not for the positive effect of inflation, and corporate stock dividends, which represent more than 45 percent of historical stock gains, most investors would have sharply smaller investment portfolios.

Now, as Baby Boomers confront retirement, and younger generations worry they will not live as well as their parents, millions of people are beginning to understand that they must get much smarter, much faster, about the stock market if they ever want to retire, pay for their children's college educations, or lead lives that eventually bear some semblance of financial ease.

1

The old ideas of coasting toward retirement by regularly investing in stocks and effortlessly doubling stock portfolio values every seven or so years as the stock market advanced are no longer valid. The Credit Crisis of 2007, and Europe's sovereign debt crisis that sparked in 2009, have unleashed new financial realities that are likely to prove true Wall Street's adage that the stock market hurts the most people, most of the time.

Yet, the future need not be as difficult as the recent past.

A well trod path exists that anyone can follow to better deal with Wall Street and the stock market. This path has quietly existed for centuries. The path was carved out, and continually refined, by a small group of people who typically avoid the financial calamities that ensnare everyone else. This group of investors has historically dominated the financial market, and quietly snickered at the widespread idea, birthed in the late nineteenth century by John Stuart Mill, that people can make rational financial decisions.

Mill called his idea *Homo economicus*. He declared his Economic Man capable of making decisions to increase his wealth. Mill's man has persisted ever since like some financial Frankenstein even though the financial markets are so complex—especially in the past 40 years—that it is increasingly apparent that Mill's man, today known simply as John and Jane Investor, has great difficulty profitably navigating the stock market.

In sharp contrast to Mill's incarnation is a small group of people who make more money than they lose. In keeping with Mill's use of Latin, think of people in that group as *Homo Indomitabilis*.

The Indomitable Man is different than everyone else in the market. He leads a life of counterintuitive thought and action that is perhaps best summed up by a simple idea: Bad investors think of ways to make money. Good investors think of ways to not lose money. Those 17 words are the most important words any investor can know. Learn the meaning of those words, and you have a chance of real success in the stock market.

The difference between the idea of the good investor and bad investor is profound. One idea ensures you eventually give back profits, and likely some, or all, of your initial investment, to Wall Street.

The other one lets you keep much of what you make. Though the good investor rule seems like common sense, it is not well known off Wall Street. This is one reason why so many people fail in the market, or are swept along with the crowd, because they lack a simple, proper, disciplined framework to make investing decisions. Most people are interested in getting rich, and getting rich fast. They try that approach again and again and again, often taking on more risk to make profits and recoup losses. Often, this ends poorly. Still, they continue to climb back up the stock market's risk ladder, chasing the higher returns of riskier investments without truly understanding the risks they are taking, or even why they failed.

The issue is not necessarily that people are too greedy for their own good, or not smart enough to understand how to navigate the stock market. The issue is that the United States very quickly morphed from a nation of savers to investors. People who once saved money in passbook savings accounts have since the mid-1970s been increasingly thrust into the stock market—even though they were, and often remain, effectively financially illiterate. These new investors use ideas that work on Main Street—but not Wall Street. The disconnect is now lethal. Rather than simply hoping the economy improves, or that another bull market erases people's financial problems, it is better to focus on the facts and ideas on Wall Street that are made truer by time, and that have long kept the best investors safe when others have stumbled.

If you think people learn anything from losing money, you are wrong. The people who lose the most money, at least in the stock market, are often the most anxious to recoup their losses. The reasoning is fascinating, and it is a key to understanding why investors are stuck in a boom-and-bust cycle. "If someone had a lot of money in the market, and then loses it, they respond by jumping back into the market because the risk of not making money is greater than the risk of losing what they have left," says Mark Taborksy, a former portfolio strategy chief at PIMCO, one of the world's largest money-management firms, who now works at Blackrock, another major firm.[1]

Gib McEachran, a financial planner in Greensboro, North Carolina, regularly deals with investors who have fallen off the risk ladder, and are eager to get back on. In late 2009, a retired couple with a $1.6 million investment portfolio came to his office for help. At the height of the Internet bubble, the couple's account was worth $2.3 million. Rather than focusing on how the money could be managed to provide them with retirement income, the man, a former engineer, wanted to know how McEachran would recoup the lost $600,000. His wife eventually told him to be quiet and listen. (Women, studies show, are more risk averse than men.)[2]

Even though there is so much anger toward Wall Street in the wake of what is now called the Global Financial Crisis that started in 2007, and that is now enveloping Europe, there is no escaping the market—only learning how to deal with it. But before learning how to deal with the market, it is important to understand how Wall Street came to Main Street.

A Nation of Stock Market Junkies

America's relationship with the stock market is actually a relatively recent phenomenon that took off in the 1990s when technology accelerated, automated, and coalesced major policy developments that had occurred over the preceding 15 years to let Wall Street invade Main Street. In isolation, none of the events seem epically important, but the sum is greater than the parts, and the succession of events, and scope of innovation, are stunning.

In 1974, the U.S. tax code was changed to create Individual Retirement Accounts (IRAs). The launch of IRAs let people invest in stocks and defer paying taxes until the money was withdrawn at retirement. This provided many people with their first taste of investing and sent millions of investors climbing up the risk ladder. The launch of the IRA also marked the end of a bear market. The next year, in 1975, the Securities and Exchange Commission (SEC) deregulated brokerage firm commissions, ending a 183-year-old practice that had protected the profits of stock exchange members and kept investing beyond the reach of many because stock trading commissions were exorbitant. Soon, discount brokerage firms, including Charles Schwab, brought

Wall Street to Main Street. To attract customers, Schwab and others dramatically lowered stock-trading commissions. Suddenly, stock trading was affordable to the middle class.

"With the sudden arrival of negotiated stock trades that were less than half the cost they had been, a major barrier to investing went away for the average American," Charles Schwab, the brokerage firm's founder, said.[3]

According to Schwab, in 1975 about $1.75 trillion of investable assets were held by individuals, and less than 45 percent was invested in securities, like stocks. Trading commissions were fixed-price and done through highly paid brokerage firms. By 2005 individuals held more than $17 trillion of investable assets, and 73 percent was invested in securities. In just 30 years, more than half of the U.S. adult population owned stocks in one form or another.

In 1975, John Bogle launched the Vanguard Group. His mutual-fund company is to Wall Street what Walmart is to retailing: low-cost. Around 1980, Ted Benna, a tax consultant, effectively created 401(k) retirement accounts that would prove to play a major role in how people saved for retirement.

Inevitably, investors who got a taste of the market in IRAs and 401(k) accounts, found they loved stocks. A massive bull market began in 1982, two years into President Reagan's first term. Conditions were ideal. It was cheap to buy stocks. It was easy to do. It was tax effective. Standing on the sidelines was inadvisable, and maybe even dumb, as the Dow Jones Industrial Average's rally would soon demonstrate. On August 12, 1982, the Dow Jones Industrial Average was at 777. The rise of the stock market would soon be chronicled in Technicolor. In 1989, CNBC was launched, which would ultimately help change the public's perception of the stock market. Prior to CNBC's launch, financial news was mostly limited to the business press, including the *Wall Street Journal* and *Barron's*. If the stock market was mentioned on TV, it was only to briefly note that the Dow Jones Industrial Average had risen or fallen during the day. Now, stock market news often dominates evening newscasts, and the front pages of many newspapers and magazines.

On Christmas Day, 1990, the Internet was effectively launched, unleashing forces that quickly revolutionized stock investing. The stock market was suddenly accessible to anyone, anytime. Buying stocks was destined to be as easy as clicking a computer mouse. In 1993, the first exchange-traded fund, the SPDR S&P 500 Trust (SPY), was created. Exchange-traded funds (ETFs) are stocks in drag. They trade like stocks, but own a portfolio of stocks like mutual funds. In 1995, as the stock market chugged higher, Dick Grasso, then chairman of the New York Stock Exchange (NYSE), let the first reporter in the Exchange's long history report live from the trading floor. Soon, reporters from all over the world joined CNBC's Maria Bartiromo at the Big Board. In 1999, the United States Congress eliminated the historic separation of investment and commercial banks, enabling the creation of mega-banks, like Citigroup and Bank of America. The late 1990s were heady times on Wall Street.

In April, 1999, the predecessor of TD Ameritrade, an online discount brokerage firm, introduced its now classic Stuart advertising campaign, and other firms followed with similar campaigns that suggested that making money was easy—and fun. Few ads captured the zeitgeist like Stuart.

Stuart was a young dude with spiky, punk rock hair and some vague office job. One day, he was copying his face on the office mimeograph machine when he was interrupted by his boss and summoned to his office. Rather than getting disciplined, the boss asked Stuart to teach him how to buy stocks on the Internet.

"Let's go to Ameritrade.com," Stuart tells his boss. "It's easier than falling in love. What do you feel like buying today, Mr. P.?"

He buys 100 shares of Kmart.

"What does that cost me?"

"$8, my man."

"My broker charges me $200 for this trade."

"Ride the wave of the future, my man."

And what a wave it was. By January 14, 2000, the Dow Jones Industrial Average peaked at 11,722.98, a gain of 1,408.7 percent in 18 years. The nation was hooked on stocks. The advance was historic. Many people effortlessly made money. And then the Internet bubble burst in 2000. But before anyone could ponder what had transpired, the Dow Jones Industrial Average delivered what was then its biggest one-day gain in history, rising 499.19 points on March 16, 2000. Naturally, many people concluded it made sense to stay in the market because the stock market had snapped back.

Amidst those wild gyrations, corporations were changing employee retirement programs. The now ubiquitous 401(k) accounts increasingly replaced pensions plans that had once guaranteed reliable retirement income after long careers. Consider IBM, whose actions are watched all over the world as a sign of how to best run a business. IBM radically changed employee retirement plans in 2006. The pension fund, which four years earlier had faced a $3 billion shortfall, was eliminated before IBM's corporate debt rating could be lowered by credit-rating agencies which would have increased the interest rates IBM had paid to borrow money. Like so many other companies, IBM shifted almost all of the retirement-plan responsibility to employees. Rather than retiring with a pension—a common benefit still enjoyed by many senior executives throughout corporate Amerca—IBM employees now invest in stock and bond mutual funds offered through the company's self-funded 401(k) retirement plan.

Kraft Foods, another major company, spent $20 billion in 2010 to buy Cadbury and create a global food beverage and candy company. But Cadbury's employees were told salaries would be frozen for three years if they did not give up their pension funds.

These changes highlight the often harsh realities of the global market, and the stock market's rising importance.

Calm Words for Wild Times

All good journeys need a tour book to help travelers make sense of the trip. The stock market's tour book was written at America's top universities. Though the ideas are rooted in complicated mathematical formulas, the conclusions are easy to understand, even during a financial crisis. The key principles are: Don't worry about stock market fluctuations. Don't try to predict the stock market. The market is volatile, but it rewards the patient and the faithful.

In 1965, long before the cult of equities swept the United States, Eugene Fama was completing his doctoral dissertation at the University of Chicago. Though he remains largely unknown off Wall Street, Fama's insights into the stock market helped give rise to the idea of buy-and-hold investing. Fama popularized the idea that the financial markets are efficient, and that it is difficult, if not impossible, for investors to beat the market. The Efficient Market Hypothesis (EMH) was the subject of his doctoral dissertation at the University of Chicago, where he still teaches. The central idea is that stock prices reflect all known information about stocks. His market was filled with "rational, profit maximizers," which perhaps was true before technology and tax code changes opened the market to Main Street. Because the stock market is a discounting mechanism, always reflecting future outcomes, Fama believed that there was no way, aside from luck, to outperform the stock market. He was nominated for the Nobel Prize in Economics in 2003. He was not chosen, but many consider him the father of modern finance.

His ideas ultimately found expression as buy-and-hold investing, which has been lustily embraced by the mutual fund industry and the parts of Wall Street that interact with Main Street. What business wouldn't want customers to always look past hardships, focus on the future, and most importantly never stop buying merchandise? Besides, many of the richest, most successful investors, were buy-and-hold investors. Warren Buffett, one of the world's richest men, was a long-term, buy-and-hold investor. Plainspoken, easy-to-like people like Buffett humanized investing by doing and saying things everyone could relate to. In 1989, another market spokesman, Peter Lynch, then manager of Fidelity Magellan, wrote *One Up on Wall Street*. In that book he introduced the idea of buying stock in things you know. His book was more nuanced than that, but the simple idea is what resonated. Clearly, Lynch's simple idea worked. He did great managing Fidelity Magellan's mutual fund, and everyone knew it. Anyone who invested $10,000 when Lynch took over Magellan, as the back of his book said, would have $180,000 10 years later—a 1,700 percent increase. Warren Buffett's results were better. A $10,000 investment in Berkshire Hathaway in 1964 was worth $80 million at the end of

2009. Of course, Lynch and Buffett are enormously skilled, and most people could not emulate what they do anymore than they could paint like Picasso or design computers like Apple's Steve Jobs. Therein lies the central problem facing most investors: Most people never think about investing in a meaningful way. Wall Street often seems intent against that.

Says Niall Fergusson, the financial historian: "Whenever I go to the Bloomberg studio in New York I seem to meet the same generic guy who has just called the bottom of the market yet again."[4] The generic man always urging others to be bullish, always urging other people to buy, is one of the stock market's timeless archetypes. You will never see a statue of him next to the famous Bull on Broadway in Lower Manhattan. He's too important to sit still. He always has a job to do, and stories to tell. He is always in demand to appear on TV, or dispense a quote or share some wisdom to help others make sense of the market. Many people reflexively accept those generalizations and rush headlong back into the market, scrambling up the risk ladder, to recoup their losses, and to make more money.

During the 2007 credit crisis, Linda Blay, a bookkeeper in Orange County, California, saw her investment portfolio lose about 30 percent of its value. By September 2009, some six months after the worst of the correction had ended, stocks were surging, and she was optimistic about the stock market. "It's got a track record," she said. "It outperforms any investment. I think it'll come back."[5] That, in a nutshell, is the hope and strategy of most individual investors, even though history shows such an approach is increasingly detrimental to their financial health.

On Wall Street, money takes the path of least resistance. Taking money from individual investors is the easiest way to make money. Dumb Money believes what it hears or reads.

"The plain truth," says Arthur Levitt, the former chairman of the Securities and Exchange Commission, "is that we are in the midst of a financial literacy crisis. Too many people don't know how to determine saving and investment objectives or their tolerance for risk. Too many people don't know how to choose an investment, or an investment professional, or where to turn for help."[6]

The most basic evidence of Levitt's lamentations is that many people repeatedly buy and sell stocks at the wrong time. They panic. They have no discipline. They have no investment style. They typically do not even understand the two primary schools of stock investing. To the amateur, value investing is buying a stock that pays a dividend, rather than finding a company that is trading at a discount to its intrinsic value. Such companies have a "margin of safety," three words Warren Buffett says contain the secret of sound investing. Growth investing, to most, is buying a stock that is rising, rather looking for companies with revenues and earnings growing faster than the market's average.

Meanwhile, Wall Street profits. Consider mutual fund growth rates. In 1960, investors had spread $48 billion among 270 mutual funds. By 2007, more than $12.4 trillion was invested in more than 8,000 mutual funds. By 2000, U.S. Federal Reserve data showed that nearly half of all U.S. households owned stock. From 1990 to 2000, the number of U.S. stockholders increased by more than 50 percent, a phenomenon described as one of the great social movements of the 1990s. From 1980 to 2005, the New York Stock Exchange's daily trading volume increased more than 3,400 percent, rising from 45 million shares to 1.6 billion shares. Over the same period, the price of a NYSE seat, which traders had to buy if they wanted to trade at the exchange, increased to $3.55 million from $275,000, up 1,191 percent.

The oft-overlooked consequence of America's reliance on the stock market is that every financial crisis impacts more people than the one that came before. The same is true if the stock market simply stalls, and people lose an all-important year of much needed investment gains. In 2010, the Standard & Poor's 500 Index was at almost exactly the same place it had been 12 years earlier. By 2011, not much had changed. The stock market ended 2011 at the same place it had begun. This makes learning to more effectively navigate the stock market, and trying to avoid future crisis, or at least minimize their impact, imperative.

Financial crises occur more frequently than is generally appreciated. The crises are stunning, not just because of the destruction caused by the bursting of a bubble, but because of the psychology of the bubble. Every financial crisis hypnotizes millions of people into believing that the implausible is plausible. Want to buy a house with no money down and no credit check? Wall Street financed that dream, and made it come true (temporarily) for millions of people around the world from about 2002 to 2007. Want to invest in a new paradigm in which the old ways of thinking no longer apply? Wall Street spent much of the late 1990s selling investors shares of Internet companies with slick ideas and no earnings that would change the world. Even in the 1920s, unbelievably high interest rates could be earned loaning "investors" money to buy stocks on margin. The "investment" was considered low risk because there was little concern stock prices would stop rising. In 1635, Holland went mad for tulips and some "investors" bought bulbs for the price of houses.

Financial crises are a permanent, frequent part of the investing landscape. History proves that, and the future is unlikely to be different. Mohamed El-Erian, PIMCO's chief executive, sees a future of perpetual booms and busts that will occur every few years. He calls this the "new normal." He is so convinced the future will be turbulent that he and his firm are challenging the fundamental ideas that have long determined how money is invested. Rather than solely diversifying investments across stocks and bonds to reduce risk, a Nobel Prize winning idea that most everyone uses to temper investment decisions, El-Erian and his fellow fund managers first focus on risk, then reward. PIMCO has essentially created a mutual fund based on the good investor rule of always thinking of ways to not lose money. The fund picks investments based on risk factors. Stocks, for example, often behave like investment-grade corporate bonds. Junk bonds are often like small-capitalization stocks. PIMCO uses its analytical expertise to decide if bonds or stocks offer the better value. The entire portfolio is then hedged with Standard & Poor's 500 Index options and other such instruments to insure investors never lose more than 15 percent of their money during the inevitable declines that hit the stock market every few years.

If, by now, you are thinking of the best spots in your backyard for burying your money, hold off for a moment. While there is nothing you can do to make the stock market a friendly, kind place, you can change how you approach the market. The *good investor rule*—thinking first of how to not lose money, rather than how to make money—is the critical first step. The second step is learning to understand the mechanics of the market. Think of the principles of judo. Size doesn't matter. Success comes to those who learn to take advantage of their opponent's weight. Well-trained judo fighters, no matter their size, regularly flip larger attackers. The same principles work for investing—but you use your mind and your emotions rather than your body. Think of Yoda, the dimunitive Jedi master, from the Star Wars movies. In a sense, investors have to become like Yoda.

Some cynics would have you believe that these recent difficulties in the market, and on Wall Street, are insurmountable, and that people are trapped. They are not. Just ask Warren Buffett. "To invest successfully over a lifetime does not require a stratospheric IQ, unusual business insights, or inside information," Buffett says. "What's needed is a sound intellectual framework for making decisions and the ability to keep emotions from corroding that framework."[7]

Bernard Baruch, who sidestepped much of the Great Crash of 1929, knew it well. "To break free of this cycle of breakdown and build up, we must free ourselves of man's age-old tendency to swing from one extreme to another. We must seek out the course of disciplined reason that avoids both dumb submission and blind revolt," Baruch wrote in 1957. "It is not mere chance that whenever society is swept by some madness reason falls as the first victim."[8]

Though Baruch and Buffett belong to different generations, they are part of the long line of people in the market, those Indomitable Investors, who live by what Buffett calls "that framework." Now, let's see how the framework is built.

Chapter 2

Greed

Most people think they are long-term investors, even though they act like bad traders. They buy stocks when prices are rising. They rarely do any substantive analysis to determine if they are overpaying for what they are buying. They buy stocks with every intention of holding them for a long time, or because they are confident prices will continue to rise, and the stocks can be sold for a profit at a later date. They never realize that those missteps define Wall Street's greater fool theory. The other equally destructive part of the theory is selling in panic stocks that were bought in confidence.

No one wants to admit they lost money. It is easier complaining that the stock market is rigged, and banks and hedge funds are corrupt, than to confront the fact that the great crowd that comes to Wall Street to make money mostly "greeds in and panics out." The crowd rarely learns much of anything from boom to bust and back again. This behavior, when viewed from a nonfinancial perspective, is peculiar. People who have been mugged, or whose houses have been robbed, would immediately try to better protect themselves. They might take a self-defense class. They would get street-smart very fast. But people get mugged on Wall Street every single day and their behavior rarely changes.

In 1984, when the United States was starting to get mad for stocks and mutual funds and the foundation was being laid for the cult of equities that now defines the United States, DALBAR, a financial research firm in Boston, Massachusetts, began tracking investor behavior. The annual Quantitative Analysis of Investor Behavior study measures individual investor returns against stock and bond benchmarks. The results are disturbing. If the stock market rises 10 percent in a year, most investors fail to see their accounts rise that much. For every year DALBAR has conducted its research, investors have sharply lagged the Standard & Poor's 500 Index, the stock market's primary performance benchmark. In some years, investors trailed the index by more than 10 points. Bond investors, who are supposedly more conservative and steady, fared no better. They trailed Barclays's Aggregate Bond Index, too.

Over 20 years of research, DALBAR has found that investors never stay in the market long enough to profit. They hold stock mutual funds an average of 3.27 years. Remarkably, fixed income investors are even less patient. They bail at 3.17 years. The asset allocation investor— someone who owns a portfolio of diverse stocks and bonds to minimize volatility and reduce risk—is a little steadier. He bails after 4.29 years, apparently never truly believing that diversification will, over time, produce superior investment returns.

It is likely that most of the people surveyed by DALBAR, if asked, would describe themselves as long-term investors. But that description more accurately describes how long they stay in the stock market— not how long they actually hold stocks or bonds. Investing in stocks for 30 years is different than holding a stock for 30 years. Most people do not see the contradiction. This is another reason why they are often out of synchronicity with the market.

On Wall Street, five years is a significant time period. It might even be the basic building block of successful investing. A market cycle is typically defined as lasting five years. A market cycle includes a stock market rally, a decline, and a recovery. Put another way: Every five years witnesses the birth of a bull market, its death, and its rebirth. Yet, most investors never stay in the market long enough to benefit from the power of market cycles. They seem to enter the market at about the same time—just as prices are nearing a peak—and panic at the same time, selling en masse, only to buy again, often en masse, when prices are rising.

Rising stock prices are seductive. It is easy for anyone to believe that a rising stock will continue to rise, especially when cheerleaders from banks and major media organizations extol the stock's virtues. Yet, when something bad happens, and the stock price sharply declines, the intuitive hope of rising prices quickly converts to the fact of lost money.

Indeed, the typical experience for many investors is buying a stock after it has raced higher and nearing the point where the price will soon decline. Somewhere around the final 20 percent or so of a stock's ascent seems to often be when the trading charts and news and commentators all say, in their respective languages, that this stock is a winner, and poised to go higher yet. At about that point, the institutional investors who first spotted the investment, when no one else did, begin thinking that this stock now exists in the best of all possible worlds. They have made the bulk of their money—oftentimes achieving returns that exceed 100 percent—and they begin to think about selling even though they know they may miss the last final surge higher. That's why some mutual funds secretly have hedge funds so they can also make money off the fumes of a peaking stock with trading strategies that increase in value if stock prices rise, or fall. The fumes of a rising stock are typically fanned into the market by media organizations, in print, online or TV, various analysts and major investors who draw attention to a stock just before it swoons. This brings in investors who do not pay much attention to critical, analytical points, such as high price-to-earnings multiple, or make any distinction between price and value. They just buy stocks on the assumption that the price will go higher because it has gone higher. Thinking any other thought is difficult because the commentary on a hot stock is almost always enthusiastic and bullish. No one worries much at the time that the commentary often proves to be like the Sirens of Greek mythology, who sang such beautiful songs that sailors on passing ships would try to reach them, only to crash their ships into the rocks.

DALBAR's research suggests that most people have no idea of how to properly buy and sell stocks or bonds. In their Quantitative Analysis of Investor Behavior of 2011, DALBAR concluded: "One of the most startling, and ongoing facts is that at no point in time have average investors remained invested for sufficiently long enough periods to derive the benefit of a long-term investing strategy," DALBAR's 2011 Quantitative Analysis of Investor Behavior concluded. See Table 2.1.

DALBAR's holding periods, when combined with the psychology of how long it takes people to believe that new regimes and patterns exist, suggest that the average investor lives in an investment world that is not synchronized with investment and economic cycles or the movement of money, but is rather paced by delayed perceptions of those cycles. To break the cycle of buying high and selling—or to at least begin to hear the real tempo of the market—requires learning to

Table 2.1   Long-Term Returns (annualized, in percent)

Year	S&P 500	Average Equity Fund Investor	Difference
1998	17.9	7.25	−10.65
1999	18.01	7.23	−10.78
2000	16.29	5.32	−10.97
2001	14.51	4.17	−10.34
2002	12.22	2.57	−9.65
2003	12.98	3.51	−9.47
2004	13.2	3.7	−9.5
2005	11.9	3.9	−8
2006	11.8	4.3	−7.5
2007	11.81	4.48	−7.33
2008	8.35	1.87	−6.48
2009	8.2	3.17	−5.03
2010	9.14	3.83	−5.31

SOURCE: DALBAR, Quantitative Analysis of Investor Behavior 2011.

do the opposite of what often intuitively seems right. You want to buy stocks when others are selling, and sell stocks when others are buying. When you buy a stock, you must have a plan to sell it.

This may seem like Alice in Wonderland logic, but it is as real and straightforward as the nose on your face. Imagine a seesaw on a child's playground. On either end of the seesaw sits buy and sell. Risk is the fulcrum in the middle that lets buy and sell rise and fall. When everyone starts to fall in love with a stock, it starts to lift the buy side of the seesaw. The higher buy rises on the seesaw, the riskier it gets. A seesaw can only rise so far before it reaches a limit and declines. The same is true for investing.

Most investors only think of buying. The only time anyone thinks of selling is when the market is declining, news is apocalyptic, and panic has replaced euphoria. Selling in panic is a surefire way to lose money.

Everyone naturally wants to make profits—even those who are focused on risk—but the finest investors think first of how to not lose money rather than how to make money. Their map of the market is based on risk, not profits. The best investors—and even the mediocre ones—keep themselves sane by using what is called a "sell discipline." It is rarely discussed, but it is a defining discipline that focuses on risk and keeping profits. By focusing on risk, investors take an important first step in breaking the perpetual boom and bust cycle that traps most investors. To be sure, Wall Street hopes you never focus on risk. Wall Street would rather you focus on the specter of profits even though focusing on profits without first thinking about risk is a way to rent investment returns, rather than own them.

"Where you want to be is always in control, never wishing, always trading and always first and foremost protecting your ass," says Paul Tudor Jones, who will always be counted among the world's greatest traders. He adds:

> I mean that's why most people lose money as individual investors or as traders because of the fact that they're not focusing on losing money. They need to focus on the money they have at risk; how much capital is at risk in any single investment they have. If everyone spent 90 percent of their time on that rather than 90 percent of their time on pie in the sky ideas about how

much money they're going to make then they'd be incredibly successful investors.[1]

Ray Dalio, who runs Bridgewater Associates, one of the world's largest hedge funds, says that successful investing is always a matter of controlling risk. "Risky things are not in themselves risky if you understand them and control them. If you do it randomly and you are sloppy about it, it can be very risky," Dalio says.[2] He says that the key to investment success is figuring out "Where is the edge? And how do I stay the right distance from the edge?" Dalio reduces risk by spreading out his investments or trades. He typically has 30 or 40 different positions. "I'm always trying to figure out my probability of knowing," Dalio says. "Given that I'm never sure, I don't want to have any concentrated bets."

Too few people consider risk when investing, just as they focus on price, never thinking of value. Such naiveté bothers no one on Wall Street. Investing is often a zero-sum game. When you lose, someone else wins. The people who win the most are the most disciplined. The banks and the keepers of the financial market could not care less what happens to ordinary investors. They need money like fire needs oxygen. And greedy, unsophisticated investors who never think about risk are the easiest source of money, because they always buy high, and, after some time has passed, they sell low. Wall Street can wait a few seconds, or years, to capture the "spread," or the difference between the purchase and sale price. You will rarely hear anyone tell investors to sell stocks and take profits. If you did, most people would probably ignore it because of the chance to make even more money, which invariably causes them to lose money, and thus the cycle begins anew.

"One of the keys to the art of successful investing is that you can't lose big," says Fred Hickey, a top technology investor.[3] One practical way to focus on risk is to think of stocks in terms of price and value. If you want, think of this as the Iceberg Principle of investing. A stock's price is like an iceberg's tip that pokes through the surface of the market. The real estimation of the stock's size, and worth, is hidden from view. To understand the stock, focus on what is hidden from view.

"Outside the world of finance, the difference between price and value is well understood and best captured in the wise saying, 'Price is what you pay. Value is what you get.' However, in finance, price and value are treated as synonyms. It is almost a matter of faith, not to mention new accounting standards, that the most appropriate measure of an asset's value is its current market price," says Christopher Davis, who runs the Davis Funds, a mutual fund company his grandfather founded in 1969.[4] When you view the market through the prism of price and value, you can begin to develop a "margin of safety." The margin of safety is an important idea that was developed by Benjamin Graham, Warren Buffett's mentor. Margin of safety is the difference between the intrinsic value of a stock and its market value. Intrinsic value is what the company is worth based on financial analysis. Intrinsic value is not the same as a stock's market price. The nomenclature of financial analysis is complicated and nuanced, but the thought process is not terribly different than buying groceries. You would not spend $50 to buy a can of beans at one store if you can buy the same can of beans for $1 at another. That simple distinction is often blurred in the stock market. In the market, analysts at several important banks would have strong buy ratings on the $50 can of beans and sell or hold ratings on the cheap stuff. The analysts would issue research reports saying that the $50 beans are the best beans in the world, the management team exudes brilliance, and consumer demand is huge and getting huger. Soon, the price of the $50 beans would surge, driving the price into the stratosphere as excitement spread about Wall Street's wonder beans.

The company that sold $1 beans would look dull by comparison. The stock would be the subject of a few analyst reports, usually around earnings reports. The reports might say the company grew earnings at a respectable clip, and returned money to investors by increasing the dividend. Simple analysis would show the stock traded at about 13 times earnings, compared to 90 times earnings for Wall Street's wonder beans. Few people would pay attention to the $1 beans. They would want to cash in on the magic beans. The magical fruit example might seem far-fetched, but it shows how market prices are set by many forces that have nothing to do with reason and everything to do with nonsense. At some banks, analysts are expected to generate trading revenues for their firms, according to one former analyst. Wonder beans are more fun to trade than the stock of a quiet company that barely budges. Market prices are influenced by emotion. Prices can be high because of fear, or euphoria, and even purely irrational behavior and thought. The value of an asset is different than price.

Price is easy to understand. Value is not. Price is a seemingly simple fact that appears next to a stock's ticker symbol. Most everyone agrees $4 or $40 is not a large sum of money. That type of superficial thinking corrodes investment decisions. The $4 stock could trade at 90 times earnings, or even have no earnings, which means that the stock is, by basic measures of value, obscenely expensive. Yet, a stock that trades at more than $200 a share, a price that many people automatically consider expensive, could trade at a price-to-earnings multiple of 10 times earnings. By comparing the price-to-earnings multiples of the $4 stock, and the $200 stock, one quickly sees that the $4 stock is expensive, and the $200 stock inexpensive.

Unlike price, determining value requires some thought, some math. The easiest way to measure value is to look at price-to-earnings ratios. P/E ratios will quickly tell you if a stock price is trading at a premium, or discount to its earnings. Earnings are critical to determining a stock's value. Look at trailing price-to-earnings multiple and forward earnings. This information is listed on most financial websites. For many investors, it is hard to justify spending more than 20 times earnings on a stock. The higher the P-E ratio, the higher investor expectations. Such stocks can tank on one bad earnings report, or news that a product faltered. Still, fast growing stocks worth owning often trade at high P-E ratios because revenue and earnings are growing faster than many other stocks, which is why it is always important to compare stocks against similar stocks, and sector indexes or exchange-traded funds. If a stock has outperformed all other similar stocks in its sector, find out why. The answer will help determine if the gain is temporary, sustainable, or a sign of something else.

Focusing on value, and not just price, must become reflexive. It must become a discipline. It is for Alice Walton, and she is an heir to the Walmart fortune, and thus one of the richest people in the world. Even on a day when she spent more than $20 million buying American art at a Sotheby's auction for her Crystal Bridges Museum of America in Bentonville, Arkansas, she thought about price and value.

"One of the great responsibilities that I have is to manage my assets wisely, so that they create value," Walton says. "I know the price of lettuce. You need to understand price and value. You buy the best lettuce you can at the best price you can."[5]

The same is true with investing. Most people rarely think about stocks in any serious, multidimensional way. They have never heard of the margin of safety concept. Because they have no real conviction based on fundamental financial research when buying stocks, they panic when their stocks tumble lower. The absence of conviction is fatal. The absence of conviction is a key reason why so many investors have such trouble staying in the stock market long enough to benefit from the market's cycles. When buying stocks, own them for three to five years and hold them for as long as the original reason for which you bought them remains valid. If the reasons change, sell them. If practiced properly, buy-and-hold investing helps investors buy mispriced companies that ultimately blossom. Discipline lets time work for you—not against you.

But it is important to understand that the stock market is not static. It changes. Facts change. Investment theses evolve. Buy-and-hold works sometimes, and other times not. Consider IBM, Procter & Gamble, and Johnson & Johnson. From April 2006 through April 2011, IBM's stock rose 103 percent, compared to 13 percent for Procter & Gamble, and 5 percent for Johnson & Johnson. Buy-and-hold worked on IBM, but not on the other two stocks. In fact, it may have been wiser to sell Procter & Gamble and Johnson & Johnson and buy IBM. This is not trading. It is still investing. The only reason to invest is to make money. The names of the stocks are secondary. If you have to sell, sell. Never fall in love with a stock.

On Wall Street, no one really engages in buy-and-hold investing— at least not in the way most people understand. Even stock market benchmarks, such as the Standard & Poor's 500 Index, the New York Stock Exchange, and the NASDAQ stock index, regularly change their minds about stocks.

Consider mutual funds that many people incorrectly think are paragons of buy-and-hold investing. Ron Baron, a well-regarded mutual fund manager, says the average mutual fund portfolio turns over every seven or eight months.[6] His mutual fund portfolios turn over every five to six years, though he has owned some stocks for 20 years or more. All stock indexes routinely sell stocks. One company is replaced with another to reflect developments like mergers or stock prices that have fallen too low and thus violate the index's membership rules. This happens so often that the rebalancing of the index—that's the euphemism used on Wall Street when stocks are kicked out of an index and new ones added—are major trading events. Everyone tries to guess what stocks will be added, and what stocks will be dumped. The New York Stock Exchange and NASDAQ stock index also regularly dump stocks. Any company that fails to meet exchange listings standards, including share price and other healthy company metrics, is de-listed. The fallen stock's ticker symbol is removed from the exchange's trading systems. It exists no more. All of these decisions are driven by rules and disciplines.

On Wall Street, selling is often a group decision based on facts, rules, and discipline, just as buying is based on the analysis of a stock or sector or market conditions. On Main Street, the opposite is true. Buying is a group decision influenced by media and Wall Street. Selling is a lonely, singular decision.

You have no risk manager watching what is happening. There is no head of trading or senior portfolio manager watching over your profits and losses. There is no voice of experience questioning an investment that seems too good to be true. It is just you and Mr. Market and the constant pressure of having to make money, or wanting to make money.

Every investor has been schooled by Wall Street to buy good stocks, and let them age like fine wine. Everyone knows J.P. Morgan's famous saying that the stock market fluctuates. Everyone also knows that time is an investor's friend. The definition of time, like friends, is increasingly subjective. Just as the first round of Baby Boomers were preparing for retirement at the onset of the twenty-first century, the stock market experienced several sharp corrections. The Internet bubble burst in 2000. The credit crisis began in 2007, and the stock market did not recover until about March of 2009. Every dollar invested in the Standard & Poor's 500 Index from December 31, 1999 until the end of 2009, when Europe's sovereign debt crisis began, was worth roughly 90 cents. Perhaps the future will be different than the recent past. But why take the risk? Many people do not have as much time as they think, or want, or need. Time is your friend, but that does not mean the stock market is a benevolent ATM machine that will be cashed up and ready for you to make withdrawals when you need the money. Think about risk. Think about your rewards.

The Hardest Decision

There are few absolute truths in the market, but this is one: Selling is the hardest decision any investor makes. In comparison, buying stocks is easy. Scores of "stock analysts" have a million reasons why you should buy a stock. Revenues are growing. Earnings are growing. A new product will soon be launched. The company is a takeover target. The stock is attractively priced. A major investor—maybe Paul Tudor Jones—is buying shares.

Selling is Wall Street's essence just as surely as buying is Main Street's. Wall Street almost never tells you to sell. That could anger corporate executives and cost banks lucrative investment banking assignments. To make money, to truly succeed in the market, you have to teach yourself how to sell. If you don't learn to be a disciplined seller, you risk losing more money than you make.

On Wall Street, the "sell discipline" defines the market's highest echelons. It is rarely discussed. Selling is a philosophical discipline as much as an expression of willpower. There is no one-size fits-all approach. The sell discipline varies according to investment styles and timelines and many other factors, including profits to be realized by selling, or losses to be limited. The market is so big that it accommodates many different styles. Some of the styles are radically different from each other, save one important similarity: discipline. Successful investors and traders disagree all the time, but they all adhere to their specific discipline. Anyone without discipline in the market is a gambler. Condition yourself to think of selling as a form of risk management. Think of it like an automobile insurance policy. You may crash your car. If you do, the policy limits your losses.

Selling is not about timing the stock market. It is about managing the risk of your own investment portfolio, and tempering your decisions. It is about maintaining constant touch with the market to ensure the reason you bought the stock—the investment thesis—remains valid. Over time, you will refine and personalize your selling discipline. Some selling disciplines are simple; others are complex. All of them have this in common: They help to limit losses and lock in profits.

The age-old approach to selling stock is telling your broker to sell your stock if the price drops by 10 percent. This is a "stop-loss order." The modern approach is entering an order with your online discount broker. If you buy stock at $50, a 10 percent stop-loss order automatically sells the stock if its price declines to $45. Some investors continually update their stop-loss orders as the stock price increases. This way they are always protected against any major market mishaps. So if the stock you bought at $50 is now worth $100, the stop-loss order is reset to $90, protecting almost all of the gains. Not everyone likes stop-loss orders, because it could lock in a loss on a stock that declined for a temporary reason—for example, the flash crash of May 2010, when the stock market quickly fell 1,000 points in 20 minutes—and is destined to trade higher.

The Iron Man

To Alan "Ace" Greenberg, vice chairman emeritus of JPMorgan Chase, selling is a simple decision. He does not philosophize or worry about how much money he might make in the future. He only worries about what is happening, and not losing. "When the market is going up, or the market stays the same, and I have something going down, I sell," Greenberg said.[7] He is extremely unsentimental. He does not fall in love with his stocks. He sells any stock if he does not like how it is behaving. He says he learned early in his long career to say "I was wrong." He considers admitting mistakes an indispensable investing rule.

This sounds easy, but it is hard. Most people have trouble confronting mistakes—especially when they have lost money. They hope that the stock will bounce back, and that they will break even. nothing is often costly. They would rather keep a bad investment and hope it recovers, than sell and lose money. Selling hurts—emotionally and financially. According to psychologist Daniel Kahneman's "loss aversion" theory, losses are twice as painful as gains are pleasurable.

One of Greenberg's first mentors, Bernard J. Lasker, an investor and former New York Stock Exchange chairman, taught Greenberg the virtues of disciplined selling. "His standing instructions were if it goes up a point, buy me more," Greenberg says. "If it goes up another point, call me. If it goes down two points, sell it. This sane simple advice became a source of enduring mystery for me. Why didn't more investors embrace it?"[8] Because it is easier to embrace hope than confront reality. Everyone buys stock because they think the price will rise. If it declines, an error was made. The collision of hope and reality are often paralyzing. Rather than analyzing their error, many people hold on to their hope. They are afraid to sell a stock because it could rise and they don't want to miss out, or they want to break even.

Selling seems straightforward. But it is a psychological hellhole. "People want perfection when they sell," said Justin Mamis, a former New York Stock Exchange trader who wrote what perhaps may be the only book ever written on selling stocks. *When to Sell* was published in 1977.[9] When Greenberg led Bear Stearns, he created a Risk Committee. The group met every Monday. The committee's purpose was to safeguard the firm's money. Greenberg required his traders to sell all losing positions. "I didn't care how nasty a hit we had to take, by 4:00 P.M. Monday all the dogs better be off the books," he said.

Greenberg did not like excuses. He did not like inaction. To safeguard against his traders falling in love with stocks or bonds, Greenberg set trading limits to limit the amount of money anyone could invest in a stock or bond.

Sometimes, Bear Stearns' traders held onto losers. They would tell Greenberg the stock was about to rise because of a pending investor meeting. On Wall Street, investor meetings are viewed as bullish events. Many investors buy stocks in anticipation of investor meetings with the plan of selling their shares when corporate management delivers good news like a new product or updating earnings guidance. Greenberg did not care.

"What do you think they're going to say? It's like asking a man what his daughter looks like," Greenberg recalled telling one of his traders.[10] He made them sell. He told them they could buy it back in a week. They rarely did. Greenberg rarely buys back stocks he sold. He doesn't believe in "dollar averaging," an old mainstay strategy that entails buying more stocks when the prices are declining. "When the company files for Chapter 11 bankruptcy, you'll be the biggest holder," Greenberg says.

Does he ever waver? No. He hates losses. He says losses interfere with the ability to think. Thinking clearly is critical to investing. "Losses are painful. People cannot think straight. It irritates you. If they own something at a loss they can't wait to get even," Greenberg said.[11]

Stress is indeed the great limiter. A 2009 study at Portugal's University of Minho suggests stress rewires the brain. Researcher Nuno Sousa exposed rats to severe stress. He shocked them. He dunked them under water. He put them in cages with dominant rats. He compared those poor rats to unstressed rats. The stressed rats could perform simple tasks like pressing a bar for food. But they couldn't determine when to stop. Normal rats could. "Behaviors become habitual faster in stressed animals than in the controls, and worse, the stressed animals can't shift back to goal-directed behaviors when that would be the better approach," Dr. Sousa says.[12]

Robert Sapolsky, a Stanford University School of Medicine neurobiologist who studies stress, says Sousa's research provides a model for understanding why people cannot escape ruts.[13] Those insights into the human condition reinforce the wisdom in having a plan to sell stocks. Bad times inevitably arise in the market. Knowing what to do before it happens is helpful.

Greenberg's discipline helped build Bear Stearns into a modern powerhouse, and one of the world's largest investment banks. His discipline also saved him from Bear Stearns' demise on his successor's watch. Greenberg didn't lose much money when J.P. Morgan bought Bear Stearns for $10 a share in 2008. True to his investment discipline, he had sold almost all of his Bear Stearns stock at higher prices.

Atlas Doesn't Shrug

Dan Rice is one of America's top mutual fund managers. He is to investing what Babe Ruth was to baseball—except Rice is a quiet superstar. When he buys a stock, he has already decided to sell. He is not looking for a gain of a few points. He wants to earn a return of 50 percent or more. He is patient. He is confident in his analysis. "We have a firm idea of what we think the company is worth and when it starts to get close to our price objective we review it closely to determine if anything major has changed. If nothing major has changed we sell," he matter-of-factly says.[14]

Rice manages Blackrock's Energy and Resources Fund. Blackrock manages over $3 trillion. Each year, Rice, has outperformed the Standard & Poor's 500 Index. Over 10 years, from mid-April 2001 to 2011, Rice's fund gained 517 percent, compared to 38 percent for the Standard & Poor's 500. Anyone who invested $10,000 with Rice in 2001 had $61,718 in 2011. The same investment in the Standard & Poor's 500 barely budged over the same period. Rice owns stocks for an average of three to four years. Rice rarely sells. He is not doctrinaire. If there is a change of circumstance that impacts his stock—such as an expected oil well that did not materialize—Rice sells. He is not bothered by short-term market fluctuations. His decisions are based on careful financial analysis. This gives him the conviction to not be scared by market moves.

"I am very fundamentally oriented," he says. "I would buy more if something blows up; 95 percent of the time it works," Rice says. "Most investors do the opposite. If something blows up, they panic and sell their stock. 95 percent of the time they lose money."

By some measures, individual investors rely less on fundamental analysis than seasoned investors. One survey found they rank technical analysis and monitoring order flow as more critical to their decisions than fundamentals.

What happens if his investments decline in value when the market rises? Not much. He does not panic. He says he is "slavishly devoted" to his models. He also pays attention to risk. Every week, he gets a report that summarizes his risk profile. What happens if short-term interest rates increase 50 basis points (one percentage point is comprised of 100 basis points)? What happens if oil prices rise or fall? What if the currency markets shift and that causes the stock market to rise or fall?

Rice is unemotional. He has trained himself to live with risk, to watch it, to study it. He is not bullied by the financial market. There is a confidence factor that perhaps is simply just another way of saying he trusts his own experience and his analysis. But if something changes, so does he. "I'm never married to a stock," Rice says. If circumstances change, he can go from having no cash in his portfolio to 20 percent cash overnight. "If I have nothing interesting to buy," he says, "my cash starts to build."

The Warrior Philosopher

Rob Arnott is a disrupter of Wall Street's sacred status quo. He is at the forefront of thinking about more effectively investing huge sums of money. He sits at the nexus where all of the old ideas about portfolio management ends, and new ideas begin. He is a confidant to Nobel Prize winners and a wise man to many of the world's top investors. His ideas are changing the way stock and bond portfolios and indexes are managed. To anyone off Wall Street, this may seem insignificant. In the financial world, portfolio management is the essence of the market.

Arnott invented an idea called fundamental indexing. The name is bland, but it upends the old order of the money management industry, and offers insights into how individual investors can make money and manage risk.

First a little background: The stock market is organized into different sectors. Professional investors measure their investment returns against various sectors of the stock market, and the Standard & Poor's 500 Index. The Standard & Poor's 500 Index is essentially based on the 500 largest stocks that trade in the United States. This is an example of a capitalization-weighted index, which means membership is based on the capitalization (the total value of a company's outstanding stock). Arnott, and his colleagues at Research Affiliates, believe that the old way is flawed. He believes—as do many of the market's most sophisticated investors—that stock prices can increase too far, too fast, and that they will ultimately return to their fair value. In other words, investors get too excited about a stock and bid up its value beyond what the stock is worth.

Another way to think of this phenomenon is to think of stock and bond prices like rubber bands. Prices stretch as hordes of investors buy them because they think the company's earnings are growing fast or some other reason. Inevitably, the rubber band snaps back—a phenomenon called mean reversion—and the high price returns to the fair value. Arnott has no problem with capitalization-weighted indexes. He even thinks they are generally decent benchmarks of the market's performance. He just does not think the old indexes are good measures of investment performance.

His methodology—fundamental indexing—severs the link between stock and bond prices and portfolio weight. Under his discipline—and it is an ingenious idea—stocks and bonds that have surged in price are sold and replaced with securities with lower prices. In essence, Arnott's methodology sells high, and buys low.

His idea is not simply based on market price, which is the primary metric most people use to evaluate stocks. Arnott's analysis is rooted in fundamental analysis of a company's financial health. Arnott's methods peer deeply into a company's financial health. He looks at five-year averages of a company's book value, revenue, cash flow, gross sales and gross dividends, and total employment. Remember the importance of five years on Wall Street. We talked about it earlier. Five years is a market cycle.

Other indexes focus on the size of a company, and that can give investors erroneous ideas. Apple and the NASDAQ 100 index are perhaps the most prominent examples of how this can distort index returns. In 2011, Apple's stock price accounted for about 20 percent of the index's movements. If Apple's stock moved up or down, so did the index. Some people may have interpreted the index's moves as an indication of the health of the top 100 technology stocks, but they were wrong. The index was overly influenced by Apple, which is why the NASDAQ 100 index was ultimately rebalanced to reduce Apple's influence.

Arnott minimizes the stock market's exuberance, which he says overweights overvalued stocks and underweights undervalued stocks. His method makes fine sense on paper, but it is psychologically uncomfortable for many people to follow. Most people would rather own high-priced stocks that are rising than low-priced stocks that are not performing as well. Data tells a different story.

Over 43 years, from 1962 to 2004, a period that included several bull and bear markets, and the bursting of the Internet bubble, Arnott's fundamental index outperformed the U.S. stock market. He tested his methods in 23 different stock markets around the world. In each market, his method proved more profitable.

Anyone can implement the principles of Arnott's fundamental indexing. Think of the process as "inefficient market trading."

"The way I would manage is to continually reassess holdings in the portfolio and ask the question what is cheap relative to long-term expectations and what is expensive, and secondly what is popular and inexpensive with the view of selling winners and buying what is out of favor," Arnott says.[15] Many sophisticated investors rebalance their portfolios every quarter by taking profits on stocks that have advanced, and buying stocks that have not. Such discipline requires a tough mental constitution.

"The notion that market price is correct seems utterly naive," Arnott says. "It's not difficult to earn good long-term investment returns, or beat the market, but I do think it is painful because you have to do things that people think are stupid. You have to be greedy when others are terrified and terrified when others are greedy."

Like Monkeys at the Zoo

Kurt Vonnegut understood the psychology of investing better than most. The writer lived through the Great Depression. In his novel, *Slaughterhouse Five*, Vonnegut imagined aliens take two people to their planet, put them in a zoo cage with a big board displaying stock and commodity prices, a news ticker, and a telephone connected to a brokerage firm on earth. The earthlings are told they have been given a million dollars to invest, and that they must manage their money from the zoo cage to insure they are rich when they return to earth. Big crowds came to watch.

"The telephone and the big board and the ticker were all fakes, of course. They were simply stimulants to make them jump up and down and cheer, or gloat, or sulk, or tear their hair, or to be scared . . . to feel as contented as babies in their mothers' arms," Vonnegut wrote.

The investors even try appealing to a higher power. "They had lost a small fortune in olive oil futures. So they gave prayer a whirl," Vonnegut wrote. "It worked. Olive oil went up."[16]

Life imitates art. Professional investors view amateur investors as Vonnegut described. This will shock many people, and perhaps offend them, too. Naturally, you likely consider yourself rational, sound, and intelligent. You probably are—in your nonfinancial life. When money is not involved, people routinely process loads of information, much of it complex. They make decisions. They solve problems. But clear thinking often falls apart when you enter the financial market. Emotion inevitably trumps reason. This happens because everyone has a plan for buying stocks, but not selling. This means most investors are little more than gamblers. They have no discipline. They are focused on the wrong side of the market. Most people fit this description, and they have for a long, long time.

Everyone battles their own greed, but amateur investors, especially the highly educated, often have great difficulty mastering this element of successful investing. Throw in a master's degree, never mind the subject, or advanced degrees from medical or law schools, and you have identified the very people who have paid for the college educations of the children of stock exchange specialists, and for thousands of family beach houses. There is a reason why—and it's not a pretty one—a specialist's clerk at a derivatives exchange can make more money than a cardiothoracic surgeon. The irony is that most people think others make bad decisions. Even after all the ups-and-downs, they still mostly think they are rational investors. If any blame is assigned, the finger is pointed to Wall Street, which is rigged, filled with thieves, and otherwise operated by gangster hedge funds and banksters. People do not really look at themselves to see what they did wrong, and why. The stock market is cunning that way. It is likely one reason why most investors, year after year, earn less money than the stock and bond markets returned. Think of the return differential as a form of financial bipolar disorder. The unseasoned investor is exuberant or depressed. The seasoned investor, our Indomitable Investor, is not easily led astray by greed or fear.

A Context

Of course, it is incredibly difficult to move opposite the crowd. We are social creatures. We find psychological sustenance in friendship and in community. Few of us are naturally wired to ever do the opposite of others. This handicaps people when they invest.

Wall Street specializes in crowd psychology. Wall Street is designed to move inventory like used cars. And as they say in the used-car business: There is an ass for every seat. On Wall Street, everything is for sale, or lease—even the buy-and-hold shares that you keep with the intention of leaving to your children and grandchildren. Your brokerage firm routinely lends those shares to "short sellers," who sell them because they think they can buy them back at a lower price and pocket the difference.

You should not expect analysts to tell you when to sell your stocks and take profits. Bank analysts rarely want to anger executives of the corporations they cover; that could cost their firms lucrative investment banking business. Besides, almost all analysts depend on corporate executives for access. Anger the executives, and you have no access. Rarer still is the bank that assigns sell ratings to stocks. Almost all stocks, all the time, are buys.

Of course, the banks know this is not always true. They worry about how their money is used. They have risk managers who monitor the investments of all of their traders. The computer systems that process these trades are all programmed to prevent major losses. This highlights a fundamental difference between Wall Street and Main Street.

The typical investor only thinks about buying stocks, and watching their prices rise. This is a key reason so many people have such difficulties in the stock market. Their ideas are simplistic and monodimensional. They are only focused on making money. "Why do you rob banks," someone once asked Willie Sutton, the famous bank robber. "Because that's where the money is." The logic is the same for most investors. This is a recipe for failure just as surely as Slick Willie was arrested and locked up. Professional investors think in risk-adjusted ways. They measure their investment performance against benchmarks. This helps control their emotions. It helps them to sell and lock in profits.

Despite the flaws with benchmark indexes, anyone who professionally manages money measures themselves against performance benchmarks that track the entire stock market, or subsectors, such as oil, technology, and pharmaceuticals. The entire market is divided into these groups. One of the most common systems is the Global Industry Classification Standard (GICS). GICS divides the stock market into 10 sectors, 24 industry groups, 68 industries and 154 subindustries. You could get lost in the details. Most people will do just fine focusing on the Standard & Poor's 500 Index as a measure of overall stock portfolio performance and sector returns. If you own stock in J.P. Morgan, you can gauge its performance against the Select Sector Financial SPDR (XLF), an exchange-traded fund comprised of different financial stocks. You can consider XLF the sector proxy; use its performance to evaluate the returns of financial stocks, and to frame selling decisions. If your stock is up 40 percent, the sector is up 10 percent, and the Standard & Poor's 500 Index is up 8 percent, you must find out why there is a discrepancy, and let that inform your decision. You might decide to buy more stock, or you might decide to sell.

The key is to adopt the discipline of regularly evaluating investments against the market. At minimum, this is done every three months. This will persuade you to give up the notion that your stocks are unique, or exist in and of themselves. Nothing is forever immune to the market's gravitational pull. Inevitably, stocks trading at premiums to peers confront such high expectations—or such widespread selling pressures—that they fall from their lofty perches.

Major premiums, or even discounts, from benchmarks are silent signals from the market to either buy or sell. Most people never get this deep. They are content checking their stock values. If their stock prices are rising, if their total portfolio value is rising, they are happy. They may pay some attention to earnings reports, investment rating changes, and sector developments. Not much else happens. They almost never think of their investment gains in a risk-based context. They need to say to themselves, "I have made say 40 percent on my investment. Now, I am risking cash profits of say $30,000 to make how much more?" At minimum, they need to think about selling enough shares to take out their initial investment. At least then they are playing with the house's money.

"If someone buys a stock at $20 and it goes to $22, they make 10 percent in two months that's like 60 percent a year," Greenberg said, "and they hold on."[17] The reason they do nothing is because they think a 10 percent surge is a sign of even better things to come. Sometimes, the good times never come. Sometimes you lose money.

When you feel yourself getting greedy, and you will, check the 10-year Treasury bond's yield. This will show you the return you would make without assuming any market risk since the U.S. government has the world's highest credit rating and never defaults on its debt. Remember, it's not what you make, it's what you keep.

The Danger of Warren Buffett

Warren Buffett is the eternal counterbalance to anyone who suggests that something might be wrong with buy-and-hold investing. The great stock investor makes buy-and-hold investing seem easy and natural—which it is, provided you pick the right stocks to buy-and-hold.

The truth is that even the Sage of Omaha sells stocks, trims investment positions, and, otherwise, changes his mind. His penchant for quotable one-liners, such as "Forever is his favorite investment period," burnishes his well-deserved halo and blurs the facts. Buffett says very little about selling stocks or bad investment decisions. He leaves that to regulatory documents that his company, Berkshire Hathaway, files with the Securities and Exchange Commission. Those reports are much drier and harder to read than his shareholder letters the financial media loves to hype.

The truth is that buy-and-hold investing is not as easy as it seems. The idea is widely misunderstood by most people, and very poorly applied.

Ideally, every time you sell a stock you will be like Bernard Baruch, who captivated the country after the Great Crash of 1929. He was another generation's Warren Buffett. Baruch attributed his success in the stock market to selling when stock prices were rising. Baruch sidestepped the Great Crash of 1929 and went on to serve as an adviser to presidents Woodrow Wilson, Franklin Delano Roosevelt, and Harry Truman.

"Men find it equally hard to take either a profit or a loss," Baruch explained in his memoirs. "If a stock has gone up, a man wants to hold on to it in anticipation of further rise. If a stock has gone down, he tends to hold on to it until an upward turn comes along so he will at least be even. The sensible course is to sell while the stock still is rising or, if you have made a mistake, to admit it immediately and take your loss."[18]

The Value of Errors

Should you sell and realize a loss, be strong and of good courage. The experience may be the best investment lesson you ever receive. That's what happened to Stephen Schwarzman shortly after he founded The Blackstone Group. He had just raised his first investment fund. He bought a steel distribution company based on a partner's advice. At the time, Blackstone had no investment process. The deal soured fast. Schwarzman minimized some of his losses, but he has never forgotten what it felt like to lose money. He even had a Lucite tombstone made to commemorate that first bad deal. He keeps it in his office. Every time he makes a decision, he says he thinks of that bad deal. His initial mistake changed his career.[19] "How you manage failure is very important," Schwarzman says. "Some people manage failure by making pretend it didn't happen and they go about their jobs and people don't pay attention. 'Oh, we lost money on that one.' I don't believe in that. I like to learn. Sometimes you learn more from your failures than you do from your successes."[20]

Blackstone, which is one of the world's top investment firms, treats failure like a major event. All failures are studied. Exhaustively. "What we do when we fail is we spend enormous time thinking through, what did we do wrong; what should we have seen; are our processes good; did we misidentify a variable that got us or did we identify it and didn't evaluate how bad that can be—we got that wrong," Schwarzman says.[21] "Or did we just simply have bad luck where there are three or four bad things that could happen and they all happened, like in a very rapid period of time?"

Schwarzman once thought his firm could make no mistakes. That is still the firm's goal, but he has come to realize that actively making decisions means that some are inevitably bad. "I think about this stuff so much—we probably get about 90 percent to 93 percent of our decisions correct, maybe a tiny bit higher, but that means we failed a lot; a 7 percent failure, sometimes we get 95 percent right but we're still making 5 percent failures across the firm so we're always struggling to improve and get that down to almost nothing," Schwarzman says. "And so failure is a really important element in learning."

Most people celebrate their victories, but the true lessons, the true feedback on investment decision-making, often comes from failure. Don't waste mistakes. Use them to refine the discipline of selling stocks to realize profits, to minimize losses, to manage risk, and reward. This will help insure you are not, as the great poet Lord Byron said, the fool of time and terror.

Chapter 3

Fear

It is an ancient fact of markets that the best investment opportunities are often draped in fear. It was true well before the Rothschilds ruled Europe's financial markets during the nineteenth century, and one of the banking family's members supposedly quipped during some long ago war to "buy when there's blood in the streets, even if it is your own."

This logic will be true 2,000 years from now. It will stay true as long as stocks, bonds, and derivatives are traded. People who learn to use their fear and that of others will make money while others lose it. This macabre market dynamic will steady you when others panic.

The logic is simple, strange, and sublime. The crowd of investors that animates the financial market always becomes too greedy, or too afraid. Just as surely as thinking about selling paradoxically protects profits, and hopefully saves you from the euphoria that creates bubbles, fear is a bullish aphrodisiac just as surely as greed ultimately ruins the party.

Consider February and March of 2009. Those were the worst two months of the credit crisis that began in 2007. They also marked the start of an historic stock rally that most people missed because the modern financial world seemed to be ending. The subprime credit crisis that began in the United States had wrapped itself around the globe, and was eroding the stability of markets in the United States, Europe, and Asia. Many investors, including some who should have known better, bought what were essentially high-end mutual funds loaded with complicated mortgages. Everyone thought housing prices would keep rising, so they looked past the risk that the fancy mortgage investments would collapse if housing prices fell. Of course, housing prices ultimately declined, and these mortgage portfolios exploded like a global chain of hand grenades that destabilized many of the world's banks and economies. Some banks failed. J.P. Morgan rescued Bear Stearns, then the fifth-largest investment bank. Lehman Brothers, then the fourth-largest bank, declared bankruptcy. Commercial banks failed all across the nation. People lost their homes. Others walked away from mortgages that were suddenly worth more than the market value of their homes. Even General Electric (GE), a company founded by Thomas Edison in 1890 that has long defined stability, was feared to be in danger of failing. Everyone was selling their stocks and bonds, and putting their money in cash or gold. The mood was so dark that Wall Street traders were e-mailing each other the link to U.S. Bunkers, a company that sells concrete and steel bunkers. Many people tapped their home equity lines because they were afraid banks would stop lending. One hedge fund manager had a massive security safe installed in his home. He withdrew $300,000 from his home equity line and put the cash in his giant safe.

The fear of economic collapse was everywhere, but some recognized it as once-in-a-life time opportunities. Many blue-chip stocks—think American Express, GE, Morgan Stanley, Goldman Sachs, and Wells Fargo—were trading in the stock market for less than they were worth. They could have been bought with the all-important margin of safety that is the hallmark of smart investing. Many companies traded at or below book value—essentially how much money a company would have left if it went out of business and paid off its debts. Comparing book value to market price is a quick trick for determining the difference between what a company is actually worth versus what the stock market thinks it is worth. Most people overlooked the discrepancy between book value and stock price. They panicked. They kept selling. Anyone who mastered their fear, and who reasoned that the worst of the worst was likely already factored into stock prices, was positioning to more than double their money.

By the summer of 2010, it was clear the worst of the financial crisis was over, due to unorthodox Federal Reserve policies, in concert with other central banks, to lower interest rates. At the time, Chris Davis, a mutual fund manager, put pen to paper. His fund, the Davis New York Venture Fund, was battered by bad investments in AIG, the global insurance company that was ultimately saved from failure by the U.S. government, and by Merrill Lynch, whose missteps led to its bargain-basement sale price to Bank of America.

He sent a letter to shareholders. He told them he could have done better for them, even though his fund's value had increased 100 percent since the stock market's low, and the stock market rose 90 percent. Davis could have let those returns speak for themselves, and no one would have questioned his acumen, but he did not. "Our costliest mistakes during this financial crisis may well be the investments we failed to make when others were panicking," Davis said.[1] He was thinking of Wells Fargo. The bank stock plummeted to about $8 per share during the worst of the credit crisis. American Express fell to about $10. At the time, many reasonable people felt financial stocks could go much lower. They did not. The prices stopped declining. "Had we added less than 1 percent of the fund to each position, we would have more than made up the cumulative losses we suffered in AIG. Such mistakes of omission are rarely discussed and yet, as the preceding example shows, they can be just as costly to long-term returns," Davis said.[2] By May 2011, Wells Fargo's stock traded at $29, an increase of some 260 percent. American Express's stock rose some 400 percent to $50. The gains illustrate how fear is often a divining rod that leads to opportunities. Fear is an investor's friend. Master fear or be mugged by fear.

Bad news panics unseasoned investors. They cease to think. They react. Individuality is gone. The crowd moves as one. All stocks are viewed as bad. No one thinks of the stocks' individual merits. In a correction, everyone rushes through the same door. Big declines change the fundamental composition of the market. People sell based on emotional reactions to the news, which is exacerbated by the crowd's behavior. Fear causes rational people to ignore the financial facts that shape the prices of stocks. When fear defines the perception of stocks rather than rational analysis, it is often a call to action. Most people want to sell. Instead, they should buy. Herein lies another market truth: Buy fear and sell confidence. That is what good traders and investors do. This seemingly odd discipline creates profits for the bold just as surely as it creates losses for investors who panic and sell. This discipline also can help minimize losses. The natural tendency is to sell in a massive market decline. But if you bought the stock for a specific reason—it pays a dividend, sales are rising, the company is financially healthy—there is little reason to panic when the crowd convulses with fear. All you are doing is selling at a low price what you bought high. Who profits? Wall Street. Who loses? You.

It is usually best to do nothing if the stock market breaks lower, and you failed to anticipate the decline. It is usually better to sit back, suffer, and wait. You will usually be rewarded for your patience and emotional discipline.

The reason is simple. Massive selling usually indicates that everyone has sold. In the absence of selling, stocks stop falling. Even the slightest amount of buying can lift stock prices. All of this might seem insane, but it describes "contrarianism," the primary intellectual and emotional discipline that runs through the financial market and defines many of the best investors.

Contrarians often do the opposite of everyone else. Some sophisticated investors argue that they are not contrarians. They say they simply do not care what other people do or think. They say they are so focused on their research and analysis that they are almost oblivious to what occurs around them.

"What's the personality of the most successful investors? They aren't affected by other people's feelings. In fact, the most empathetic people I know are the worst investors," says William Bernstein, a neurologist, who manages money for Efficient Frontier Advisors.[3] As a foundation, as an emotional anchor in the stock market, contrarianism is a good starting point. You will ultimately customize your approach as you learn more about the markets, and how you react to pressures, and analyze opportunities. Contrarianism will help temper you against fear and alert you to greed like sonar in a submarine.

Learn this way of thinking and you just might break yourself of the habit of panicking and selling based on the stock market's knee jerk reactions. DALBAR's research shows investors are perpetually out of step with the market. Contrarianism can help you understand the market's rhythms and how to invest according to its beat.

Understanding contrarianism will save you money. It will keep you from making the mistakes and emotional reactions that harm most amateur investors. "Most people react after the fact. If they see on the cover of *Time* magazine that the market is going up, they buy, and when there's a correction, they panic and sell," says Glenn Dubin, portfolio manager of Highbridge Capital, a hedge fund.[4]

In the markets, it rarely pays, at least not for long, to be like most people. Rather than selling when everyone else is selling, a contrarian buys. When everyone is buying, a contrarian sells. The idea works. As Humphrey B. Neill, the father of contrarian investing, is wont to say: "the public is right during the trends, but wrong at both ends!"[5]

Remember the dark days of February and March 2009. The Standard & Poor's 500 Index was at its lowest level of the credit crisis. Almost every investor in the world was panicked. Daily news reports were so gloomy it seemed the very fabric of modern society was unraveling. Major banks, including Goldman Sachs, and even General Electric (GE), were increasingly identified as being in danger of failing. Everyone seemed to be selling. But far from the crowd, legions of contrarians were asking themselves how much worse could it get? If everything was priced for failure, they reasoned failure was not probable. It was unlikely that GE would fail, or Goldman Sachs, or Morgan Stanley, or hundreds of other companies whose stock prices had fallen to unusually low prices. Those prices reflected panic—not the fundamental earnings power of the company.

Contrast this widespread feeling of fear with the mood in July 2007, when the Dow Jones Industrial Average first crossed 14,000. Many investors thought stock prices would go even higher. They waited. They hoped. Very few sold to take profits. They didn't want to miss the next surge, and the chance to make even more money. They held on even when the stock market fitfully tumbled lower. And when the market finally fell with a thud, millions of investors panicked and sold their stock.

Seasoned investors stayed calm during the darkest hours. They bought as much stock as they could. They reasoned the stock market was unlikely to fall any further. After all, how much worse could it get? The bad news created an unprecedented buying opportunity. The stock market soon began an historic rally. The Standard & Poor's 500 Index rose 86.3 percent from its March 11, 2009 low of 721.33 to a February 18, 2011 high of 1,344.07. Many investors missed much of the rebound because they sold at the wrong time.

"You want to be greedy when others are fearful and you want to be fearful when others are greedy. It's that simple," Warren Buffett says.[6] The irony of Buffett's statement is that he made it on national TV in early October 2008, during the worst of the financial crisis. Anyone who heard the interview, and millions likely did, had time to reflect and act. It is clear that very few paid attention as investors continued to panic and sell for another six months. The stock market finished convulsing sometime in March of the following year. To this day, Buffett remains frequently quoted, and rarely imitated.

The Theory of Contrary Opinion

Though contrarianism may seem like a way to time the stock market simply by doing the opposite of everyone else, it is not. Simply going against the crowd is being disagreeable for the sake of disagreeableness. Sometimes the crowd is wrong. Sometimes the crowd is right. Contrarianism is best used to add nuance to your thinking and as a tool to always question the crowd's thinking and actions. In an endeavor like investing, which invariably involves lots of people, you have to learn to deal with the mob to avoid being trampled by the mob. You have to develop mechanisms that help you question the mob's behavior. You need to retain your sanity against what former Federal Reserve

Chairman Alan Greenspan called irrational exuberance, the impulse that leads you to cease to think and mindlessly react and follow the crowd.

Bernie Schaeffer has spent decades studying contrarianism. His firm, Schaeffer's Investment Research in Cincinnati, Ohio, has made contrarian investing a hallmark of their investment process. Schaeffer says the central principle of contrarian investing is very basic, and very difficult to dispute. "When everyone is bullish, buying power has been exhausted. A top is at hand, and the next major move is down," he says. "When everyone is bearish, selling pressure has been exhausted, a bottom is at hand, and the next major move is up."[7]

The commentary that frames these market moves often offers great clues into the future. By reading newspapers, for example, you can tap into the mind of the mob. Kent Engelke, the chief economic strategist at Capitol Securities Management, says bull markets always end when there is not a cloud in the sky. He adds:

> I vividly remember some past "end of Bull Market statements" such as the economy has entered into a "new paradigm" where the business cycle is dead. Or Wall Street has diversified risk away via synthetic investment products and complicated asset management strategies. At the end of all bull markets the vast majority are euphoric and to heck with risk. Conversely bear markets end in great fear, lack of conviction and paralysis in making any investment decision outside of cash.[8]

Disagreement is a sign of a healthy bull market just as surely as sick markets are defined by unanimous opinion. The natural urge for most people is to join the comfort of the crowd. It feels good to effortlessly make money, and ride stock prices higher. It is somewhat addictive, but it always ends in tears.

Contrarianism will help you maintain a healthy skepticism. It will not give you a system to beat the stock market. It is not a crystal ball. It is nothing more than a way of thinking.

In other words, forget about being a bull or a bear. Find that which is right and proper based on the analysis of stocks and probabilistic thinking. Remember the old saying about playing poker. You are never playing for money. You are playing odds. If you are sitting around the poker table and you cannot figure out who the fool is, it is you. The same applies to investing.

A contrarian mind-set tempers widespread euphoria. It is a form of immunization against irrational exuberance.

Contrarianism is a way to help you think about the ends of trends. The twists and turns away from widespread enthusiasm for a stock, or a market, tend to be where many people stumble and falter, and give profits back to the market.

When the market turns, most people react too late because of a lack of sell discipline. They want to sell at the highest possible price—the ever-elusive last eighth. As Jesse Livermore, who in the 1920s was one of Wall Street's great speculators, has said: "One of the most helpful things that anybody can learn is to give up trying to catch the last eight—or the first. These two are the most expensive eighths in the world."[9]

When everyone thinks stock prices will continue to rise, it is a sign that just about everyone has spent all of their money buying stocks. When everyone is fully invested—they have no money left to spend on stocks—stock prices decline. The opposite is true when everyone is bearish and afraid that stock prices will fall. When everyone sells their stocks, it tends to happen all at once, as is indicated by sharp declines. After such widespread selling, stock prices tend to stall, an event called "bottoming," or "oversold." In the stillness after a major decline, stocks tend to bounce higher simply because the slightest amount of buying will lift prices and that again attracts some investors eager to catch the hoped-for recovery. Stock rebounds after a major correction are a well-known phenomenon in the market. It has a colorful name: dead-cat bounce.

"The difficult part lies in correctly identifying these situations and doing so in real time rather than after the fact," Schaeffer says.[10]

Exile on Wall Street

Many seasoned investors view the public as a reliable indicator of what not to do. "The masses are asses," one strategist said.

"The stock market is where smart people think of ways to take money from dumb people," a trader said.

"The majority must lose for the minority to win," a trader said.

"The stock market is a field of dreams," another strategist said.

"Losers always come back to Vegas," an options market maker said.

Those are harsh assessments, but they are backed by experience. The irrational crowd is a mainstay in financial history. The development of organized, financial markets helps magnetize the mob. The stock exchanges provide the architecture to support the mob's scope. Mass media increases the mob's velocity and ensures that everyone knows how much money can be made without much mention of how much could be lost. As Bernard Baruch noted in 1932:

> All economic movements, by their very nature, are moti-
> vated by crowd psychology. Graphs and business ratios are, of
> course, indispensable in our groping efforts to find dependable
> rules to guide us in our present world of alarms. Yet, I never
> see a brilliant economic thesis expounding, as though they
> were geometrical theorems, the mathematics of price move-
> ments, that I do not recall Schiller's dictum: "anyone taken as
> an individual is tolerably sensible and reasonable—as a mem-
> ber of a crowd, he at once becomes a blockhead."[11]

This has been proven for hundreds of years. The first financial bubble arguably began in Holland, in 1634, over tulips of all things. The tulip, whose name according to Charles Mackay, the great chron- icler of crowd hysteria, was taken from a Turkish word that means tur- ban, became very popular with the wealthy in Holland. The flower was de rigueur for anyone who aspired to be a person of wealth and taste. Soon, the rage reached the middle class, Mackay says, and mer- chants and shopkeepers wanted to own the rarest tulips.

In 1634, the rage among the Dutch to possess tulips was so great that the ordinary industry of the country was neglected, and many peo- ple got into the tulip trade. As the mania increased, so did prices, By 1636, tulips traded on the stock exchanges of Amsterdam, Rotterdam, Haarlem, Leyden, Alkmaar, Hoorn, and elsewhere. In small towns that lacked exchanges, tulips were traded in the main tavern. Eventually, tulips also traded on London's stock exchange, and Paris, though the Dutch paid more than anyone.[12] Stockbrokers sensed opportunity. They manipulated the market and drove prices higher and lower. They made great profits buying when prices fell, and selling when they rose. The amount of money that was being made was fantastic. People began doing everything possible to raise money so they could buy tulips. The mania jumped Holland's borders and spread throughout Europe. Soon, tulip-mad speculators began pouring money into Holland. Everyone was involved, from the chimney sweeps to the nobility. Finally, and seemingly suddenly, Mackay says the rich stopped buying expensive tulips for their gardens. Dealers panicked. Prices plummeted. Mackay says:

> Many who, for a brief season, had emerged from the humbler walks of life were cast back into their original obscurity. Substantial merchants were reduced almost to beggary and many a representative of noble line saw the fortunes of his house ruined beyond redemption.[13]

When all seemed lost, people who had lost money asked the Dutch government for help. The government's rescue plan entailed canceling all contracts prior to November 1636, which was when prices peaked, and that every deal made thereafter would have its price adjusted to 10 percent of the agreed price. Naturally, there were breach of contract lawsuits. Ultimately, the matter was sent to the Provincial Council of The Hague. Not much really came of that; prices tumbled lower, and soon people forgot how much the tulips had once been worth. Now tulips are mostly remembered for their beauty, and few people remember that tulip mania provided a framework for all the other manias and bubbles that were yet to come.

These manias have been well catalogued elsewhere, but let us not forget that prior to the Great Crash of 1929, few thought that stock prices could decline. Many people back then bought stocks on margin, effectively borrowing money from banks, because they thought that stock prices would keep rising. In 1929, nearly $4 of every $10 that banks loaned were spent on stocks. Corporations even

made stock loans, including General Motors and John D.
Standard Oil. By October 1929, everything came crashing ᴜᴜ

Since then, the crowd has gone mad for Internet stocks, whicn
would supposedly change the world, and houses, which everyone
could afford to own and whose prices would never decline. All crises are different, but they share an important characteristic, which
MacKay identified after a study of manias:

Men, it has been well said, think in herds; it will be seen that they
go mad in herds, while they only recover their senses slowly, and one
by one.[14]

Robert J. Shiller, a Yale economist, is something of a modern-day
Mackay. He wrote a well-known book, *Irrational Exuberance,* on the irrational exuberance of investors. Shiller thinks financial bubbles should be
diagnosed like mental disorders. Just as psychiatrists use the *Diagnostic
and Statistical Manual of Mental Disorders* to better understand patients,
Shiller has created a methodology to diagnose financial bubbles.

- Sharp price increases, such as occurred in real estate or Internet stocks.
- Great public excitement about those price increases.
- A media frenzy.
- Stories of people making lots of money, causing widespread envy among others.
- Public is increasingly interested in the asset class.
- "New era" theories justify unprecedented price increases.
- A decline in lending standards.[15]

The Media Is the Message

Woe often awaits investors when a major magazine makes a bold statement on its front page.

The classic example is *BusinessWeek*'s "Death of Equities" cover
story from August 1979. The cover story marked the beginning of a
massive, historic bull market. The article pulled together the collective
wisdom of another generation's market pundits as it confronted massive
inflation—oil prices had increased by 60 percent, and inflation was on

the rise. Housing was identified as the most popular inflation hedge in America. The world was upside down. Before inflation took hold in the 1960s, *BusinessWeek* reported that the total return on stocks had averaged 9 percent a year for more than 40 years, while nearly riskless AAA bonds rarely paid more than 4 percent. "Today the situation has reversed, with bonds yielding up to 11 percent and stocks averaging a return of less than 3 percent throughout the decade."[16]

The cover story seemed sparked by a change in the previous month, to the rules that governed pension funds. The U.S. Department of Labor, which regulated such things, was allowing pension funds to invest in assets other than just listed stocks and high-grade bonds. For the first time, pension funds could invest in the shares of small companies, real estate, commodities futures contract, and even gold and diamonds. *BusinessWeek* recognized that the change could lead to higher investment returns for pensioners whose accounts had suffered from years of inflation. The primary drawback to the decision, according to the magazine, was that it was yet another bad development for the stock market.

Sound, serious men fretted.

Robert S. Salomon Jr., a general partner at Salomon Brothers— that generation's Goldman Sachs—told the magazine: "We are running the risk of immobilizing a substantial portion of the world's wealth in someone's stamp collection."[17]

The article's dark conclusion was that "the institutionalization of inflation" and structural changes in communications and psychology— killed the U.S. equity market for millions of people.

The article's author told readers that "the old attitude of buying solid stocks as a cornerstone for one's life savings and retirement has simply disappeared. To support his assertion, he anonymously quoted a young U.S. executive. "Have you been to an American stockholders' meeting lately? They're all old fogies. The stock market is just not where the action's at."[18] The magazine's cover story marked a turning point. At the time, the Dow Jones Industrial Average was floundering around 850. "It was virtually the bottom of one of the most spectacular equity rallies in all history," says Art Cashin, UBS' director of floor trading at the New York Stock Exchange.[19] From 1979 to 2000, the Dow Jones Industrial Average increased more than 1,076 percent, peaking around 10,000, when the Internet bubble burst amidst another generation's conclusion that the old rules no longer applied and that we were living in a new paradigm in which technology made it possible for the economy to grow far faster than the historical 3 percent growth rate.

Interest in *Business Week*'s "Death of Equities" story peaked again during the 2007 to 2009 credit crisis. It was then much in vogue to say that equities were dead. Bloomberg, which had bought *Business Week*, reposted the article on the Internet on March 10, 2009—which coincided with the start of a massive two-year stock market rally.

Cashin says ideas that get too popular, or too conventional, get tripped up. "That's part of the contrary basis of the contrary axiom that once an idea makes the 'cover' of a popular magazine that idea is about to be reversed," he says.[20]

One Florida stockbroker takes the magazine cover indicator to a new level. He uses the *Economist* and *Business Week* to help him sort out smart money and dumb money. When the magazines arrive at his office, the broker rips the covers off, throws away the actual magazines, pins the covers to his wall, and uses them to track investor sentiment. The *Economist* offers the upscale view; *Business Week* serves the dumb money.

Media Misreads Google

Consider Google and the press coverage of Google's 2004 initial public offering (IPO)—when it sold stock for the first time. It is surprising to see how much skepticism existed on Wall Street and in the financial press. Weeks before the IPO, Stephen Wozniak, a cofounder of Apple, told the *New York Times* that he would not buy Google stock because experience proves that a few people make out big, and that he didn't think the stock's price would likely rise much in the future. Google's stock was priced at $85 for the IPO. The offering raised $1.67 billion and valued the company at $23.1 billion. The *New York Times* warned readers of Google's "bubbly" valuation. "Only time will tell if the company can fend of efforts by Yahoo! and Microsoft to build superior search engines," the *Times* intoned in an editorial. By 2011, Microsoft and Yahoo! were practically has-been stocks compared to Google.[21]

Time magazine warned readers before the IPO: "Google's IPO: Buyer Beware." *Newsweek* confidently said: "This price is insane. And anyone buying Google as a long-term investment at $109.40 will lose money."[22]

Wall Street's analysts, who are often the primary sources for most financial news reports, were just as bearish. On October 13, 2004, when the stock was trading above $140, only 30 percent of the analysts who follow Google stock rated it as "buy," while 60 percent rated the stock as "hold," and 10 percent rated the stock as "sell." Schaeffer said:

> What we had here was a classic case of investor disbelief, despite the acknowledged strengths of the company and despite very strong post-IPO price action that quickly left the offering price of $85 in the dust. Of course, as the shares continued their amazing ascent and the company continued to outgrow expectations, we moved fairly quickly into the acceptance stage and ultimately to euphoria.[23]

By late May 2005, Google was at $260 and 80 percent of analysts rated the stock as "buy." By early March 2007, before the stock peaked at $747, every analyst who followed Google rated the stock at "buy."[24]

Schaeffer said the sweet spot for a contrarian bullish position was from the August 2004 IPO to November 2004, when less than half the analysts rated Google as "buy." He says the stock could have been held even longer on the grounds that Wall Street was catching up with the facts driving Google's stock, but the exit sign was hung over the stock when everyone rated it at "buy."

Paulson's Gamble

Media effectively calls market tops, or bottoms, because it is an information sponge. When reporters call the so-called experts, the experts pontificate. This is a type of show business. The same market commentators are often quoted over and over by the financial press. This is one reason why many financial stories are similar in tone, and thrust. This is why it is important to look for the footprints in the market that pave the way toward consensus which, history shows, inevitably collapses under its own weight.

One could write a book about market indicators, and some have, but at some point one must take a stand or fall victim to having so much information as to be able to justify or rebut any point of view. Shiller's bubble checklist is a good starting point, but the best contrarian indicator is common sense. Common sense is usually the most uncommon virtue among investors.

When John Paulson, at the time an unknown hedge fund manager, began questioning the rapid rise of U.S. housing prices in 2005, people thought he was nuts. When he made $4 billion in a year, people thought he was brilliant. His journey from ass to Adonis is the perfect parable for investors developing a contrarian discipline.

Paulson made the single and perhaps greatest contrarian investment in the history of the free market because he did not believe Wall Street's status quo opinion that U.S. housing prices never experienced a nationwide decline. He decided to check it out for himself. He examined housing data. He found the data Wall Street used to justify its view on housing prices only went back to World War II. He went back further. "You had to go back to the Great Depression to find a period when home prices declined nationally. They were not factoring that scenario into their analysis."[25] He asked the banks about this. They told him that even if housing prices reached zero, that it was likely to be a temporary aberration and that housing price growth would soon resume. So, Paulson reviewed the very methodology Wall Street had used to analyze the housing market. He learned the data relied on nominal prices—which is misleading because it includes inflation. Nominal growth was high in 1970s because of double-digit inflation, but Paulson says real growth was low. When he converted nominal prices into real prices, and took that back 25 years, he found that home prices, at least in his recorded history, never rose as fast as they did in 2000 to 2005. "Our opinion was they were overvalued and they were going to correct and that the quality of mortgages was very poor and the losses would be rather likely very substantial," he said.[26]

He began assembling his own complicated investments that would increase in value if the housing market imploded. After the crisis crested, Congressional investors asked him if he ever shared his views with banks or rating agencies. His answer shows the inner works of his investment mind. Paulson said:

I was not after convincing the research department that they're wrong, I'm right. I was trying to do our own analysis to make our own conclusions to make investment decisions for our firm and try to understand why other people had contrary view-points. My goal was not to convince them that I'm right or they're wrong but to understand what they were doing and how we thought things differently and what the rational for that was. Most of them, when we did express our viewpoints, thought we were inexperienced, were novices in the mortgage mar-ket. We were very, very much in the minority. If I said we were 1,000 to 1, we were the one; that would be the scenario. Even friends of ours thought we were so wrong they felt sorry for us.[27]

The Financial Crisis Commission investigators asked him why everyone thought he was wrong. Paulson said:

There had never been a default of an investment grade mort-gage security and I'll qualify that except I think for manufac-tured housing in the early 90s in California. Aside from that small datapoint there had never been a default of investment grade mortgages and that house prices had never declined nationally so they just didn't see. And the actual loss rates in the time period were so far below the level that would impair any mortgage security they just didn't see any problem at all in the sector.[28]

The natural question is why did Paulson even think to doubt the consensus view of the housing market. Mostly, it had to do with a sense of history. He was born in 1954. He had lived through enough financial history to recognize cycles. He saw the 1990 credit default cycle triggered by Drexel Burnham Lambert's failure. The firm, which was dominated then by Michael Milken, invented high-yield bonds. He remembered bond defaults of Enron and Worldcom, too. "Going through cycles and being slightly older, I subscribed to the view that both the credit market and the housing market were cyclical and both housing and credit appeared to be at a peak in terms of quality and pricing and could be ready for a fall," Paulson said.[29]

Buffett's Goldman Trade

Not everyone has the skill to bet stocks, or markets, will fall. Most people are more comfortable betting that prices will rise. Placing wagers in the midst of a crisis scares most people. In late September 2008, during the height of the credit crisis, when no one wanted anything to do with banks, Warren Buffett invested $5 billion in Goldman Sachs. At the time, Lehman Brothers, the world's fourth-largest investment bank, had declared bankruptcy. The U.S. government had taken over Fannie Mae and Freddie Mac, and bailed out American International Group. In a two-part deal, Buffett's company, Berkshire Hathaway, spent $5 billion on "perpetual" preferred shares that paid a 10 percent dividend. Buffett also got warrants—essentially contracts that convert into stock—to buy $5 billion of Goldman common stock at $115 a share. At the time, the $115 price was 8 percent below Goldman's $125.05 stock price. The *Wall Street Journal* heralded the investment as "one of the biggest expressions of confidence in the financial system since the credit crisis intensified early this month." When Goldman repaid the loan in March 2011, Buffett's profit totaled $1.7 billion, or about $190,000 a day. It pays to buy fear.

Fading the News

Not all trades must be made in environments of pure fear. Chris Davis selectively makes contrarian investments in his Davis New York Venture Fund. "These often involve controversial situations where the market is discounting a company's share price to reflect a perception of risk we think is greater than the probable economic risk to the business's long-term fundamentals," Davis says.[30]

Sometimes, his clients have trouble understanding the logic because the companies are often the subject of negative newspaper articles and broadcast media reports. "But it is precisely because so many other investors automatically sell companies with near-term challenges, however surmountable, that the potential for high returns exists in many such instances," Davis adds.[31]

Consider Moody's, a major credit ratings agency. The company was perceived to be at the center of the credit crisis, and it was the subject of many critical news stories. The company rated mortgage securities, many of which proved to be not nearly as safe as the ratings suggested. Yet, some investors thought that others were overreacting to the bad news and near constant stream of negative headlines—a phenomenon known as headline risk. But anyone who could look past media coverage could see that Moody's business fundamentals were sound, and the company was financially healthy. Besides, Moody's was one of the few firms anywhere in the world that offered credit rating and related services. As traders took advantage of the negative news flow, and jerked around the stock, fundamental investors had a chance to buy when everyone else was afraid.

Moody's stock did indeed ultimately recover. The cloud of bad news hovered above for a long time, but sooner or later investors began to conclude that all of the bad news was priced into the stock. This shift in sentiment even protected the stock from an April 2011 report of the U.S. Senate Permanent Subcommittee on Investigations that concluded the rating agencies tried to win business prior to the financial crisis by offering the most favorable ratings to complex mortgage products. The report was ancient news to investors. They had reached that conclusion long ago, reacted appropriately, and readjusted that strange concoction of fear and greed that is so critical to the final determination of stock prices.

Chapter 4

The Anatomy of Information

S hortly after Al Qaeda terrorists flew jetliners into the World Trade Center, Donald Rumsfeld, then President George W. Bush's Defense Secretary, was at a press conference. A reporter asked him for evidence Iraq was providing weapons of mass destruction to terrorist groups. The reporter said reports suggested no evidence of direct links between Iraq's government and terrorists. The Rumsfeldian response:

> Reports that say that something hasn't happened are always inter-esting to me, because as we know, there are known knowns; there are things we know we know. We also know there are known unknowns; that is to say we know there are some things we do not know. But there are also unknown unknowns—the ones we don't know we don't know. And if one looks

throughout the history of our country and other free countries, it is the latter category that tends to be the difficult ones.[1]

Wall Street immediately took ownership of Rumsfeld's informational taxonomy. Ever since, it has ordered the mass of information on Wall Street.

A known known is information already known about a stock. This includes previous earnings reports, Securities and Exchange Commission filings, historical stock performance, investment ratings, shareholder information, ongoing litigation, historical financial ratios, including return on equity, book value, and all the other mathematical formulas that measure stocks. In short, anything easily learned about a stock is probably a known known. Known knowns are typically harmless, historical facts that are as well known by serious investors as their own birthdates. Known knowns are found by looking at publicly available information on a company and its stock. This is the bedrock of all financial decisions. Specialized financial data companies own and operate massive databases to provide investors with known knowns, for instance, price-to-earnings ratios, dividend yields, earnings estimates, and historical earnings reports. Known knowns are the foundation of a stock's price, and are already reflected in the price. If you understand the past, you have a better chance of predicting the future, which is the primary focus of investing.

Known unknowns are more exotic than known knowns. Most of Wall Street's efforts are focused on determining if known unknowns are bullish or bearish. Known unknowns are events expected to happen in the future that will make or lose you money. Known unknowns include pending corporate earnings reports, investor meetings, new product launches, retail sales data, Federal Reserve interest rate decisions, economic reports, including gross domestic product (GDP) reports, employment data, inflation data, housing prices, Institute for Supply Management reports, and just about anything else known to occur but whose outcome is unknown. Known unknowns are the primary concern of all investors. Figuring out what may happen when a company reports quarterly earnings or how the stock market might react to economic data is the essence of trading and informed investing. Enormous intellectual firepower is applied to this endeavor. Tens of thousands of people are engaged in gathering corporate information, and all matter of financial and economic data, to figure out what might happen. These financial facts are instantaneously incorporated into stock and bond prices, or dismissed as financial flotsam. When a known unknown becomes a known known, stock prices are quickly adjusted. "Buy on mystery, sell on history," is the lyrical description of the process in London's financial market. The world's great diseases, including cancer, would probably be eradicated if a fraction of Wall Street's brainpower was diverted to humanitarian endeavors.

Increasingly, the business of reacting to known unknowns is done by computer programs that also buy and sell stocks, and futures contracts, based on keywords in news stories. These algorithms operated by hedge funds and market-making firms convert words into computer codes that are devoid of emotion and able to make decisions on patterns the human mind has difficulty tracking. The news algorithms know that 10 negative news stories cause a specific reaction in a stock. They know this because many major news organizations have sold their news archives to investment firms that have then parsed them with computers to find hidden patterns.

Unknown unknowns are waking financial nightmares that defy human imagination. Examples include the 9/11 attacks that toppled the World Trade Towers in 2001, the 2008 bankruptcy of Lehman Brothers, Japan's 2011 nuclear disaster caused by a tidal wave that was triggered by an earthquake, and the 2010 flash crash when the Dow Jones Industrial Average dropped some 1,000 points in about 20 minutes. Unknown unknowns are also called black swans. Nassim Taleb, the chronicler of coal-colored cygnets, describes them as profound impacts understood after they happen. Such was the case of Long Term Capital Management (LTCM), a hedge fund that was destroyed in 1998 by a black swan despite the fact that it was advised by Nobel Prize winning economists and a portfolio manager who was then considered an exceptionally shrewd trader. All of their collective brainpower and experience was compressed into a computer program. The computer formulas profitably predicted most market movements, yet it never anticipated that a major nation, such as Russia, would default on its debt. When Russia did just that, the black swan emerged, toppling LTCM. That unknown event turned

LTCM's trading positions into a Gordian knot that not even the best traders and most advanced computer programs could unravel. The U.S. Federal Reserve and Wall Street banks rescued the fund, and saved the world's markets from a massive crisis. No one seemed to learn anything constructive from the experience. The main lesson taken away by Wall Street's leaders seems to be that they could pursue profits and let others worry about the risk should trades explode. Many of the Wall Street leaders who rescued LTCM were among the great tragic actors of the 2007 credit crisis.

Since the credit crisis, black swan spotting has become a cottage industry on Wall Street.

The challenge for investors is focusing on known unknowns, and preparing for unknown unknowns. This is essentially what Robert Rubin, the former Goldman Sachs chief and U.S. Treasury Secretary, calls probabilistic thinking. It is actually quite common to many seasoned investors who have insatiable appetites for information and learning. They read everything and this helps them focus on what they don't know and to assign odds to the outcome.

The Doors of Perception

Wall Street's accumulation, and application, of financial information rivals, and quite possibly exceeds, the efforts of major news organizations, and even many governments. It has been this way for centuries. The Rothschilds famously realized that information was better than money in the 1800s. They constructed a network of carrier pigeons and couriers to gather and ferry information across Europe. The Rothschild network was much faster than diplomatic and royal mail service. The family supposedly first learned Napoleon had been defeated at Waterloo, which naturally produced prodigious profits. An ingenious system also existed in revolutionary America.

In the earliest days of the United States, Philadelphia was the nation's financial capital, and the site of the nation's first stock exchange. European ships, laden with goods and market-moving information, docked in Manhattan some 85 miles away. The road to Philadelphia was often congested with speculators, stock-jobbers, agents of foreign investors, and others anxious to make use of the information at the Philadelphia Stock Exchange before anyone else learned the news. This was problematic for exchange members until, in 1790, the exchange's leaders implemented a clever solution worthy of Benjamin Franklin:

> The coups scored by these early commuters led a group of Philadelphia brokers to set up signal stations on high points across New Jersey. The signalmen watched through telescopes as coded flashes of light brought news of stock prices, lottery numbers and other important information. Relayed from station to station, the information could move from New York to Philadelphia in as little as 10 minutes, more quickly than any coach horse could run, so the system sharply narrowed the advantage of New York speculators. It remained in use until the arrival of the telegraph in 1846.[2]

Much has changed since then, save two critical facts: Information remains asymmetrical and the speed of information still influences profits. The asymmetry of information simply means someone always has more information than you. In any given market, or sector, there are probably 20 to 50 people who know everything that will happen before it occurs, or before it is announced. Those people have a global, multidimensional view. They can be executives, traders, investors, investment bankers, or a few very fine analysts that understand their companies' financials and dynamics as well as the executives who run the firms. Many of these people rarely speak publicly.

At the top of the information food chain are major investors, including top hedge funds and institutional investors, and some strategists and analysts at major banks, particularly Goldman Sachs, whose clients tend to be the world's top investors. That group tends to spot economic and corporate developments days, and often weeks, in advance of others. Speed of information matters. It provides a time-and-place advantage by allowing investors to be the first ones to invest or trade, and to benefit from the ensuing increase in prices that follow as others connect the dots and see the full picture. "Information is everything," says Dennis Davitt, a hedge fund manager. "The faster the market moves, and the faster trades travel over electronic wires, the more valuable good information becomes."[3]

Anatomy of Information

Market information mostly spreads through well-known, closely watched conduits. Corporate earning reports, economic reports, and corporate regulatory filings with the Securities and Exchange Commission are primary conduits. Financial media and bank analysts often amplify these reports just before they are scheduled for release, and after they have been reported. Of course, timing is everything. Even the analyst reports that are so widely remarked upon by financial media, and play such critical roles in the decisions of individual investors, are terribly dated. The reports are typically released on a tiered schedule. The best clients get the reports first. They get to trade first. Then the reports are sent to other clients. The media get the report the next day, or 15 minutes after everyone else, which in these fast, electronic markets means the next day. The media often bring in individual investors who buy and create opportunities for the bank's best customers to sell.

Information seeps into and through the market in various ways. Wall Street's information is organized in databases and news engines by stock ticker symbols and subject codes. A few keystrokes on a Bloomberg terminal instantly reveal everything known about a stock. Most people do not have access to Bloomberg terminals, which can cost $2,500 or more a month. These terminals can be standalone or part of the trading terminals customized by banks and hedge funds. They include 24/7 financial news services, among them, Dow Jones Newswires, Bloomberg, and Reuters.

The key information at the banks does not necessarily come from research reports produced by analysts. Increasingly, the best information on Wall Street comes from trading desks that trade stocks, bonds, and derivatives.

Unlike the typical analyst report that often focuses on historical information, trading desk reports usually includes the all-important look ahead. An analyst note might summarize what is expected ahead of a corporate earnings report. A trading desk note will reveal if investors are bullish or bearish and what they are doing in anticipation of the earnings report. Trading desk notes are rarely shared with ordinary investors, media, or anyone else. Banks send trading desk reports to their best customers. The reports are distributed each day, and often throughout the day, detailing what is happening in the market and how clients, or competitors, are positioning their accounts in the stock, bond, and options markets. Everyone wants to be on those distribution lists (DLs). The reports are often e-mailed by traders via their Bloomberg terminals. The Bloomberg terminals are universally used as Wall Street's central database. These e-mails often bear no resemblance to media and analyst reports.

In comparison to trading desk notes, news reports often seem like noise, which actually is an economic term that describes information with no value. Some investors and traders will not read newspapers or watch TV. They think they are a distraction. Instead, they use news services, such as Street Account, which sends email bursts of information to BlackBerry devices. Traders, strategists, and analysts can then respond to the information in real time by bringing to bear their knowledge of stock trading, volatility, credit default swaps, bonds, and other specialized information that will give them—and their best clients—an edge over everyone else. Even this pales in comparison to the high-speed computers that parse the news and take the numbers or facts and themes and use them to update highly complex computer models used to buy and sell stocks and bonds and commodities, like some Wall Street version of Watson, the IBM computer that can reason and beat someone at *Jeopardy*. The mistake many investors make is overly relying on most of the business press to safely point the way. There is no magic formula, no alchemist's amulet, that anyone can offer you to give you free and unfettered passage through the markets. As one hedge fund trader said: If you put a big pot of money across the room, traders will find the fastest way to get there. Usually, this means they run right over you.

Real-Time Library

Both the stock market and successful investors function like an online library that is constantly cataloging and updating information. The sum total of human knowledge on endeavors spanning from agriculture and automobiles to energy and retailing to technology and finance and medicine and pharmaceuticals is found in the market. These views are expressed in the price of stocks, bonds, commodities, and derivatives. Risk is also a measure of the totality of an investor's knowledge. The more one knows, the better able risk can be assessed. The more you know, the easier it is to recognize value. And that helps determine if the market price is attractive or not. By the time anything is discussed, or reported, by financial media, price has typically trumped value. Think of value like a gold mine. Value is invisible to most people. Value is quiet, it is not flashy, and it is uncovered by analysis much like miners digging for gold. Value is not the purview of financial media. The media is concerned with prices and events that have happened, or are known to be happening in the near future. By the time a stock is featured in a major media story or broadcast, value has all but disappeared, and momentum has taken control.

Twitter

It is easy to be overwhelmed by financial information. The key is knowing who to listen to, and who to ignore. Twitter, a social media network, helps investors separate good information from bad information. Launched in the summer of 2006, Twitter is changing the way Wall Street communicates. Tweets, as posts are called, are limited to 140 characters. The brevity encourages sharp, concise thought. Unlike newspapers or TV, Twitter tends to quickly convey the key points, while offering the chance to click through embedded links that lead to longer pieces. This makes Twitter especially useful for sorting and identifying data. Better still, you can control your information streams by deciding who to follow and who can follow you. Better yet, Twitter seems to encourage intelligent dialogues among users. Twitter lets you share information with other people with similar or diverse interests. This takes a bit of fine-tuning, but you can almost recreate the instant-messaging network hedge fund and investment bank traders use to communicate with each other throughout the day. In fact, many traders, strategists, influential bloggers, and even Jack Welch, the former chief executive of General Electric are on Twitter.[4] If you think this is stuff for kids, you are wrong. Twitter influences stock and options trading. "Since brokers have to save instant messages and e-mail, but thus far have no such mandate for tweets, well, you can guess that the far more discreet traffic is on Twitter," says Jon Najarian, of Trademonster. com, a brokerage firm. For example, Najarian first heard on Twitter news that Matrixx Initiatives' Zicam nasal spray allegedly damaged people's sense of smell. "Guys started tweeting and the stock dropped from $19 to $13," he says.[5]

Though some companies are trying to mine Twitter as an indication of investor sentiment than can be used to wager if stocks will rise or fall, most people are just best served using Twitter to get smarter about investing and tap into a potential gulfstream of useful financial information. If you still think Twitter is irrelevant to the market consider that the Federal Reserve Bank of New York in September 2011 solicited proposals from companies to monitor social media platforms, including Twitter, Facebook, blogs, forums and YouTube. The Fed wanted to track social media in different languages, and different countries, and geographical regions. The Fed wanted to monitor social media conversations and posts as they occurred. The social media listening platform, as the Fed detailed in a request for proposal, would monitor "billions of conversations and generate text analytics based on predefined criteria. They can also determine the sentiment of a speaker or writer with respect to some topic or document."[6]

The Future Is Now

While it is important to look to the past to contextualize the stock market, it is vitally important to realize that the stock market is a discounting mechanism. That odd phrase means that the stock market, and therefore sophisticated investors, always focus on the future, on the known unknowns. The market continually assigns odds, or discounts, the outcome of various events. The purpose of life in the market is trying to discern today tomorrow's price, and learning to recognize when fear and greed trump fundamentals. This bedrock fact, so commonly known by so many seasoned investors, is an unknown unknown for most others. Figuring out what tomorrow may bring is an all-consuming endeavor. At any moment, likely even now, thousands of computers are searching for invisible, profitable patterns hidden in trading data that exceed the computational ability of the human mind. Some investors are so determined to invest with an edge—some skill or piece of information that will give them an advantage over others—that they pursue potentially privileged information, as the 2011 trial of hedge fund manager Raj Rajaratnam proved. Rajaratnam, while working as Galleon Fund manager, used relationships with a Goldman Sachs board member and employees of technology companies to learn today tomorrow's corporate news.

The market always looks forward. Financial news frequently looks backward. By the time news media write an article, or prepare a broadcast, the optimal opportunity to invest or trade has passed. This is not necessarily the media's fault. Much of the developments occurring before major events are so specialized as to be mind-numbingly boring. Few people want to read about the filing of legal briefs or the machinations in a pharmaceutical drug approval process. They just want to know who won the lawsuit, if the Food and Drug Administration approved a drug, or if a company's earnings disappointed or exceeded expectations. Seasoned investors are different. They use each incremental advance to modulate their investments. They are focused on the process of events. This is how they monitor risk and maximize reward. They operate in real time, making decisions ahead of, and in reaction to, all of the links that form the chain of an event.

On Main Street, it is usually the exact opposite. Most people are unaware that a massive lag exists between the release of quality information and its arrival on Main Street. By the time John and Jane Investor read anything in the press or listen to it on TV, the game has changed. That is the tragedy. People think they are making smart, rational decisions in response to information. They rarely realize they are chasers of smoke. This is another reason why people perpetually buy high and sell low. They let news reports greed them into investments, and allow news reports to panic them out of investments. What separates the rock stars from the groupies is the time spent constantly pursuing information related to investing. That's all that seasoned investors do: They are informational vacuums that suck up data and news. They refine what they find. They put it on a scale, and they use it to instantly adjust the prices of stocks, bonds, credit default swaps, and all the other financial instruments that coalesce to create the modern financial market. Almost everyone else reads and reacts.

"I keep a running list of known unknowns that could roil specific stocks, or change the dynamics of a sector," says Steven Sosnick, the equity-risk manager at Timber Hill, one of the world's largest trading firms. "I factor these risks into our prices and positions. The list is updated daily. We know that some events—unknown unknowns— will occasionally surprise us, which is why we constantly focus on risk and avoiding significant losses."[7]

Most financial news reports—including earnings reports and economic data—relay the conclusions that Wall Street has long expected. So, by the time you read a news article, it is old hat on Wall Street. The bigger the event, the truer the old-hat rule is. Corporate earnings reports are wagered upon days, and sometimes weeks, before the reports are actually released. Wall Street analysts are in constant contact with major hedge fund and mutual fund managers. The reflex among many investors, especially hedge funds, is to use put and call options to speculate on an event. This creates a wave of bullish or bearish sentiment in a market that most investors do not follow. So when the actual earnings report is released, the options wave crashes into the stock market, often sending stock prices sharply higher or lower. The same pattern, with or without options trading, occurs for most every event that occurs in the stock market, including the outcome of court cases, the approval of pharmaceuticals, the introduction of new technologies, and just about anything else in the life cycle of a stock.

You must desensitize yourself to the news. You must learn to use the news and not let the news use you. You must be skeptical. Rarely is news a leading indicator that predicts what will happen. If you failed to anticipate the outcome, do not react violently to the results when they become known. Don't chase stock prices when they are sharply higher, nor panic and sell when prices are sharply lower. This is how seasoned investors operate.

Consider Warren Buffett's decision in August 2011 to invest in Bank of America. Prior to his investment, the stock was trading near its 52-week low. Investor sentiment was so negative that rumors crisscrossed the stock market that the U.S. Federal Reserve was committing $100 billion to bail out Bank of America, provided it agreed to merge with J.P. Morgan, with its fortress balance sheet. Media coverage of Bank of America prior to Buffett's deal was almost universally negative. Some traders even advised clients that Bank of America would be forced to raise as much as $50 billion to cover bad mortgages. In short, no one wanted to buy Bank of America stock. It was too risky. Bank of America was a piñata, and the bank's chief executive was widely mistrusted. A week or so prior to Buffett's investment, a major shareholder, Fairholme Capital, had arranged a conference call. Some 6,000 investors dialed in to ask Brian Moynihan, the chief executive, questions. That was highly unusual. No new information was thought to have been shared. The stock sank.

Yet, on the day Buffett's investment was announced, the media heralded his deal and the stock price gained more than 20 percent in intraday trading. The *Wall Street Journal* concluded that Buffett's investment was a vote of confidence in the bank's management. Perhaps, but the deal's terms were phenomenal. For $5 billion, Buffett got 50,000 preferred shares that paid a 6 percent annual dividend, and can be redeemed at a 5 percent premium. He also got warrants to purchase 700 million Bank of America shares at $7.14 each over the next 10 years. The financial details are dry and complicated, and the coverage reflected that. Still, investors bought the news and chased Buffett. Bank of America shares ended the week with a gain of more than 10 percent. Of course, since then, the shares promptly sank.

Show Business

Like any complicated enterprise, nothing works all the time—even the market's famed ability to handicap the future. Sometimes stuff happens that demands immediate action. Sometimes you will have to respond to news if the information changes the basic premise of why you bought a stock. You must use news reports as an opportunity to ask yourself one of the central questions of investing—is the reason you bought the stock still valid? Reports of criminal enterprises, a failed drug approval of a one-drug biotechnology company, and anything else that seriously harms a stock's viability are reasons to bail and take your loss or realize profits.

On Wall Street, there is a show business element to speaking with media. Lawyers and public relations people try to manage the process. Most often you hear bland, overly general statements about the stock market or specific companies.

Consider what happens when chief executives appear on CNBC. After CNBC publishes its broadcast schedule, unsophisticated investors sometimes bid up the stock because they think the CEO will say something meaningful. The CEO's stock price gains 1.86 percent in the two days leading up to the interview, according to J. Felix Meschke's research, an Arizona State University business school professor. Meschke studied 3,641 interviews of CEOs of 1,491 companies from 1999 to 2001. "The actual information content of these CEO interviews is usually quite low," he said. Ten days after the interview, the stock price declines 2.78 percent. "These results," says Meschke, "support the conjecture that enthusiastic public attention may move stock prices away from fundamentals and are consistent with the popular notion of media hype."[8]

He calls this "strong mean reversion," a key financial concept that describes how prices eventually return to their more normal patterns. Remember the rubber band theory of prices that was previously mentioned? When the rubber band is stretched, it snaps back, or reverts to the mean to use financial jargon. Prices and news events are similar. The news cycle often takes money from dumb investor who hear or read something and get excited and decide to buy something. Seasoned investors are more than happy to sell high, and wait for Dumb Money to inevitably panic and sell low that which they had bought high. In academic parlance, the Dumb Money is known as "noise traders." These are people with no special insights or skills who believe they have some advantage over professional risk-averse investors and traders. The natural question is how does the news influence stock trading patterns and what do investors need to know to make smarter decisions. The usual pattern is that bad news prompts a stock decline, then the stock price may soon resume its normal patterns, or stall. If the reason for the initial decline was not apocalyptic, investors and analysts eventually calm down and reapply a long-term view to the stock. Good news often sends stock prices sharply higher. Like bad news, prices typically normalize the next day or so; therefore, it is better to wait until after the surge of buyers to invest because the price often ebbs lower when the surge of buying is done. To act in the middle of the process is usually a mistake that demonstrates a misunderstanding of how the market operates.

Remember, invariably initial selling pressure gives way to bargain hunters who see opportunity in battered shares knocked down in price because momentum traders, or more aggressive investors, exited the scene when some expected outcome failed to materialize. The same is true with buying pressure. Sooner or later, buyers and sellers run out of money and stock prices stop rising or falling. That metric should be used with every news story that triggers an investment or trading idea. What's left to drive trading after an event has been confirmed or an anticipated outcome refuted? If the answer is nothing, wait and let market forces collide. Afterward, the stock price will likely settle. This common reaction is misunderstood by many people, who consistently lose money by greeding in or panicking out.

Words Are Weapons

The reflex to buy stocks at the wrong time for the wrong reason is well understood by seasoned investors. They use it to their advantage. They use it to minimize their own market mistakes. They use it to pawn off their bad investments to people who don't know any better. One of the most frequent tricks is *rumortrage*, a ruse that coincides with the rise of the Internet and inexpensive trading commissions. Rumortrage lets sophisticated investors buy low and sell high. To do this, they start a takeover rumor. This is surprisingly easy to do, and it is irresistible to naive investors. The chance to buy stock in a real takeover target is like winning the lottery on Wall Street because the acquiring company typically pays a premium price. Financial news organizations should be sophisticated enough to quash the rumor, but rumortrage takes advantage of the mechanics of the news business. No news organization wants to be scooped by competitors. A takeover scoop is a major win. Reporters know this, and so do rumortragers who insure that their hustle has several ingredients that satisfy legitimate news standards: unusual trading volume in the options and stock market, the requisite "no comment" on market speculation from the "takeover target," and at least one, but preferably two, people, often traders, who acknowledge the rumor's existence. Ideally, the rumor-stock occurs in a sector in which there was a recent merger. In such sectors, it is commonly understood that other companies often need to merge to regain pricing power, or compete against a bigger competitor. These traits add legitimacy to rumortrage.

A key way to distinguish rumortrage from real takeover trading is when the rumor hits the market. By Friday, after rumortragers have spent the week building their positions in stock and options, the market fills with stories that the rumor-stock company will be taken over by another company sometime over the weekend. Someone may contact a reporter or a specialized trading news services. Perhaps the options trading volume will be so large that it appears on unusual trading volume screens that scan the market, which is often enough to propel rumors into the market. Invariably, unusual options trading, which in the late 1990s emerged as a reliable predictor of corporate takeovers, is mentioned by a mainstream news service like Dow Jones Newswires, Bloomberg, or Reuters. Even before the story is reported, it has likely circulated across Wall Street on various services that cater to traders, including TradetheNews.com or Theflyonethewall.com. When a reporter calls someone to ask about the rumor, the person probably heard about it on one of those services, and, voila, the rumor is confirmed, it has legs, and soon the naive pay top dollars for the calls or stock that rumormongers had bought earlier in the week at sharply lower prices. On Monday, in the absence of a merger, the stock price drops. It is true that takeovers are often announced on Mondays, but real takeover deals are rarely leaked to the press.

"There are many unscrupulous traders who will circulate a rumor merely for the purpose of unloading an unwanted position to other unsuspecting traders," says Larry McMillan, president of McMillan Analysis Corporation, a Morristown, New Jersey, firm. "This is especially true after a stock has had bad news, if one then sees takeover rumors springing up. Some wire services require independent confirmation of a 'story' before it can be run, but I'm not sure all do. So there is always the chance that, if a stock appears as a rumor on one of the 'boutique' services, that it has been touted to that service by sellers. Hence, it is not a good idea to trust isolated, single-day rumors, but it is important to keep track of them."[9]

McMillan says three takeover rumors that occur close together are often a sign the takeover rumor might be true. Similarly, if a company says it is exploring "strategic alternatives," that often means the company's investment bankers are trying to sell the company.

Trust, but Verify

Information is a weapon on Wall Street. Words are used as artillery or camouflage. They attack and deceive. George Orwell's observation now applies to business. "Political language," he wrote in 1946, "is designed to make lies sound truthful and murder respectable, and to give an appearance of solidity to pure wind." Such is the language of business and Wall Street.[10]

Sharing information is not the purpose of language on Wall Street or corporate America. In commerce, where one invariably loses and someone else gains, language discloses information, and that is different than providing context or meaning.

According to Arthur Levitt, the former SEC chairman, most financial disclosures are designed to protect the provider of the information—not to inform readers. Levitt says this is because most issuers of equities, debt, and other investment instruments are afraid that if they wrote plainly, someone might understand what was at stake. "Imagine what would happen if a stock prospectus said: 'You could lose your shirt if you buy this'." Levitt adds:

This precise problem sparked some of the great scandals of the last financial crisis. Investments were packaged and sold without the kind of forthright disclosure that would have made plain their riskiness. They came with volumes of documentation, footnotes and disclaimers, but at the cost of clarity and focus. Generally, one could predict that the more documentation necessary to explain an investment, the more likely it was to fail.[11]

In other words, risk is inversely related to how much information is given about any investment. The more information provided about an investment, the riskier the investment.

Companies, and this includes anyone selling investment products, only say what is needed to protect themselves from lawsuits and to comply with regulatory requirements. Language often reflects the minimum standard mandated by regulatory bodies, such as the SEC. Even market regulators often misunderstand what actually transpires at the very companies they regulate. Congress knows this. Congress' investigative arm, the General Accounting Office (GAO) has even performed landmark studies that show the SEC is ill equipped to effectively regulate the markets. The SEC is chronically understaffed and at a major informational disadvantage to the companies it regulates. Some critics contend the SEC does not fully understand the impact of the trading rules that it passes, especially electronic trading systems. This has contributed to the enormous advantage some institutional investors have over everyone else.

The SEC is unable to approve basic exchange rules in a timely fashion, much less to determine if corporate reports are truthful or not. This is your problem, and that of every investor. Parsing language for clues into what is actually transpiring may seem extreme, perhaps paranoid, but even paranoids have enemies. Parsing language is simply recognizing that corporations use spin-doctors and corporate lawyers that, apparently, have a deep prejudice against clear and concise language. This mucks up public statements to the point that readers must have specialized knowledge to understand meanings revealed between the lines. Even annual reports, considered the key to understanding a corporation's regulatory filings and operations, are part public relations, part fact. The front of the report is little more than marketing material. The facts are buried in the financial statements and revealed in Management's Discussion and Analysis (MD&A).

The media often has a hard time scratching beneath the surface. Journalists must maintain relationships with sources. The number of people available to discuss a company is always limited. This is why many reporters speak to analysts at banks. The analysts follow companies in ways most reporters cannot. They tend to have closer relationships with companies than reporters. The analysts often talk the company line. This is a kind of silent trade. They get better access to information, or at least have the ability to clarify information, and they get executives to come see their clients and tell the story. Road shows—also called marketing trips—crisscross the globe each and every day. Companies know which analysts understand their point of view, or share the view. They sometimes try to guide reporters to those analysts, and create a feedback loop that reinforces the company line. Anytime you hear an analyst echoing the company line, make a note. It could be a sign that the analyst is trying to curry favor with the company. Good reporters and analysts avoid this. They try to peer deep beyond a company's mumbo jumbo to understand supply chains and customers and to contextualize corporate speak.

After the credit crisis, it was common on Wall Street to think of corporate executives as pathological liars. Such was the experience with Lehman Brothers, which allegedly used accounting tricks to mask its true financial condition, and with many other companies that tried convincing investors of their long-term merits despite the short-term perils. Ultimately that proved insurmountable. Clearly, some executives are liars. The honesty problem in corporate America has likely to do with how executives are compensated. The bulk of their compensation is in stock options—if the stock rises the executives are worth more money.

This may explain why many CEOs seem like Narcissus of Greek mythology. The boy was so enamored with his beauty that he stared at his reflection in a pool of water, only to fall in and drown. Executive compensation has seemingly done the same for the senior management of many companies, especially chief executives. They often seem increasingly like stock promoters, more focused on the short-term stock movements of their stocks than the long-term performance of their companies. By some measures, the CEOs of a Standard & Poor's 500 company keep their jobs for about five years, which happens to also be the length of a stock market cycle. CEOs are compensated with stock to supposedly align their interest with shareholders. It is not clear that really happens. Instead, the primary outcome appears to be the creation of a massively wealthy cadre of corporate executives whose lives bear no resemblance to most, including the bulk of their shareholders. It is likely that some CEOs fall in love with their stocks and lose perspective. Because many CEOs lead their companies for only one stock market cycle that witnesses the birth of a bull market, its death, and its rebirth, it seems logical, and entirely human, that CEOs are heavily focused on their own compensation, especially their company's stock price. The stock price ultimately impacts the value of what may prove the most lucrative time of their career. The common CEO complaint that Wall Street's suffers from short-term focus, not long-term results, rings hollow. Current compensation practices seem to insure that CEOs are as focused on short-term stock movements, as any institutional investor who measures success, and thus his own compensation, in increments of three months to a year. The cycle is vicious. Executive stock compensation can arguably turn corporate executives into boiler-room stock salesmen in expensive suits. Carefully scripted by public relations and investor relations specialists, CEOs ultimately focus only on the best attributes of their companies, and downplay any risks. Rather than communicating, they convince. Rather than candidly discussing issues facing their companies, they spin. Think of this as the Kool-Aid theory of business. Corporations brew their Kool-Aid to serve to investors, analysts, regulators, and other constituencies. Corporate communication takes on the tint of a political campaign. The only nod to something other than a rising stock price is the safe harbor disclosure, a boilerplate that essentially says the future is uncertain. After near continual repetition of corporate talking points and the pageantry of office, the corporate Kool-Aid seemingly becomes reality. Bad things often follow. Almost 60 years ago, C. Wright Mills, an astute sociologist of power, worried about the corrosive effect of dissembling facts for popular consumption. In *The Power Elite*, his classic study of power, he noted:

> Moreover, most American men of affairs have learned well the rhetoric of public relations, in some cases to the point of using it when they are alone, and thus coming to believe it.[12]

In the midst of the credit crisis, Wachovia, the nation's fourth-largest commercial bank, replaced its chief executive. Bob Steel was hired in 2008 to steady the place. Steel was a former Goldman Sachs banker, a deputy undersecretary of the U.S. Treasury. One of Steel's first acts as Wachovia's CEO was recording a video that was prominently displayed on the home page of Wachovia's corporate Internet site. Steel also bought a lot of Wachovia stock. At the time, many people feared Wachovia might collapse. Wachovia was involved in aggressive banking and loans. Steel's video message did not portray this. "So although the nation's financial news lately has been a bit troubling, and Wachovia certainly isn't immune, I want you to know that our company is on exceptionally sound footing," Steel said on his video.[13]

When Steel was appointed, Jim Cramer, the host of CNBC's *Mad Money*, called him brilliant, a visionary, a hard worker, someone who gets it, someone who knows the banking system is in big trouble. Cramer said Steel knew Wall Street and Main Street. He even recommended that his viewers buy Wachovia's stock. Cramer disclosed that he worked for Steel at Goldman Sachs. By October, some three months after Steel recorded his video statement, Wachovia reported a $24 billion loss. At that time, the stock had lost 87 percent of its value over the past five years. Wachovia was ultimately taken under by Wells Fargo for $7 a share.

The story was similar at Lehman Brothers. Dick Fuld, Lehman Brother's chief executive, was unequivocal about his company's financial health during what turned out to be Lehman's last conference call to discuss quarterly finances. Fuld was a long-serving chief executive who had built Lehman Brothers into a global powerhouse. He reportedly owned somewhere north of $1 billion of Lehman Brothers stock. "We have what we believe will be a strong and clean balance sheet that will allow us to serve our customer business," he said.[14] The keyword in Fuld's statement was "believe" just as "exceptionally sound" was for Steel's statement. At the time, Fuld was one of the most respected men in the global financial market.

People naturally want to believe that chief executives and political leaders are honest and worthy of respect. Some are. Some are not. What is certain is that an epic tug of war exists between corporate

executives and investors. Executives are increasingly rewarded for saying everything is fine, and if not fine now, fine soon. Invariably, it is
fine for them. The rest are left to fend for themselves.

Words + Numbers = Reality

To be sure, the market speaks loudly if you know how to listen. You
must learn to think in numbers because Wall Street's primary language
is mathematical. Numbers determine the tone of the tape. Securities—
stocks, bonds, and commodities—are ranked according to how well
each company and sector is positioned to make or lose money. The
rankings are based on price-to-earnings multiples, revenue and earnings growth, and myriad other facts. It is more important to focus on
the numbers, and data, than on what Wall Street says. Investment ratings assigned by stock analysts, such as Strong Buy, Buy, and Hold, are
not terribly meaningful. Since 1997, the majority of Standard & Poor's
500 Index stocks carry bullish ratings by bank analysts, according to data
from Zack's Investment Research. In 1999, before the Internet bubble burst, 395 stocks were rated buy, 37 were rated strong buy, 68 were
rated hold, and not one was rated sell or strong sell. Even before the
credit crisis of 2007, most stocks carried bullish ratings. Yet, the best-
performing stocks typically have the worst investment ratings.

There are so many bits of information, data, and indicators that are
leading, lagging, and coincidental, that you could go mad. So much
information defies the ability of most people to process it and make a
decision. Yahoo!, whose finance site is one of the most visited financial news sites, limits how much information it displays on its Internet
pages. "In our research with users, we found that the more information that was displayed on the page, the greater the anxiety," says James
Pitaro, who at the time was vice president of Yahoo!'s audience group.
He said Yahoo! uses the "Apple model" of simplicity and clean looks to
avoid "overburdening our users with too much information per page."
He said Yahoo!'s research found that too much information on the page
made users anxious.[15]

Note he did not use the word *readers*. Users and readers clearly
interact with information in different ways. Readers focus on facts and

substance. Users arguably focus on imagery. Gustave Le Bon, a nine-teenth century French sociologist who wrote *The Crowd: A Study of the Popular Mind*, believed crowds thought in images. He believed crowds were susceptible to "contagion," a term now commonly used to describe the transmission of economic fear from one country or from one financial sector to the entire market. The father of contrari-anism, Humphrey B. Neill, who was influenced by Le Bon, says:

> Because a crowd does not think, but acts on impulses, pub-lic opinions are frequently wrong. By the same token, because a crowd is carried away by feeling, or sentiment, you will find the public participating enthusiastically in various manias after the mania has got well under momentum. This is illus-trated in the stock market. The crowd—the public—will remain indifferent when prices are low and fluctuating, but little. The public is attracted by activity and by the moving of prices. It is especially attracted by rising prices. Thus, in former days, a "crowd" could be tempted into the market when a manipulator made a stock active and pushed its price higher.[16]

The American Association of Individual Investors Survey (AAII) offers investors a chance to use those ideas to calibrate their investment decisions. Each week, AAII requests that its members complete a survey asking if they expect to be bullish, bearish, or neutral about the stock market during the following six months. AAII says their survey is unique because it represents the upper echelon of active, hands-on investors. AAII's average member is male, in his late 50s, has a graduate degree, and an investment portfolio of at least $500,000. The survey's extreme-readings of investor sentiment often represent stock market turning points. Extreme fear or exuberance is a classic contrarian market signal. As Neill says: The public is right during the trends but wrong on both ends! History backs this up.

On November 16, 1990, when Iraq invaded Kuwait, AAII's bull-ish sentiment reached an all-time low of 12 percent. Investors had reason to feel bearish. At the time, Wayne Thorp, AAII's financial analyst, said oil prices were rising, the U.S. economy was weak, and the Standard & Poor's 500 Index had fallen almost 5 percent over the past three months.[17] Within 12-months the Standard & Poor's 500 Index rose some 26 percent. Similarly, extreme bullishness is often a contrarian clue that the stock market may decline. Less than two months before the October 1987 market crash, AAII members were very bullish about stocks, and for a seemingly good reason. The Standard & Poor's 500 Index was up almost 20 percent in three months prior to August 21, 1987. Of course, the stock market soon came crashing down and 1987 was etched into financial history as the year of a great crash.

When AAII readings register extreme bullishness, or bearishness, pay attention. If you see AAII at all-time highs, or lows, the stock market is likely at a turning point. One indicator is not fool proof, but it can be helpful in weighing news reports, and sifting through market data to see if the crowd is too bullish or too bearish. AAII e-mails alerts every time the survey is released. Sign up.

To avoid getting sucked into the crowd, investors must create a fortress of data amidst the chaos of the market. First, follow the Standard & Poor's 500 Index. This index is comprised of the 500 largest U.S. stocks. When it moves up or down, it tends to influence all other stocks. The Dow Jones Industrial Average is better known, but less important. The Dow is comprised of 30 stocks, and it is not much of an indicator of anything, because it measures too few stocks. The Dow's primary value is as a gauge of investor sentiment because so many nonprofessional investors use the Dow to define the market. If the Dow rises or falls, you will know if investors feel scared or confident. Every Dow point represents about nine points on the Standard & Poor's 500 Index. The NASDAQ 100 index is the proxy for the NASDAQ stock market. (The two primary exchanges are the all-electronic NASDAQ stock market and New York Stock Exchange.) The NASDAQ tells you what is happening with technology stocks. The Russell 2000 Index tracks small-capitalization stocks—typically defined as companies with market capitalizations (total number of outstanding shares) less than $5 billion. The Russell 2000 Index is often considered a pure play on the U.S. economy because most small companies typically lack the scale to operate globally. Follow the yield of the 10-Year U.S. Treasury Yield, and use it as an indicator of the risk-free return in the market. Each market cycle is different, but if the 10-Year U.S. Treasury Yield offers a substantial return without risk, likely investors will sell shares and buy high-yielding bonds.

These indexes gauge surface activity and they help reveal the footprint of investors.

To understand what is transpiring beneath the surface of the stock market requires journeying into the options market. The options market is the heartbeat of the stock market, and also its probability lab. It is here that the best investors regularly reveal what they expect to happen to stocks, and the entire stock market.

To monitor the sentiment of sophisticated investors toward the stock market for the next 30 days, focus on the Chicago Board Options Exchange's Volatility Index (VIX). The VIX is comprised of options on the Standard & Poor's 500 Index. The VIX usually moves in the opposite direction of the stock market. When VIX rises, stock prices should be falling. When major investors are afraid, they buy S&P 500 puts to hedge their stock portfolios. When VIX declines, stock prices should be rising. Sometimes the relationship between VIX and the stock market breaks down. If the stock market is rising, and so is VIX, it could mean that smart investors are afraid the rally will end badly. Ideally, VIX functions like a canary in a coal mine, offering a good warning sign prior to a correction or crash. Mostly, VIX works best in the midst of a correction as a true measure of fear whose extreme readings typically mark the end of a correction. A simple saying captures VIX's contrarian logic: When VIX is high, it's time to buy. When VIX is low, it's time to go.

Options, also called equity derivatives, are based on the price of the underlying stock. Investors buy and sell calls or puts. Calls increase in value when stock prices rise. Puts increase in value when stock prices decline. Puts and calls have different expirations. You can buy puts or calls that expire in a month or anytime out to two years or so. Because one options contract represents 100 shares of stock, and because puts and calls cost a fraction of the price of associated stocks, sophisticated investors routinely use options to express their views. An increase in bullish call options, or bearish put options, is often an indication smart investors are preparing for a stock to rise or fall.

Puts and calls also will help you size up stocks. Focus on options that expire in one to three months. If an earnings event is scheduled, investors usually buy calls if they are bullish, or puts if they are bearish. The options market is not always 100 percent accurate, but it will provide you with enough information to filter the news, and sharpen your probabilistic thinking. You can get more granular by filtering trading activity at the Options Clearing Corporation's (OCC) web site. The OCC issues and settles all options contracts. The OCC has a volume query function that lets investors sort trading volume by stock ticker and customer type. This is a critical analysis that recognizes that all investors are not equal. In the options market, orders are split between customer, firm, and market maker—denoted by C, F, and M. Customer can include individual investors and hedge funds, who are customers of banks. Firm order flow is typically reserved for professional investors, including proprietary trading desks at banks, hedge funds, and other very sophisticated investors. Market makers are dealers. When analyzing order flow, ignore market makers because they are almost always trying to hedge, or eliminate the bullish or bearish direction of the order flow that they have interacted with. Look at customers. See how many bearish puts have traded compared to bullish calls. Compare that number to firm order flow. In essence, this gives you a back of the envelope, quick trader's trick to measure Smart Money versus Dumb Money. This is not a 100 percent accurate measure; nothing is in the market. But it is one of the best ways to determine what is taking place deep inside the market. Do those calculations and you will have better information than most investors.

Chapter 5

Chaos

At the start of the twentieth century, a young Winston Churchill, very much on the make, led a group of other young House of Commons members dubbed the Hooligans. Every Thursday, they invited a political eminence to a dinner discussion of the day's important issues. Joseph Chamberlain, then a giant of British politics, joined them in July 1901. Chamberlain had a jolly good time. As he was leaving, he decided to repay his young hosts with the wisdom of experience.

"You young gentlemen have entertained me royally, and in return I shall give you a priceless secret. Tariffs! These are the politics of the future, and of the near future," Chamberlain thundered. "Study them closely and make yourselves masters of them, and you will not regret your hospitality to me."[1] Churchill immersed himself in tariffs, ultimately rejecting the idea of protecting an economy by levying extra taxes on imported or exported goods. His decision encouraged the growth of free trade, and helped set the cornerstone of what would be called globalization some 100 years later. Now, at the onset of the twenty-first century, investors must contend with the indigestion of Churchill's long-ago dinner. Volatility is globalization's destructive side effect. Volatility has become the wings of the "black swan." The black swan always hovers over the modern market's horizon.

Money Never Sleeps

The world has evolved—some critics might say devolved—into a giant flowchart for capital. Rivers of money meander from one investment to the next, from one country to another. Since 1990, global capital flows have increased faster than the world's gross domestic product (GDP).

If you could look upon earth from outer space, and somehow illuminate all the capital flows, you would see huge oceans and rivers of money in the United States, Europe, and Asia. Smaller seas, chopped with waves, would be evident in emerging markets, such as Vietnam. At different times of day, the money pools would glow red as markets opened and closed. The amount of money in these oceans and rivers—what is called liquidity—is ever shifting. The growth of cross-border capital flows demonstrates that the world is intoxicated with investing. All of this money—harnessed by stocks and bonds—coils around the globe.

Everything is touched by derivatives contracts that sit in all the spaces between bond and stock markets, essentially unifying all the world's markets so that if one part stumbles, the problem infects other markets like a super virus. This makes volatility a constant market hobgoblin, and one that is increasingly violent, as the world's largest, most sophisticated investors are increasingly chasing fewer and fewer opportunities to make high returns on money.

Perversities

More money chasing less investment opportunities creates *crowded trades*, a buzzword increasingly used in the modern market. It is also a sign of potential volatility. An idea that once attracted $500 million now attracts $1 billion. A $1 billion trade may attract $5 billion. This money is invested in stocks, bonds, and derivatives. The money may stay put for a few days, months, or years. When the money exits the opportunity, volatility often follows. These crowded trades suggest major investors increasingly lack original thought. This is not insignificant. It may encourage perverse behaviors that harm many people.

In 2005, when Raghuram G. Rajan was the International Monetary Fund's chief economist, he penned a paper raising concerns that revolutionary changes to the financial system since 1975, including technology and the creation of complicated financial products, were making the world riskier. Rajan was mostly denounced, but he was vindicated two years later when the subprime credit crisis began in the United States in 2007 and soon engulfed the world financial markets. Rajan, who is now a professor at the University of Chicago's business school, was concerned that it was easy to induce "a variety of perverse behavior" among investment managers. Herein lies the perversity:

> The knowledge that managers are being evaluated against others can induce superior performance, but also a variety of perverse behavior. One is to take risk that is concealed from investors— since risk and return are related, the manager then looks as if he outperforms peers given the risk he takes. Typically, the kinds of risks that can most easily be concealed, given the requirement of periodic reporting, are risks that generate severe consequences, but in return, offer generous compensation the rest of the time. These risks are known as tail risks. A second form of perverse behavior is the incentive to herd with other investment managers on investment choices, because herding provides insurance the manager will not underperform his peers. Herd behavior can move asset prices away from fundamentals.[2]

If the group is startled, changes its mind, or learns that one of the key points of its analysis is flawed—like the idea that housing prices had never before declined in the United States—it can set off a volatility explosion deep in the market. In those moments, everything behaves like everything else because everything is increasingly interconnected. When correlation increases, stock picking is of little consequence.

This would not be so significant if these issues were isolated. But they are not. The trading models at top funds and major banks are constructed like giant chains. Each link in the chain may include bonds, stocks, commodities, and derivatives. Any sudden, unexpected movement in one link causes the chain to ripple. Links can snap and the chain can break if the movement is sharper than expected by the financial models that gauge the chain's tensile strength.

Sophisticated trading, and global economic forces, always seem like abstractions to anyone simply trying to make a living. Once, it was possible to ignore global economic forces: not anymore. The ease at which money moves around the globe exposes everyone to the complexities—and inevitable calamities—of high finance. There is no longer any guarantee of safety simply buying quality stocks and making what would historically be considered conservative financial decisions.

Just before the credit crisis began in 2007, the U.S. Treasury acknowledged in a little known document widely shared on Wall Street that the growing institutionalization of the capital markets was making it difficult for investors to "properly evaluate their risks" because they did not fully understand the risks of the complicated products in the first place. This would not pose any problems for anyone else if the products existed in carefully controlled, segregated areas of the market that could not infect stocks and bonds if they failed. Of course, no such safety exists. The firms who buy securitized products, like the ones that figured prominently in the subprime credit crisis, instead often use loads of borrowed money (leverage) and correlated trading strategies that insure problems in these fetish markets impact the broad market—which, as the U.S. Treasury prophetically noted—"with the potential for broad market disruptions."

This phenomenon is exacerbated by the rise of exchange-traded funds and Wall Street's decision to market futures trading to Main Street investors interested in assets that are supposedly not correlated to stock prices. ETFs are mutual funds in drag that trade like stocks. When you buy an ETF, the ETF effectively buys a basket of stocks so it can create the ETF units bought by investors. Futures are similar. When you buy a futures contract on the Standard & Poor's 500 Index, you are essentially placing an order for the 500 stocks. Because so many people, especially hedge funds, use ETFs and futures to benefit from trading trends, and to quickly dart in and out of the market, it is difficult to beat the market. This helps to increase correlation and volatility. In June 2011, the *Wall Street Journal* reported ETF assets totaled $997 billion, up from $65.6 billion in just a decade. ETF trading volume has spiked in recent years and could even overtake mutual funds as a primary investment for many people.

After the credit crisis, trading with futures was increasingly touted to investors as a wonderful addition to portfolios, because it is a type of trading that is not correlated to the stock market. Of course, that will likely change as more people trade futures. The continued increase in futures volumes will likely lead to even more violent movements between the stock market and other assets. So the idea that owning staid blue-chip stocks is enough to protect you from less conservative behaviors occurring in other parts of the market—or elsewhere in the world—is simply not true. Your investments, chosen with care, presumably characterized by advisers or your own research as conservative, or aggressive, push you squarely into the middle of a complicated game increasingly dominated by major investors who essentially operate in private markets that are beyond the understanding or reach of regulators. A Swahili saying perfectly expresses the paradox: When elephants dance, the grass is crushed.

The Black Swan's Calling Card

To avoid getting crushed, you have to make friends with volatility. Volatility is the mascot of the modern financial market. Volatility is so important that several of the world's largest Wall Street banks, including Goldman Sachs, have published landmark research reports telling their best clients that they should consider volatility an asset class—just like stocks and bonds.

Indeed, volatility is closely tracked by the world's most sophisticated investors. Volatility is everywhere. For a moment, forget the world is filled with people and cultures and cities and towns. Imagine the world is just a giant stock market, and nothing more. Now, picture a globe of the earth hanging in the air in front of your eyes. Now, imagine that globe is crisscrossed with lines that look just like longitude and latitude grids. The lines are volatility. They are the invisible and inevitable byproduct and measurement of the financial market's movement. The volatility lines are primarily influenced by the movement of stocks, bonds, and credit default swaps, volatility is so sensitive as to capture movements in many different markets and areas of the economy. Sometimes volatility is benign. This happens when the market has enough liquidity to absorb movements in and out of stocks, or between asset classes. Sometimes, volatility is fierce and destructive. This may happen when everyone decides to sell all at once, or maybe everyone wants to buy—although, no one is much bothered by sharply rising stock prices even though that, too, is an example of volatility.

Map of the Market

Volatility is the stock market's central nervous system. Every stock and every index is measured in volatility. At any time, you can check the volatility of, say, Apple, or Goldman Sachs, or the Dow Jones Industrial Average, or oil, or gold, or almost any stock or index that you own or want to own. These data points are in such demand among sophisticated investors that the Chicago Board Options Exchange (CBOE) has created a big business making volatility indexes, all of which are available for free on its website.

Volatility is, of course, what happens when the Dow Jones Industrial Average rises or falls by a few hundred unexpected points. But volatility is also a mathematical idea that represents how much a stock's price has changed in the past, and how it might change in the future. Volatility is expressed as a number. From 1991 to 2011, the Standard & Poor's 500 Index has had an average volatility reading of 20. A utility stock, such as the Southern Company, typically has implied volatility of 12 percent. That means the stock barely moves. A biotechnology stock could have implied volatility of 140 percent or more. If a stock has low realized volatility, but high-implied volatility, it indicates that the most sophisticated stock investors expect the stock to make a big move. The only drawback using volatility to analyze and predict stock prices is that implied volatility only reveals if a stock is likely to move. It doesn't tell you if the stock will move up or down.

Just as Churchill studied tariffs, investors must study volatility. There are two types of volatility. Historic volatility—also called realized volatility—is concerned with the past. The measure of how much the price is expected to change in the future is implied volatility. Implied volatility and realized volatility bookend stock prices. Volatility can range from zero to more than 100 percent.

Volatility changes throughout time. The duration of volatility typically spans from one week to two years. This tracks options traded on stocks and indexes at exchanges. In the private, over-the-counter market, banks will create products to let wealthy investors speculate on volatility movements for much longer, or even much shorter, periods.

A small army of traders and investors, including Warren Buffett, trade volatility. They risk billions of dollars wagering if the stock market will rise or fall today, tomorrow, or on a certain date 15 years from now. Volatility trading is complicated, and anyone who trades volatility is part of an exclusive club.

For a moment, imagine a calendar. The calendar measures days, months, and years, like an ordinary calendar, but its pages have a simple line that increases just a little bit as each day, week, month, and year passes. The line called "term structure" measures volatility. The line increases because the future is unknown. What is unknown is often volatile. This calendar overlays the stock market, and that creates the opportunity for volatility trading.

Anyone who buys a variable annuity product, from a broker or insurance agent, is involved in the volatility market. The way insurance companies guarantee annuities against losing value is by hedging them in the volatility market. The insurance companies typically buy puts on the Standard & Poor's 500 Index that expire in 10 to 15 years. A put option increases in value when an associated security declines in price. So, if the

Standard & Poor's 500 Index declined in value, the put would increase, and the variable annuity would not lose any value. Very few investors have the creditworthiness, or resources, to commit huge sums of money for more than a decade. Only a few major investors, for instance, pension funds and Warren Buffett, are rich enough to play that game.

Because everyone knows the insurance companies must buy those contracts, puts that expire in 13 years tend to be unusually expensive, and thus a good sale provided the stock market is not convulsing in chaos around the time that the contracts are due to expire. Warren Buffett reportedly often sells 13-year volatility on the Standard & Poor's 500 Index. According to a 2008 report from J.P. Morgan, more than $1.5 trillion are invested in variable annuities, and more than 60 percent of those contracts are invested in stocks.

The easiest way to track volatility is checking the options market. The CBOE has a franchise in volatility gauges. The most famous one, the Volatility Index (VIX), tracks the Standard & Poor's 500 Index. If the VIX is low, it suggests investors are confident about the stock market for the next 30 days. If the VIX is high, it means they are nervous. Often called the fear gauge, the VIX is really the sum total of a very complicated formula that uses the implied volatility of a strip of bearish puts and bullish calls on the Standard & Poor's 500 Index to come up with a simple number that all can understand even if they cannot tell a put from a call. The VIX is designed to tell investors what the most sophisticated investors think will happen in the stock market over the next 30 days. For the past 20 years, a VIX below 20 has been interpreted as a sign investors are optimistic about stock prices. A VIX above 20 has been interpreted as a sign investors are nervous that stock prices could decline. Contrarian investors know that unusually high VIX readings are a sign that smart investors should do the opposite of the crowd. When the VIX peaked at about 90 during the worst of the credit crisis in 2008, it was a sign that the stock market was soon to rally. Why? Because it meant that everyone was selling stocks and buying defensive puts. Extreme fear is bullish.

All stock investors should follow the VIX. It is to investors what canaries are to coal miners. The VIX will alert you to dangers in the stock market.

Don't Get Skewed

The VIX's primary shortcoming is that it only provides a 30-day snapshot of fear and greed.

To increase the accuracy of volatility analysis requires looking deeper in the market. The key message for determining if the stock market will rise or fall is "skew." That odd little word describes the implied volatility of put and call options that will increase in value if a stock index makes a sharp move higher or lower.

Remember, put options increase in value when stock prices decline. Call options do the exact opposite. Calls increase in value when stock prices rise.

When sophisticated investors fear the stock market will decline, they tend to buy bearish puts that will increase in value if, say, the Standard & Poor's 500 Index declines. To save money, sophisticated investors tend to buy puts that will increase in value if the stock market declines by 10 percent. Because declines are not always one-day affairs, sophisticated investors tend to buy options that expire in three months so that they can maximize protection. Knowing this quirk of sophisticated investors lets other investors monitor the hidden crash protection market. The key is comparing the implied volatility of bullish calls and bearish puts. If the put volatility is at 37 percent, and call volatility is at 20 percent, it is a sign that the options market is preparing for the stock market to decline. That conclusion is evident because volatility—which is concerned with how likely a stock, or index price, is to move up or down—is higher for bearish puts.

The key fact in all of this complicated stuff is to remember that the options market is driven by fear. The stock market is driven by greed. This is an oversimplification—but not by much. Bearish put buying heavily influences implied volatility. To safeguard profits, or to make money on stock market declines, sophisticated investors buy defensive puts. The dealers who sell the puts respond to the buyers by raising the implied volatility of the puts. The dealers do not know who is buying the puts, or why, but that does not matter. All they really need to know is that someone—who is obviously sophisticated enough to hedge stocks—probably has better information than the derivatives dealers who live and die by mathematical models that sum up the history of the stock market.

Anyone can track skew. Barron's publishes a chart that details skew for the Standard & Poor's 500 Index and the NASDAQ 100 index. The CBOE has a Skew Index. You can enter the symbol SKEW into most financial websites and get a reading. The SKEW Index ranges from 100 and higher. When the SKEW Index is at 100, it means that the probability of a steep stock market decline is minimal. When it rises above 100, the odds of a sharp decline increase. On March 21, 1991, the SKEW Index reached an all-time low of 101.09. This was close to the end of the recession that had begun in July 1990. During the Russian debt crisis in October 1998, and the surprising move by the U.S. Federal Reserve to lower interest rates, the SKEW Index reached an all-time high of 146.88. The SKEW Index was also high in March 2006, just before the housing bubble burst and the stock market experienced its worst crash since 1929.

Apathy and Fear Are Your Friend

Investors regularly use the SKEW Index and VIX with great impact. Consider the 2011 nuclear disaster at Japan's Fukushima power plant as an example of how investors use volatility's ebbs and flows to better navigate the stock market's inevitable rise and fall. In the week before the nuclear reactor meltdown, implied volatility as measured by the CBOE's VIX was declining as the stock market sharply advanced. This is a normal event. The VIX and stock prices are supposed to move in opposite directions. Prior to the meltdown, the VIX hovered below 20, and as low as around 15. Many investors thought VIX was too low, and more arcane measures of volatility were even lower. They felt volatility was ignoring the problems in the U.S. economy and the risk of owning stocks, suggesting nary a concern that some unknown event, some black swan, would derail the stock market. In the midst of this, many traders and investors bought index puts. The positions were adjusted and readjusted as volatility ebbed lower and lower. These traders effectively *black swanned* their stock portfolios simply because the fast rise in stock prices had dramatically lowered the price of bearish puts on the Standard & Poor's 500 Index. Prior to the meltdown, the VIX hovered around 15. When the tsunami hit, the VIX quickly doubled. Those investors who had bought index puts, of course, never imagined an earthquake would cause a tsunami that would damage a nuclear reactor that would raise fears that many key factories in the global supply chain might be temporarily knocked out of commission, which would disrupt global trade and even interfere with Apple's ability to produce iPads. All those investors knew was that it is prudent to buy volatility in the form of index puts when the VIX falls to low levels because experience proves that inexpensive volatility inevitably becomes expensive. So when the nuclear disaster happened—and no one could predict that—other investors panicked, and sold stocks or rushed to pay top dollars to buy puts that would increase in value if stock prices declined even further. The wise traders who had bought index puts simply because of inexpensive prices were able to sell their black-swan hedges at enormous profits.

To some, profiting from tragedies and suffering of others will seem distasteful. But Wall Street has two emotions. Sorrow is not one of them. All good traders know it pays to be greedy when everyone is afraid. The opposite is also true. The massive profits realized in the aftermath of Japan's nuclear disaster prove that. Of course, not everyone has the time or inclination to continually track and analyze volatility and stocks. Fortunately, you can hire someone to do it for you.

Fear Not Black Swans

Since the credit crisis of 2007, *black swanning* investment portfolios has become a cottage industry as Wall Street firms have sought ways to reconnect with frightened investors. Firms have created black-swan funds that may simply buy defensive index puts, or use stop-loss limit orders, to ensure investors never lose more than 5 percent or 15 percent of their money. PIMCO, one of the world's largest money management firms, is at the forefront of black swanning investment portfolios. The firm introduced the Global Multi-Asset mutual fund in 2008, during the worst of the financial crisis. The fund personifies the good investor rule of focusing first on risk, then reward. The fund's methods are so innovative that it might one day change the way everyone handles their investments.

Rather than relying on historical returns as the basis of investment decisions—which is the traditional approach—PIMCO deconstructs asset classes—stocks, bonds, and so forth—into *risk factors*. PIMCO uses those risks to make a map of the least risky ways to make money. Sometimes the fund might invest in bonds, rather than stocks, commodities, or derivatives. At all times, the fund buys financial instruments that will increase in value if the fund's holdings, or the broad market, decline. The goal is to protect investors against losing 15 percent or more of their money, while making long-term returns of 8 to 12 percent each year.

Thinking about investing in terms of risk, rather than investment gains, is a radical departure from the typical approach. Rather than dividing the world into investments that advanced or declined sometime in the past, PIMCO's risk-factors approach is designed to manage volatility, and protect investors from big losses.

The fund's premise may seem like common sense, but it is a revolutionary idea on Wall Street—and not without controversy. PIMCO is not alone in this approach.

Several other firms, including Blackrock and Goldman Sachs, offer similar multi-asset allocation funds.

Is MPT MIA or KIA?

For an endeavor as nuanced as investing, the basic idea about how to manage stock portfolios is surprisingly rigid—and slow to change. Modern Portfolio Theory (MPT), as the theory is called on Wall Street, was developed in the 1950s, when Dwight D. Eisenhower was president, Apple's Steve Jobs was just a toddler, blacks and whites were widely separated, man had not yet walked on the moon, derivatives barely existed, and the New York Stock Exchange loomed large because the NASDAQ stock market would not be created until 1971.

The issues now defining the market barely existed in the 1950s, when Harry Markowitz began his life's work. Back then, World War II was still a recent memory. The United States was emerging as the world's only superpower. The Internet did not exist. People wrote letters, not e-mails. The majority of stock trading occurred on the floor of the New York Stock Exchange. To even gain admittance to one of the regional exchanges required character references. At the Philadelphia Stock Exchange, three people were needed to vouch for a prospective member, including a minister. Electronic stock trading did not exist. There were no algorithms that traded stocks, bonds, and commodities in milliseconds. Many people did not even own stocks. In the 1950s, the European Union did not exist. Jean Monet, the architect of the European Union, was barely laying the foundation to unify Europe's economies—the European Union was not formed until November 1, 1993.

MPT, Markowitz' idea about how portfolios should be managed to minimize risk, is fiercely defended, and much honored. Markowitz earned a Nobel Prize for Economics in 1990 for his idea that diversifying investment portfolios with a mixture of stocks and bonds reduces the overall risk of the portfolio.

MPT is a wise idea, backed with intensive math, that is often applied by practitioners with a simple age-based formula. Subtract your age from 100. The answer represents the percentage of bonds that you should own. If you are 40, your portfolio should include an allocation of 40 percent bonds and 60 percent stocks. Someone who is 50 years old, for example, would have a portfolio that is 50 percent stocks and 50 percent bonds. A 20-year-old who has all the time in the world to recover from the stock market's inevitable rises and falls would have 20 percent in bonds and 80 percent in stock—although a 100 percent stock allocation is fine.

The logic of MPT was seemingly unassailable until 2007. In that year, when the global markets began the start of a two-year collapse due to the subprime-credit crisis in the United States, some of the world's top investors began concluding that MPT was KIA. The crisis perfectly coincided with the publication of Nassim Taleb's book *The Black Swan*, which has been translated into 30 languages since it was first published in 2007. In a financial market that never sleeps and simply follows the sun around the world from the United States to Asia to Europe, MPT is arguably no longer adequate all by itself.

Correlation, which means that stocks move like each other despite their differences, has sharply increased. All of the world's stocks and bonds often trade in tandem as if there was no real difference between U.S. stocks and European stocks, or Asian bonds and U.S. bonds. In fact, in the past 10 years, cross-asset correlation has doubled since 2001, according to J.P. Morgan research. This contributes to the stock market's chronic risk on and risk off trading patterns that can be triggered by a rising or falling U.S. dollar or other currencies or gyrations in the commodities or bond markets. Some investors believe high cross-asset correlation is a sign of systemic risk. If everything behaves like everything else, then simple diversification between stocks and bonds may not effectively limit risk.

Yet MPT's central idea that investors can maximize returns and minimize risk by investing in a diversified portfolio of stocks and bonds continues to reign supreme as if the world had stood still. The theory heavily relies on historical volatility and correlation patterns that measure the movement of assets. Sometimes, certain assets, like stocks or bonds may outperform one another. MPT contends this will not last because stocks and bonds are *mean reverting*. The rule of mean reversion means that if stocks have historically returned, say, about 9 percent since 1929, and stocks rise 40 percent one year, those stock returns will inevitably revert back to their normal behavioral pattern. Mean reversion is a massive concept in the markets. A simple way to think about mean reversion is to imagine a rubber band that is stretched out. The rubber band always snaps back. That is mean reversion.

Many strategists and academics say diversification, which is a key part of MPT, is the only free lunch in the market. Of course, diversification was of no use during the credit crisis of 2007 to 2009, which provided evidence of what happens to MPT when all the forces and financial products that did not exist when MPT was developed collide with the concept. The credit crisis proved yet again what all seasoned investors know: TANSTAAFL. The phrase is the abbreviated yawp of economist Milton Friedman, who once famously said, "There ain't no such thing as a free lunch."

During the crisis, the supposed free lunch of diversification proved useless. Stocks and indexes all over the world traded alike; correlation was extremely high. Volatility moved to apocalyptic levels. Stock prices crashed. The Dow Jones Industrial Average dropped from a high of about 14,164 in October 2007, and then lost about 50 percent of its value for about 17 months.

To protect against a recurrence, PIMCO's Global Multi-Asset Fund is designed to never lose more than 15 percent of its value, and to try to consistently make annual returns of 8 to 10 percent in good times, and bad. The fund is always hedged with a basket of defensive index put options on the Standard & Poor's 500 Index or other indexes or assets. If the index declines, the value of the puts increases. The fund's managers include Mohamed El-Erian, now famous for coining the phrase the "new normal" that now seems to increasingly define these modern times of erratic, but limited economic growth and financial gains.

The idea behind PIMCO's fund is a more muscular evolution of Modern Portfolio Theory. MPT is a good idea as long as the financial markets adhere to historical performance and volatility patterns. If something happens that history has not anticipated, MPT breaks down.

"It is a very elegant approach, but it doesn't really work that well," admits Mark Taborsky, a former PIMCO strategist, who previously helped manage the endowments of Harvard and Stanford universities. Taborsky now works with Blackrock, another of the world's major money-management firms.

When investment portfolios are traditionally modeled—and this is the process that occurs when you give your broker money to manage—they use asset allocation models that look back on historical asset class performance patterns. You have probably seen these models in proposals from brokers. They appear as one-page grids filled with different colored squares. One year, the top square might be small-capitalization stocks. Another year, it might be large-capitalization stocks. Still another, it could be bonds or real estate. Brokers use these charts to justify why you should own so many different mutual funds. Brokers will tell you that you can never beat the market, so you have to diversify. This always benefits the broker. Brokers make money on the sale of every mutual fund, or whenever a money manager is hired to manage your investments. Meanwhile, it is no longer evident that the approach is as beneficial to investors as it once was.

Taborsky says:

The traditional approach to asset allocation relies on looking back in history to what asset classes returned. There is a huge reliance on mean reversion. There is a huge reliance on historic volatilities and correlations. We think people can use their views of the world. Are they worried about inflation? Inflation is a risk factor. Do they think interest rates are going up? That's a risk factor. Are they worried about the dollar? That's a risk factor. If they can think more precisely about those things, then trying to think at the 30,000-foot-level about asset classes, we think they will get much better results with their portfolio.[3]

Rather than just dividing the financial market into asset classes—stocks, bonds, real estate, and the like—PIMCO thinks of asset classes as if they were building blocks. Imagine a box of Legos. Each Lego piece is a different color. Each color stands for something different, such as risk, volatility, correlation, interest rates, or even time.

"When we invest," Taborsky says, "we try to isolate how many yellows are in this block, how many blues, how many reds. Each color represents a factor. Sometimes, when we invest, volatility is a factor we are investing in. Sometimes it's duration. Sometimes it's the equity factor. Sometimes it's currency," Taborsky says.[4] In essence, PIMCO uses risk factors that define assets to create a map that it can follow to create consistent returns while minimizing the chance to lose money.

Taborsky adds:

We have a good sense of what happens in big systemic shocks. We know that risky assets, like equities, do poorly. We know that credit spreads widen. We know that yield curves steepen because monetary authorities cut rates at the short end. We know that long-duration riskless assets do well. Our argument is that we know what is going to happen; we just don't know when. So if we can own a portfolio of assets that do well when risky assets don't, and if we can own them in an option-like format, this will always protect us. We use this in combination with asset allocation, because when volatility is very high, this nice basket of assets that does well when risky assets don't can be very expensive. So we use a combination of asset allocation in our tail-risk portfolio to manage risk.[5]

Just as "new normal" is a popular phrase on Main Street, "tail risk" is much in vogue on Wall Street. Tail risk is the clinical financial description of a black swan. When investors are modeling investment returns for an asset, for instance, stocks, they tend to use Value at Risk models (VaR, in shorthand) that visually represent returns and volatility. Imagine the letter U flipped upside down, and stretched. The long, thin lines on the side are tails. The tails represent risk. The area in the middle—the bell curve—represents normal investment returns. Wall Street's most accomplished practitioners see a future filled with tail risk.

800 Years of Crisis

The concept of black-swanning investment portfolios is in the nascent stages of mainstream acceptance, even though the idea has been adopted by the upper echelon of the financial market.

The credit crisis, the first black swan event of the twenty-first century, makes clear that the old ideas of managing money, and limiting risk, need to evolve because the future is likely filled with even more financial calamities.

"We know we have crises every five or ten years," Jamie Dimon, J.P. Morgan's chairman and chief executive, said during congressional testimony in January 2010."[6] The pattern has, by some measures, existed for 800 years. Since 1980, the financial markets have repeatedly been leveled by financial crises. Each new crisis seems more intense than the one that came before. In 1982, Mexico defaulted on its bonds, sparking an international debt crisis. In 1987, the Dow Jones Industrial Average dropped 22.6 percent in one day. In 1989, the markets contended with the U.S. savings and loan crises and the Latin American debt crisis. This led to a European monetary system crisis in 1992 and 1993, and a Mexican peso crisis, requiring a $50 billion U.S. guarantee in 1994 and 1995. In 1997 and 1998, Asia experienced a financial crisis that required a $40 billion rescue organized by the International Monetary Fund. In 1998, Russia defaulted on its debt, and Long Term Capital Management, the U.S. hedge fund, nearly toppled the global markets. In 2001 and 2002, Argentina defaulted on its debt, the Internet bubble burst, and terrorists toppled the World Trade Towers. In 2007, after years of low interest rates in the United States, the world became embroiled in a global financial crisis that began in the U.S. housing market.

"With globalization increasing, you'll see more crises," John Meriwether, the former LTCM hedge fund manager, prophetically said in August 2000.[7] Seven years later the world learned just what he meant when the subprime credit crisis started in the United States, and then wrapped its way around the globe. Mark Mobius, the executive chairman of Templeton Asset Management's emerging markets group, believed another financial crisis is inevitable. "There is definitely going to be another financial crisis around the corner because we haven't solved any of the things that caused the previous crisis," says Mobius, who oversees investment portfolios exceeding $50 billion. "Are the derivatives regulated? No. Are you still getting growth in derivatives? Yes."[8]

By his tally, the total value of global derivatives exceeds total global GDP by 10 times. With that volume of bets in different directions, volatility and equity market crises will inevitably occur yet again.

Fear Gray Swans

The market is impacted by more than just what occurs within its own confines. The market reflects the world.

Demographics shifts also may contribute to volatility spikes that will roil the stock market. By 2050, the world's population is expected to grow by two billion people. The total population is expected to exceed nine billion. By some measures, about one billion working-age adults will join the workforce. The number of people older than 60 will grow by 1.25 billion. The number of people younger than 25 is projected to remain stagnant at about three billion, according to the United Nations. Some fear that this could prompt countries to default on their debt payments as older voters are expected to vote to protect government-sponsored benefits, including health and retirement funds. European nations with generous social benefits experienced rioting when financial problems prompted them to consider austerity measures to save money. In 2010 and 2011, France erupted in riots as the Senate prepared to meet to raise the retirement age to 62 from 60. The United States faces similar challenges. Social Security, which accounts for a substantial portion of retirement income, may run out of money, according to various calculations. This could create considerable political pressure on the U.S. government.

Europe's difficulties balancing budgets in 2011 and 2012 show that such news causes stocks to decline and volatility to increase. For months, Europe's financial problems taunted U.S. markets. On many days, problems with the debt ratings of Portugal, Italy, Greece, and Spain pushed stock prices lower in the United States. The problems are not isolated to the federal level. Many states, including California, Illinois, and New York, face great economic difficulties. This could also hurt state budgets, which would hurt municipal bonds that are widely owned by older Americans.

Says Ali Alichi, an economist for the International Monetary Fund:

> As the number of older voters relative to younger ones increases around the globe, the creditworthiness of borrowing countries could decline—resulting in less external lending and more sovereign debt defaults. Because lenders cannot easily confiscate a government's assets in the case of a default, they must rely almost completely on the creditworthiness of a sovereign in deciding whether to make a loan. To the many factors affecting a nation's credit-worthiness—such as macroeconomic strength and past debt-payment record—lenders must add aging. Studies have shown that a country's willingness to repay is as important as whether it has the resources to repay. This willingness deteriorates as voters age because they have a shorter period to benefit from their country's access to international capital markets and become more likely to opt for default on current debt. Moreover, older voters generally benefit more from public resources—such as pension and health

care benefits, which could shrink if debt is repaid. If the old are a majority, they might force default, even if it is not optimal for the country as a whole. Lenders will take this into account and reduce new lending to an aging country.[9]

Alichi's view is dismal. It may or may not prove true. War could reduce populations. So could famines and disease. Yet, the graying of the world looms as another potential cause of massive spikes in volatility should prove to impact sovereign debts.

Of course, such world views are rarely discussed by financial advisers, or money mangers. It took a Congressional inquiry to get J.P. Morgan's Jamie Dimon to admit that the stock market frequently experiences a crisis, a fact that everyone on Wall Street intuitively knows, and wants you to ignore. Wall Street wants you to focus on how much money you can make in the market because it helps Wall Street sell you bonds, stocks, and other products. Wall Street "helps" guide your decisions—and protects itself from litigation—by preparing thick packets of documents that almost no one reads, much less understands. The only information in the packet that is comprehensible is how much money you can make if you follow the recommendations.

The packets are always filled with lots of papers with graphs, bullet points, and reams of fine print that say the past is not the future. Yet, without any sense of irony, with no feelings of self-consciousness, your money is invested as if the past is the future—even though all the fine print in the packet of information that is too familiar to your broker says otherwise. You will rarely, if ever, see a chart in the portfolio allocation packets that shows you what will happen to your money if volatility spikes, correlation increases, or if something happens that no one expected, such as a country in Europe deciding to stop making payments to its debt holders. And yet there you are, with all of your money, with all of your hopes and pressures of life, tied up into an idea that turned 60 years old in 2012.

Says Taborsky:

Anyone who has done it (MPT) more than a year recognizes how far off their estimates of expected returns are by asset class and how far off their expectations of volatilities and correlations are. The other thing is that everyone using it uses the exact same information. Everyone looks at the same volatilities and correlations, and everyone is comparing notes on what expected returns they have. So you end up with lots of people—and you see this in the endowment/foundation world—with very, very similar allocations. That tells you that using one approach can be dangerous because people will move in and out of asset classes and investments at the same time.[10]

PIMCO tries to avoid the crowd by using an approach that is simple to understand, but difficult to implement. The fund's managers formulate views on major forces that influence the financial market, including inflation, economic growth, credit spreads, and interest rates, to forecast investment returns. The fund's managers think in terms of the drivers of returns, rather than trying to forecast what an asset class might do. In essence, PIMCO is always asking, always checking to make sure that it is getting paid to take risk. Most investors simply take risks that they do not understand. "If you are going to give me 25 percent returns, am I taking on too much risk for that? Is the probability that I may end up with a goose egg at the end of three years too high for me to handle? People have talked about risk-adjusted returns for a long time," Taborsky says, "but I don't think they paid attention because you can't eat a lower-risk portfolio, but you can eat the higher returns."[11]

Indeed, the return of capital, more so than the return on capital, should be the precise focus of every investor. Too often investors chase returns, think too little of risk, and suffer dire consequences.

Chapter 6

Diogenes' Lantern

This is a true story. In 2007, a couple sold a townhouse in Park Slope, a neighborhood in Brooklyn, New York. The price of the townhouse had more than doubled in the five years since they bought it. It was a nice townhouse, on a wonderful block, with magnificent neighbors. But a more than 100 percent return in less than five years was too good to be true. Besides, the kids were getting older. They needed someplace greener and safer to play. So they sold the townhouse. The couple, their two kids, and their pug dog, moved from the city. They bought a rambling house in the country. They lived beside a river. They missed the city. But they enjoyed the extra space, the clean air, and the wad of cash they had received thanks to the real estate sale and some fortuitous business dealing. They were also lucky. The couple sold their townhouse right as the real estate market peaked. The money was too much to handle alone. Soon they got a call from a stockbroker offering to help. The stockbroker called himself a "financial advisor." The couple's private banker had introduced him. The private banker had worked for the husband's parents for many years. She was trusted. The stockbroker was likable. The stockbroker soon presented a plan after a few telephone calls.

The bulk of the money was invested in six or seven mutual funds. A few hundred thousand dollars were invested in a "bond ladder." The idea was that stock mutual funds would increase in value as the stock market advanced, and the bonds, which were laddered to mature at different times, would provide a steady stream of cash to pay the mortgage, which happened to be with this well-known bank.

The new plan worked great—for a few months. It was early 2007. The Dow Jones Industrial Average was surging toward 14,000. Stocks seemed like they would never decline. Banks would lend anyone money. By spring, the stock market began convulsing. The market was not sinking, but it was volatile. Stock prices moved higher and lower with such speed that it was scary to watch—even though prices often ended the day higher. The husband was experienced in the markets. He knew extreme market volatility was a sign of an unhealthy market. He called the stockbroker. They scheduled a meeting to discuss market volatility. The stockbroker also wanted to meet to discuss developing a full financial plan. The meeting was a disappointment. The stockbroker said he had computer problems. He had not prepared any of the expected reports. The husband raised portfolio volatility with the stockbroker. The stockbroker said something along the lines that stocks fluctuate, and dismissed the concerns. The husband asked the stockbroker to prepare a report on why their accounts were behaving so erratically given that they owned a diversified stock portfolio that should reduce risk. Sometimes the total value rose and fell by 5 percent in a day. The stockbroker was asked to develop a plan to lower portfolio volatility. A week passed—still no volatility report. And another week passed—the report never came. The husband called the stockbroker. He told him to sell all the mutual funds and all the bonds. The stockbroker did not like that. He was no longer so affable. He sharply said no one had ever told him to sell everything. He was confrontational. He accused the husband of being emotional. He said the stock market would end the year higher and that the husband was the only the person he knew who thought otherwise. The husband was not moved. The stockbroker was instructed to sell everything at the close of trading that day and to call to confirm that everything had been sold.

About four weeks later, the stockbroker called the husband's office. The stockbroker told the husband how much money he would have made if he were still invested in the stock market. A few months later, the stock market collapsed. The husband's and wife's money was serendipitously safe in a money-market fund. The husband wanted to call the stockbroker. He wanted to ask how the accounts would be doing now. The wife said no. Instead, they took advantage of the fear of other investors who were selling in sheer panic.

When corporate bonds were at historic lows, they bought corporate bonds. They rode them higher, and sold. They then bought municipal bonds at historic lows. They sold those higher, and started buying stocks in February and March of 2009, as the stock market began to recover from the worst crash since 1929. The couple did not lose any money during the credit crisis. They actually made quite a bit in profits. But that was not the experience of most of their friends, or their friends' parents, or most people who relied upon stockbrokers and mutual funds companies. But one good thing happened during the financial crisis it is that Wall Street's pleasant veneer was stripped bare. People got a deep, intimate look at ugly business practices. The experience laid bare the canard that stockbrokers and highly paid fund managers have some magical understanding of the market. The market crash made many people realize how little they know about investing and Wall Street. If they thought that they had access to expert financial advice and insights, they realized that they were mostly alone. They were scared. Some stockbrokers took excellent care of clients. Those stockbrokers often catered to wealthy families or businessmen. Some good stockbrokers work with people not dripping in wealth, and there are good mutual fund managers—but finding them is often difficult, if not possible, for most people. Just as Diogenes roamed ancient Athens during the day with a lantern, searching for one honest man, most investors are on a similar path on Wall Street and they don't even know it. Diogenes lived in the streets of Athens. He had a simple home. He lived in a barrel. It is better to know of Diogenes than be like Diogenes.

Performance Is Relative

These are facts worth knowing, and doing something about: Most mutual funds fail to outperform their performance benchmarks. The funds may track the Standard & Poor's 500 Index, or some other benchmark, but they rarely achieve returns that are higher than the benchmark index. Yet, mutual funds charge a complex array of fees that investors must pay even if the fund fails to beat the benchmark. Trying to track mutual fund performance is a task worthy of a lawyer. More than 50 percent of all mutual funds are merged with other funds, or closed, within 10 years after they have been launched, according to data from Morningstar, a mutual-fund analysis firm. Those facts are not frequently discussed. Neither is the immense wealth generated by mutual funds for mutual fund companies. The main beneficiaries of mutual funds are mutual fund companies. Overtime, mutual fund fees cripple, if not destroy, investment returns, but they do wonders for the mutual fund company's stock price. Consider T. Rowe Price Group, a top mutual fund company. From 1990 to late October 2011, T. Rowe Price's stock dramatically outperformed the Standard & Poor's 500 Index and the Dow Jones Industrial Average. The stock gained about 4,000 percent, compared to about a 400 percent gain for the Standard & Poor's 500 and Dow indexes. Shares of Franklin Resources, another leading mutual fund company, similarly outperformed the Standard & Poor's 500 and Dow indexes. What accounts for their financial strength? Fees paid by investors.

Fee income is vital to financial companies. Fee income is relatively steady. Many uncontrollable forces, such as the economic cycle, by contrast, influence investment-banking revenues. Trading revenues are volatile, and sometimes the source of significant losses. Fee income rises and falls based on how much money the fund companies manage, but fee income is otherwise reliable, and not as temperamental as other sources of money on Wall Street. The same metric applies to stockbrokers. This is why many major banks actively recruited stockbrokers during the credit crisis. Many banks paid huge, multimillion signing bonuses to stockbrokers for leaving their firm and bringing their clients to the new bank. Fee income is that important.

Death by a Thousand Fees

Finding a good stockbroker, or reliable mutual fund, entails luck and considerable effort. But there is one critical part of the investment process that is easy to control and that will immediately increase investment returns: fees.

Fees can prove to be the difference between a comfortable retirement, or not. The issue is significant in a low-return environment such as has existed in the United States for more than a decade, and which some pundits believe could exist for a decade longer as the nation, and world, struggles to emerge from the credit crisis. If a stock portfolio annually advances 5 percent, and an investor pays 1 percent in fees, they are giving away 20 percent of their return. No one thinks that way—but they should.

It is not realistic to expect financial products will be free of fees or transaction costs. There is a cost in running banks, exchanges, and even in organizing and selling mutual funds, and operating a stockbrokerage office. Stockbrokers deserve to be paid for their time. But it is important to be realistic about fees. Fees can influence decisions that stockbrokers make for clients.

If you are a self-directed investor, and make your own decisions, and do your own research, online discount stockbrokerage firms that charge low fees are irresistible. Vanguard's low-cost index funds and exchange-traded funds (EFTs) are hard to ignore. But most people inevitably turn to, or are recruited by, stockbrokers who work for firms such as Merrill Lynch, Wells Fargo, or UBS.

The president of a brokerage firm, who has asked to remain anonymous for reasons that will soon be apparent, says investors must determine if their stockbroker works from left to right, or right to left. That quizzical phrase is how the stockbrokerage chief thinks about stockbrokers and customers. A stockbroker who works from the left to the right first considers how much fee income he will earn off the customer. Fees then determine what products are sold to the customer.

A stockbroker who works right to left focuses on making the right decisions for customers. Telltale signs that a stockbroker cares more about themselves than their clients are recommendations to invest in mutual funds that charge high management fees, or that have high sales commissions, known as loads. Expensive stock commissions are another sign, especially if the stockbroker frequently recommends buying and selling stocks. Frequent trading can be a sign that your stockbroker is "churning" your account to generate sales commissions. That is a red flag. Something is always wrong if your stockbroker earns more money managing your account than you earn through your investments.

Most people spend their financial lives stuck between the underperformance of mutual funds and the overpromising of stockbrokers. Most people enter the market by first buying mutual funds. The familiarity with mutual funds leads them to climb the risk ladder into stocks, and maybe even options. When they have saved enough money, they usually seek—or are sought by—stockbrokers. Having a stockbroker is a rite of passage for many people. When you have enough money, you have a stockbroker. If people are very lucky, they find a good, honest stockbroker who will treat them, and their money, as if it was their own in the best sense of the phrase. If they are unlucky, or have average luck, they meet stockbrokers who treat the clients' money like their own in the worst sense of the phrase.

The brokerage firm president knows this. He is torn between overseeing the firm and working as a stockbroker. He believes he could make more money managing clients' accounts, because investors are desperate to work with honest stockbrokers who work right to left. He says too many stockbrokers think about their own interests over the interests of clients.

Stockbrokers generate fees for their banks, and for themselves, based on the size of their "books." The book is Wall Street lingo that describes a stockbroker's assets under management (AUM). The more money a stockbroker "manages," the more money the stockbroker makes. Most investors pay their stockbrokerage firm a 1 percent annual management fee. The stockbroker shares some percentage of that 1 percent fee with his or her employer. A 1 percent fee may not seem like a lot, but it represents $1 million for every $100 million that a stockbroker manages. It's hard to say what the average stockbroker earns, but a stockbroker with a decent sized book could make $300,000 to $400,000 each year. The best stockbrokers make more, and they are worth every dime, plus their weight in gold.

If you have access to the top stockbrokers, and top banks, you get the best of all possible worlds. If you have a small account, and just have a few hundred thousand dollars, very few stockbrokers will take the time to work with you. They won't make enough money. The median account size, according to industry sources, is about $88,000. An account that small maybe merits an annual, hour-long meeting.

The size of the book is an asset for brokers. Books are bought and sold. Sometimes by other brokers. Sometimes by other brokerage firms. Every seven years, some stockbrokers switch firms because they can sell their books and get a big check.

If a stockbroker brings a "book" to a new firm and stays seven years, it is common to get a check for three-times revenue. If a stockbroker has a $450,000 income and generates $1 million a year in commissions or fee-income, that stockbroker can get a $3 million check by moving to a new firm. That's a big enough number, especially when kids are going to college, weddings need to be paid for, or retirement looms.

Fees are not as salubrious to the financial health of investors. Over time, mutual fund fees, for example, devour investor returns.

According to Vanguard, an important mutual fund company, minimizing costs are critical to long-term investment success. This is a counterintuitive point because many people equate high prices with quality. That logic does not always work in the financial industry. Sometimes, high fees are charged simply because they can, and because the people paying the fees do not understand what they are doing. David F. Swensen, the well-regarded chief of Yale's pension fund, is a sharp critic of the mutual fund industry. He believes individual investors should own index funds, and avoid actively managed funds that charge higher fees. "Instead of pursuing ephemeral promises of market-betting strategies, individuals benefit from adopting the ironclad reality of market-mimicking portfolios managed by not-for-profit investment organizations," Swensen says.[1] He believes the mutual fund industry exploits investors. He thinks the U.S. government should intervene.

Vanguard mutual funds, which satisfies Swensen's dictum, notes that there are five main factors that determine investment returns: dividends/interest income; operating costs; transaction costs; and taxes.[2] Of those five factors, operating costs are the only ones that are fairly predictable.

Those costs cover fees paid to the fund manager and administrative, recordkeeping, and reporting costs.

Vanguard cites a February 2002 study performed by the Financial Research Corporation that shows that expense ratios are the most reliable predictor of future performance. Expense ratios overshadowed past investment performance and Morningstar ratings. Vanguard, which specializes in low-cost mutual funds, has a website tool that shows how much money investors lose because of mutual fund fees. A $250,000 mutual fund investment in a Vanguard fund whose average expense ratio is 0.21 percent, and which rose 8 percent annually, saves investors a significant amount of money compared to a mutual fund that charges a 1.15 percent fee. Over 20 years, investors saved $192,675 if they picked the fund with lower fees.

The difference is even more dramatic over 30 years.

A $200,000 investment split between two identical mutual funds that earned 8 percent annually respectively, but that charged different expenses ratios proves the point. An investor would earn $242,079 more by investing in Fund A that charged an expense ratio of 0.2 percent, compared to Fund B's 1.19 percent expense ratio.[3] The double insult for investors is that most mutual funds fail to beat their performance benchmarks. For every Dan Rice at Blackrock who continually beats the market, most fail to keep pace. This means investors often pay top dollar for substandard performance. This is a tricky area. Mutual fund companies often market their hot funds. Many investors chase after those hot mutual funds. The irony is that this year's hot funds are often next year's duds. This is because the funds tend to attract so much money that managers have a tough time investing the same way as before—or it means the managers just got lucky. But most mutual fund companies—and therefore most investors—focus on one-year market performance—and not enough on low costs and long-term investment results.

An August 2010 study performed by Morningstar confirms Vanguard's assertion that expense ratios are a "primary test" in fund selection. Russel Kinnel, the analyst who performed the study, found that fees are the most dependable predictor of performance. When picking funds, he recommends focusing on funds in the cheapest, or two cheapest, quintiles.

"In every single time period and data point tested, low-cost funds beat high-cost funds. Expense ratios are strong predictors of performance," Kinnel found. "In every asset class over every time period, the cheapest quintile produced higher total returns than the most expensive quintile."[4]

For example, the cheapest quintile from 2005 in domestic equity returned an annualized 3.35 percent versus 2.02 percent for the most expensive quintile over the ensuing five years. The gap was similar in other categories, including municipal bonds and taxable bond funds.

Just as dividends are an historically important—and often overlooked—part of the profits investors earn when buying stocks, fees are an important reason why investors often do not earn as much money as implied by the return of certain mutual funds or even entire swatches of the stock market as measured by the Standard & Poor's 500 Index.

As an exercise, compare your mutual fund's performance to similar ETFs. ETFs are like mutual funds except they trade on the stock exchange. ETF fees are typically much lower than mutual funds. ETFs are not always superior to mutual funds. Someone who makes small investments each month is probably better off with mutual funds. But someone who has a chunk of cash and is investing in a sector, or even the broad stock market, should consider ETFs—or low-cost index funds. If your mutual fund manager cannot consistently beat a benchmark index, or similar ETF, there is no reason to own the mutual fund. Why pay top dollar for substandard performance?

Stockbroker Pay

The destructive effect of fees on investor accounts is widely known on Wall Street. The subject is never really discussed in great detail, though occasionally an entity like Morningstar produces a report that shows how fees kill returns. Even then the report must compete with the day's events for news coverage. In the normal pace of things, a story on a study about fees is inevitably buried deep within a paper, or lost on a financial news website. Stockbrokers know all about fees.

That's a major contributor to their income. Fees sustain stockbrokers' lifestyles. Fees are tentacles that wind and wrap through the stockbrokerage industry and all of Wall Street.

A former hedge fund salesman with extensive experience dealing with stockbrokers says the first question many ask about investment products is: "How much does this pay?"

Understanding the full extent of stockbroker compensation is more difficult than learning Sanskrit. Compensation information varies widely. A top stockbroker in Manhattan, New York, says his branch manager—a stockbroker who handles administrative duties at a stockbrokerage office—has a hard time understanding his compensation structure. Stockbroker payouts are based on money management, plus some sales commissions, plus different commission rates for different products. Some stockbrokers are paid monthly. Some are paid quarterly. All of them make money mostly the same way, though they get different percentage payouts.

Increasingly, most investors are put into *wrap accounts*. They pay a flat, annual fee, usually 1 percent to 2 percent of total portfolio value. The wrap is apparently sometimes negotiable and sometimes not. The total wrap fee is split at varying percentages between the stockbroker and brokerage firm.

By itself, a 1 to 2 percent management fee seems benign. If the stock market is rising, the fee seems inconsequential. But it is incorrect to look at fees in isolation. Fees must be contextualized. Karl Rozak, an Oppenheimer & Company stockbroker in Manhattan, thinks about client accounts through what he calls the 3 percent guideline. If a client withdraws 3 percent or less from an investment account, the account's value will continue to increase. If the client withdraws 5 percent from the account, the account will not increase in value. If the client withdraws more than 5 percent, the customer has triggered a process that will inevitably deplete the account. Through Rozak's prism, a 1 to 2 percent management fee is anything but innocuous. Rozak is a rare stockbroker. Diogenes would have stopped looking for an honest man had he met Rozak.

Think of fees as important parts of your cost of capital (C-of-C). Professional investors always monitor their C-of-C because the less money they spend for something the more money they keep. Seasoned investors are always trying to maximize their gains and minimize anything that reduces their profits. Over time, investment fees might be the difference between a relaxing retirement, or a financial crisis at a time when you are least able to work, and most need money.

The wrap fee traditionally covers all transactions. Think of the wrap account like an all-expense paid vacation where most everything is covered. The wrap account has increasingly replaced transactional relationships as the primary income source of stockbrokers. This shift reflects the rise of online, discount stockbrokerage firms that let anyone trade stocks for inexpensive rates, for instance, $6.95, compared to the several hundred dollars that can be charged by full-service stockbrokerage firms. The shift also reflects the deregulation of stockbrokerage commissions that occurred in May 1, 1975. May Day, as the event is known on Wall Street, eliminated fixed transaction commissions and introduced competition into an area that had none. Stockbrokerage firms all charged high transaction fees. Some stockbrokers still make a living off transaction fees, but wrap accounts are the primary income source. In a wrap account, or separately managed account (SMA), stockbrokers create a portfolio of mutual funds. Investors then buy these mutual funds, hopefully creating a portfolio that reduces the risk of the stock market and maximizes return. A certain percentage of money is invested in value stocks of varying sizes, and also in growth stocks that meet similar criteria. A value stock typically pays a dividend. A growth stock typically generates returns by increasing in value. Apple is a growth stock. Utility stocks, such as Southern Company, are value stocks. By owning small-, mid- and large-capitalization stocks that are bundled together in mutual funds, oftentimes with bond mutual funds and international mutual funds, investors—or so the theory goes—reduce their risk and maximize gains. Some investors with portfolios that exceed $500,000 are often invested in SMAs. The SMA is similar to a mutual fund, but different. Money is given to a mutual fund company whose manager essentially creates a mutual fund for that one client. Which is better? Some stockbrokers say it is better to own mutual funds. Others like SMAs. Both types of accounts generate account management fees of, say, 1 percent annually. Sometimes stockbrokers earn additional money for whatever else they get customers to buy.

Every morning, at every Wall Street firm, begins with a conference call. Investment strategists discuss the day's events, and, along with stock analysts, talk about stocks, whose ratings or earnings estimates have been raised or lowered. At varying degrees, these conference calls ripple throughout the firm and can be used by stockbrokers as the basis of telephone calls, or meetings, with clients.

Firms also regularly create and sell structured products that might guarantee investors certain rates of return over time. Those funds are typically loaded with fees and high commissions that are invisible to clients, because the fees are hidden into the purchase price. A $10 product, for example, could contain $4 of fees. Those recommendations are not always the best. Consider variable annuities. These insurance products are increasingly popular on and off Wall Street in the wake of the financial crisis. Unlike stocks and bonds that fluctuate, variable annuities offer guaranteed rates of return. Variable annuities also pay stockbrokers commissions of 6.5 percent to more than 14 percent. A $500,000 variable annuity with a 10 percent sales commission generates a $50,000 commission for a stockbroker. Somewhere, the fees are often disclosed, but typically in incomprehensible legal language and in small print. The disclosure documents are rarely read by anyone but lawyers hired to write them. Mostly, people do what Wall Street has trained them to do. They focus on the future benefits like guaranteed income provided by a variable annuity.

"There is a misalignment of incentives," says Stephen Solaka, a partner of Belmont Capital, a Los Angeles investment advisory firm. "Stockbrokers are not incentivized for the client. Higher risk products pay better. Fixed income pays stockbrokers a small amount of money like 30 basis points, but equity pays 1 percent. A lot of stockbrokers are tilted toward riskier things because they get paid more."[5] Solaka's clients pay a fee, rather than ongoing commissions. This is a key difference between Registered Investment Advisors (RIA), of which Solaka is one, and stockbrokers. Advisors, also known as RIAs, bill for their time much like lawyers or accountants. Fees are always transparent, but in return for that, clients often must pay upfront for their services, though some advisors do deduct fees from assets under management just like stockbrokers. Advisors, however, are typically only paid for their advice. They are often not compensated for selling financial products.

Stockbrokers rarely, if ever, disclose the extent of their compensation beyond the 1 percent annual management fee, or commissions charged to sell stocks. They rarely make clear that investors also are charged management fees by the mutual funds that are sold by the stockbrokers. This is a problem for the brokerage industry. Trust is a rare, and a premium commodity, between Wall Street and its clients. The inability, or unwillingness, to fully and simply illuminate brokerage compensation is a remnant of a time and place that no longer exists. If accountants, lawyers, and doctors routinely provide bills or statements of service, the same can and should be expected of stockbrokers. Until that type of transparency is imposed on Wall Street's sales practices—particularly for individual investors—most people are well served to think of stockbrokers (and Wall Street) like car salesmen or hustlers. That view is overly harsh, but it conveys the point. The job of a stockbroker is not mysterious. They are intermediaries who help people buy or sell various products. Understanding what they do, and how they do it, should not be draped in mystery and half-exposures.

Perhaps, your stockbroker helps you manage fees. If that is true, you likely have a good stockbroker. That is good because fees ultimately devour investor returns. This is especially true when investors buy mutual funds and other products that simply rise or fall with the stock and bond market and have no mechanism to offset losses. Stockbrokers often disclaim responsibility for losses. They prefer to take credit for investment gains.

Remember, stockbrokers are salesmen. A financial consultant is a salesman. Whatever name they go by at their firm, stockbrokers work for their firm's sales divisions. They are always selling. This is why they are often the last to realize what is happening in the financial market. Stockbrokers are paid to be bullish. Bearish stockbrokers starve. If you are not invested in stocks, or holding cash, stockbrokers do not make as much money, and may not make any money.

In October 2011, for example, when the world's stock markets were declining because of fear that a new dangerous phase was beginning in the global financial crisis that had begun in 2007, some stockbrokers faced difficult choices. A few confessed that if they told their clients to sell mutual funds, and buy high-dividend paying stocks that ultimately offered shelter from the storm, the stockbrokers would lose money because they would not receive fees from mutual funds. Once you buy a stock, and pay the commission, that's it. Stockbrokers often make more money off mutual funds than stocks.

Hidden Fees

Mutual funds typically have various fees, hidden and explicit. In addition to management fees, funds charge sales fees called loads. These loads are confusing, and there is more than one kind. Class A shares typically charge a front-end load of about 5.75 percent. Class B shares charge a fee when the fund is sold. Class C shares charge a fee for the entire time an investor owns the fund. Some funds have even more share classes.

Many mutual funds also charge a 12b-1 fee. This lets mutual fund companies deduct expenses supposedly related to marketing and running the mutual fund. At least, that's how 12b-1 fees were originally used. The fees are now widely used to pay stockbrokers for selling funds. Sometimes the money is credited back to clients. Sometimes it is not.

Each mutual fund share class has a different 12b-1 fee. In addition to the sales charge, Class A shares often have a 25 basis point 12b-1 fee. Class B shares have no up-front fee, but they can charge a 25 basis point to 1 percent 12b-1 fee, which happens to be the maximum allowable amount a fund company can levy. When Class B shares are sold, investors often pay a fee, though that fee declines in value the longer the fund is owned. Class C shares also often charge a 1 percent 12b-1 fee. Those tiny percentages add up to big money. In 2007, mutual funds collected $13.3 billion in 12b-1 fees, though that number declined to $9.5 billion in 2009.

Beware of New Products

Wall Street continually develops new financial products. Investors should be wary. The products can be expensive roach motels: easy to buy, hard to sell. New products are sometimes sold to unsuspecting investors because institutional investors are trying to unload difficult positions. One top municipal bond dealer introduced several ETFs during the worst of the credit crisis when no one wanted to buy municipal bonds. The ETFs let the dealers sell positions to unsophisticated investors that sophisticated investors would not touch. Remember that story when considering buying a new financial product. Find out why the product is being sold and who is behind the effort. If you understand the motivation behind the product, you better understand the risk.

A key risk, at least initially, to all new products is that they typically have little liquidity. Many seasoned investors avoid new products for at least six months, or until the new product has average daily trading volume of at least 1 million shares, or some other volume level that indicates the securities can be bought and sold without impacting the price. Liquidity simply means that there are buyers and sellers. Look at IBM's stock. It trades millions of shares each day. You can buy and sell IBM stock without any problem. An order to buy or sell 100 shares, or 10,000 shares, will not change the price. It's the opposite with many new financial products. They are often easy to buy and hard to sell.

An Uncomfortable Conversation

Skepticism is a critical attribute for investors. It is a critical mind-set for dealing with stockbrokers and anyone else on Wall Street. Second-guessing someone as personable as most stockbrokers will seem rude, and perhaps even paranoid, to some people, but you must remember that you have a relationship with your money—not your stockbroker. That might seem cold, but that is the relationship Wall Street has with you. Wall Street does not care if you live or die, make or lose money. Wall Street only cares about how much money it makes from you. This unemotional view recognizes an important fact about Wall Street and stockbrokers that too few people understand.

A Funny Aside

Jokes offer insights into people and places in ways that are sometimes more direct than analysis, or even conversation. Jokes reveal cultural mores. Here are two good ones told by stockbrokers.

A stockbroker dies. He gets the chance to visit both heaven and hell and then decides where he wants to spend eternity. He picks hell first. He expects to see demons with pitchforks, but all he encounters are beautiful women, great food, fine wines, and parties. Heaven is filled with little angels strumming harps. The stockbroker chooses hell. In a flash, he is standing before the devil. All around are fires and screams of torment. The stockbroker asks the devil what happened to all the beautiful women, great food, wines, and parties. The devil laughs. "That," he says, "was the prospectus we use to sell hell."

In another joke, a stockbroker dies and goes to heaven. There is a huge line at the Pearly Gates. The stockbroker walks to the front. He asks St. Peter if he can help get the line moving. St. Peter agrees. Suddenly, hordes of people start running toward hell, and the stockbroker is first in line.

"What did you say, my son, to get everyone to move?"

"I told them there was a hot-stock deal in hell," the stockbroker said.

Suddenly, the stockbroker turned on his heels and ran toward hell.

"My son, my son, where are you going!" St. Peter yelled.

"To hell."

"But why?"

"Because it might be true," the stockbroker said.

Another Punch Line

Stockbrokers typically do not have fiduciary responsibilities for their clients. A fiduciary standard requires stockbrokers to put their clients interests first. The SEC recommended in January 2011 that the fiduciary standard should be applied to stockbrokers, but nothing much has since happened. Stockbrokers are still mostly covered by a suitability requirement. This means stockbrokers are required to make sure that they do not sell, or recommend, products that are improper for a client. A retiree who lives off Social Security should not trade derivatives and own a portfolio of risky growth stocks. That client is better suited for conservative stock and bond investments that generate income.

Suitability Requirement

Stockbrokers are supposed to ensure that financial recommendations are consistent with, or suitable for, an investor's age, investment objectives, and financial status. A retiree living on a fixed-income with a relatively modest portfolio, for example, is likely to be ill suited to trade options and have all of their money in stocks. Those risks are much higher than owning a mix of bonds and stocks. But the riskier choices can generate higher commissions for stockbrokers. Besides, some stockbrokers get frustrated being stockbrokers. They want to be traders or money managers. They may think that they have a feel for the market, or what is hot, or will be hot, and they move money around to chase trends. Managing money to the market—rather than the investment goal—is wrong. Stockbrokers should help clients stick to an investment strategy. That is why it is always important to ask to see the firm's recommended portfolio allocations to judge your account against the firm's recommended model. The two need not match, but neither should they be diametrically opposed. Of course, everyone completes a client questionnaire when they open a brokerage account. The form usually asks information about assets, income, risk tolerances, and experience. In practice, the form seems to function more as a document that protects a brokerage firm against investor suitability complaints than anything that really helps an investor.

According to an SEC study, three approaches to suitability have developed in the courts, SEC enforcement action, and the Financial Industry Regulatory Authority (FINRA), which licenses stockbrokers, among other duties. Reasonable basis suitability means stockbrokers must investigate and have adequate information about recommended securities or strategies. Customer-specific suitability means stockbrokers must make recommendations based on a customer's financial situation and needs. Stockbrokers must obtain relevant—and current—information from customers about their financial situations.

Quantitative suitability applies to stockbrokers who have actual, or de facto, control over a customer account and must have a reasonable basis for believing the number of recommended transactions within a certain period, even if suitable when viewed in isolation, is not excessive and unsuitable for the customer when taken together in light of the customer's investment profile. This includes activities such as excessive trading.

Fiduciary Standard

Never forget that stockbrokers work on commissions. They are salesmen. They work for the sales divisions of banks. They are increasingly given names, to mask the fact that they are salesmen. Unlike RIAs, who have a fiduciary duty to clients that dictates that they act in the best interest of their clients, stockbrokers operate under different regulatory rules. This is an important distinction. It is not a fatal distinction, but it is widely misunderstood. The SEC issued a January 2011 report on RIAs and stockbrokers that recommended the fiduciary standard be imposed on stockbrokers. Naturally, this is an incredibly controversial issue, and nothing has happened. In the report, the SEC said that the fiduciary standard applies to an investment advisor's entire relationship with clients, and even prospective clients. Advisors have an obligation to disclose all material facts, and an obligation to use "reasonable care to avoid misleading'" clients, and anyone they want as clients. The fiduciary standard imposes the "duty of loyalty and care" that requires an advisor to serve the best interests of clients. The SEC report says this duty obligates advisors not to subordinate the clients' interests to their own interests. Advisors must make a reasonable investigation to determine that recommendations are not based on inaccurate or incomplete information.

When advisors select or recommend something to clients, they must reveal payment deals and business relationships. The advisor must explain how the conflicts are handled.

Advisors are required to disclose to clients how they are paid for their services. Advisors must detail in their firm's brochure how they are compensated for advisory services, provide a fee schedule, and disclose if the fees are negotiable. SEC staff believes fiduciary duties mean that advisors must charge fees that are fair and reasonable, and disclose if those fees are higher than others. Sounds pretty good, doesn't it?

Shakespeare's Rule

These types of discussions about how Wall Street makes money invariably invoke strong emotional reactions on Wall Street. This is why the Shakespearean rule of investing is helpful: "Me thinks thou doth protest too much." The intensity of Wall Street's criticism of an issue is typically inversely related to the amount of good that any proposal or idea will do for John and Jane Investor. Many people at the highest levels of Wall Street know this, yet they do little to nothing because there is little to be gained standing up for a group that generates a small amount of money. If you still think banks do not think about fees, you are wrong. In the midst of the financial crisis, a sales trader at a top international bank accidently e-mailed a confidential client form to a group of investors. The e-mail identified confidential information about a hedge fund client. The e-mail included the number of years of experience of the hedge fund trader, and the amount of annual fee income that trader paid to the bank. The amount was $250,000. That is real money, and that is where Wall Street directs its attention. Individual investors are road kill. Harsh words. True words. And it is a reality that many sophisticated people actively monitor.

A senior executive at one of the world's top exchanges is so concerned with making sure he doesn't get mugged by Wall Street that he pays a financial planner to supervise his brokers. He says he wants to make sure that the brokers are not trying to get away with anything.

Appeals to Common Sense

Not all brokers are bad. Many stockbrokers are very good. When you find a very good stockbroker, stay loyal. Refer friends and family to them. They work hard, and deserve to be paid well. Most people never get near those types of stockbrokers because their accounts are too small, or they have rotten luck. Most people get stockbrokers who are often trying to sell, sell, and sell. The most dangerous and disingenuous of the lot make common sense appeals that seem logical, but are not always straightforward. Common sense sales appeals always have a whiff of truth. A common ploy is to liken declines in the stock market to sales at department stores. That's a good point, of course, but it leaves out the most important point that the stockbroker usually did not tell the client to sell some or all of his holdings before the crash. The stockbroker would rather the client invest even more money because, after all, as the stockbroker may note, it pays to own stocks for the long-term. Of course, that may be true, but perhaps only for people who live for 100 years and never need access to their money. Naturally, the conversations rarely touch upon matters of risk and loss. The conversations can even be manipulative, or ignore difficult market facts like diversification is supposedly the antidote to risk, but correlation is the enemy.

Consider this from an e-mail received in the midst of the credit crisis in 2007. "We as investors have been lied to over and over again," a reader wrote. He was desperate. His stockbroker told him to buy Wells Fargo stock. When the stock began to decline, he asked his stockbroker what should he do. His stockbroker told him to sell his stock if he thought Wells Fargo would go out of business. If not, he should hold his shares or buy more. "How," he asked, "does the average investor make a decision?"[6]

Clearly, things are often not what they appear to be. Stockbrokers like to accept responsibility when clients make money, but investment losses prove President Kennedy's observation that success has a thousand fathers and failure is an orphan.

Trust but Verify

Never give your money to a stockbroker without first checking FINRA's BrokerCheck website or calling (800) 289-9999. This will tell you if anyone has filed complaints against the stockbroker, and if the stockbroker is involved, or has been involved, in any customer disputes or regulatory actions.

All stockbrokers are registered with the Central Registration Depository. You can find out if stockbrokers are properly licensed in your state and if they have had run-ins with regulators or received serious complaints from investors. You will also find information about the stockbrokers' educational background and work history. It is also important to check with state securities regulators who often have more comprehensive information—especially about investor complaints. Contact information for the state securities regulator is listed on the North American Securities Administrators Association website.

Never give money to a stockbroker or advisor who is not covered by the Securities Investor Protection Corporation (SIPC). SIPC is like the Federal Deposit Insurance Corporation, which protects people if a bank fails. If you give money to a non-SIPC member, you may not get your money back if the firm goes out of business.

Most people never ask about their stockbroker's qualifications or experience. They just hand over huge sums of money on the expectation that it will be invested responsibly. This always marvels the brokerage firm. The president says the first thing he would ask any broker who wants to manage his money is to share his most recent stockbrokerage statement and personal financial statement. This brokerage chief says it's important to see how a stockbroker handles his own finances before letting him handle yours. If the stockbroker balked—and most will—the brokerage chief said he would find someone else to handle his money. A better solution might be for stockbrokers to complete the new client questionnaire that all clients are asked to complete when opening an account. That way clients could get a sense of their stockbroker's financial personality, experience, and assets. Some people might feel uncomfortable being so direct, but it is far more uncomfortable to lose money because you failed to conduct basic due diligence.

At minimum, you want to know how long stockbrokers have been at a firm and if they plan to move in the next 24 months. Ask to see their resume. Ask about their families and goals. Ask them for the average account size, and median account size that they manage. You don't want to give someone your account if they mostly look after larger accounts, or smaller accounts. If they typically manage large accounts, small accounts may not get much attention. If they manage small accounts, they may not have the experience to handle a large account.

Ask the stockbroker how long clients stay with them. By some measures, stockbrokers only manage to keep clients for about two years. Ask stockbrokers to describe their worst investment mistake and shrewdest investment decision. What did they learn? Ask to meet their boss. Ask the stockbroker to give you a list of 10 clients that you can call as references. A list of three clients is not enough. Everyone has three friends. Ask them how their investor accounts were positioned before the 2007 credit crisis and afterward. You need to understand how they view market volatility and risk. If they say stocks fluctuate, be concerned. Such nonchalance could be a sign of a stockbroker who always effectively tells clients "don't be sore, buy some more." Ask stockbrokers how they define a successful relationship. Ask them if they measure their own performance, or client accounts, against a benchmark such as the Standard & Poor's 500 Index. The old college try does not cut it in the investment world. If it cannot be measured, it does not exist. You need to know how to measure investment results. A 10 percent gain is not good enough if the relevant benchmark index rose 20 percent. Again, all numbers, including all fees, must be contextualized and measured against something else. Find out if your account is designed to track the Standard & Poor's 500 Index, or a bond index, or something else. That is the measure that should be used to determine if the account is successful or not.

Ask stockbrokers how they manage clients. Ask how you can reach them if you have a question. You will, from time to time, need to have money transferred in or out of your account. Find out how long that takes. Ask them about how they are paid and how those rates or commissions compare to competitors.' In short, understand what you are getting for your money and who you are giving your money to. If it makes you uncomfortable to ask such pointed questions, at minimum ask your stockbroker to complete a Financial Advisor Questionnaire developed by AARP that you can find on the Internet. The more information you have, the better.

Active versus Passive Fund Management

The discipline of constantly questioning how your money is managed applies to all areas of your financial life. A healthy skepticism will serve you well, especially when picking funds or ETFs. Most investors with account balances under $100,000 should probably only buy ETFs or mutual funds that charge low management fees. If you must choose actively managed mutual funds, look at more than one year's performance. Compare fund fees. At minimum, see how the fund fared over five years. Ideally, review a fund's performance over its entire lifecycle. If the fund changed managers, look at how each manager performed. A lot of changes might indicate trouble at the fund. It is probably a good idea to initially avoid mutual fund rankings like Morningstar's star system. Do the work yourself. Develop your own opinion, and then compare it to Morningstar or other companies that rate funds.

The idea of owning indexes or ETFs that track the market is scary for many investors. Indexes rise and fall with the market. Actively managed funds have someone at the helm who hopefully buys low and sells high. Yet, some two-thirds of all mutual fund managers fail to beat their benchmarks.

Standard & Poor's put the question to the test. The company found that 71.9 percent of actively managed, large-capitalization mutual funds failed to outperform the S&P 500 from 2004 to 2008. The number was even higher for the S&P MidCap 400; 79.1 percent of mid-capitalization funds failed to outperform the Index. The number was even more dramatic for small-capitalization mutual funds; 85.5 percent of those funds failed to beat the S&P SmallCap 600 Index. Fixed income and international funds had similar performance. The results were similar in the 1999 to 2003 market cycle.

"The belief that bear markets favor active management is a myth," wrote Srikant Dash and Rosanne Pane, Standard & Poor's analysts in an April 2009 report that compared S&P indexes versus active funds scored in April 2009. [7]

Standard & Poor's has a vested interest in shaping perceptions about index funds and actively managed funds. The company makes loads of money licensing its indexes to mutual funds and other financial groups.

But the Massachusetts Pension Reserves Investment Management Board does is not similarly conflicted. The fund has a simple mandate: increasing returns on the almost $47 billion under management.

In August 2008, in the midst of the credit crisis, the pension fund fired five active-fund managers for poor performance. Money was taken from Legg Mason, Gardner Lewis, NWQ Investment, Mazama Capital, and Ariel Capital and invested in a Russell 3000 Index and a variety of hedge funds.

"We've been managing money here for 24 years and our approach utilizing traditional long-only equity managers has not added value over that span," according to Michael Travaglini, who at the time was the pension's executive director.[8]

The pension fund's decision attracted little attention off Wall Street. Dennis Gartman, publisher of the influential *Gartman Letter*, read by top hedge funds and banks, felt compelled to alert his subscribers to the decision's importance. He wrote:

"We strongly suggest that long-only equity managers read, and re-read and re-read again Mr. Travaglini's comment for we fear that this is the death knell for the long-only stock fund manager. His/her age has passed. The era of paying managers to be long of the equity market only, and to recompense them and to applaud them for relative performance is dying," Gartman wrote. "Money, in the future, will pay only for performance beyond a very small fixed fee, and it will be quite happy to pay well for excess performance. At the same time, it will be swift in culling those managers who do not perform positively."[9]

Indeed, Travaglini explained his funds decision by saying the pension fund wanted to create a structure that "consistently added value"[10]— and that is precisely the key issue that all investors must remember when dealing with stockbrokers and mutual funds.

Chapter 7

Cycles

Three major cyclical patterns influence the stock market's activity. Seasonal patterns influence monthly trading tones. Secular patterns, also called secular markets, occur when a stock or sector creates its own reality independent of the overall market. Apple is a famous example of a secular bull market as it has created new markets and new trading patterns after launching the iPhone and the iPad. Infamous examples of secular patterns include the rise and fall of real estate stocks and the Internet sector. Economic patterns, the third cyclical pattern, reflect the economy's growth and contractions. All three cycles function like ocean tides, or the rising and setting of the sun.

Every month in the stock market has a distinct personality. Some months are bullish simply because they coincide with events that impact trading, including the April 15 tax deadline, or the end of mutual fund fiscal years. Some months are bearish because historic declines have tended to occur in that month. These seasonal patterns have developed over 100 years. Wall Street uses seasonal patterns to frame trading and investment decisions. These seasonal patterns influence stock trading like magnets attract slivers of metals—except for when they don't. Major exogenous events—economic recessions, major bank failures, and the like—can override seasonality, which is why seasonality is mostly used as a prism to better focus the market, rather than as a foolproof trading system. Of course, the only people who believe in foolproof systems tend to be fools.

Time moves to a different meter in the market. A year has 256 trading days—not 365. Days are six-and-a-half hours long—not 24. The stock market, in New York City, opens at 9:30 A.M. and closes at 4 P.M. Anything that occurs before or after market hours exists only in relation to market hours. Even the hours of the trading session are not equal. The most critical times are usually the first and last half-hours of trading. In those 30-minute windows, the business of the day is handled, and everything else in between, barring major news events, is often uneventful.

Understanding each month's seasonal personality keeps investors synchronized with the stock market. The patterns provide an informational advantage over those who do not understand them. The patterns are like a doctor's stethoscope. They help identify and listen to the market's tempo.

Why these monthly patterns exist is a mystery, even though they are market facts. Facts are different than the truth. An idea supported by market data is a fact. Any idea not supported by data is speculation. Facts indicate where the truth lies. Facts are a market compass, and nothing more. When seasonal patterns work, they reinforce the idea that the stock market is somewhat predictable. When they fail, they are often an important indicator that something is wrong and forces are potentially brewing deep within the market that will soon roil the surface.

The Year in Stocks

January is a month of excitement as investors redeploy money after having sold money-losing stocks in December so that they can claim losses on their tax returns. In January, the Dow Jones Industrial

Average has risen 1.01 percent for the past 100 years and 1.2 percent for the past 50, and it has been flat for the past 20 years, according to Bespoke Investment Group, a research firm that advises institutional investors.[1] January is often filled with much emotion. If the past trading year was difficult, hope springs eternal in the New Year. If the past year was good, there is always hope the New Year will be even better. At the start of each year, all banks issue strategy reports predicting what will occur in the stock market. The reports are almost always universally bullish. The notes are widely distributed via massive e-mail distribution lists, institutional salesmen who call on major investors, and even by stockbrokers to their clients.

Two of the market's most important seasonal patterns occur in January: the January Barometer and the January Effect.

The January Barometer, according to the *Stock Trader's Almanac*, is a good predictor of the entire year. If the stock market advances in January, it is usually a good omen for the rest of the year. This has been accurate 78 percent of the time since 1950. The *Stock Trader's Almanac* says that every time since 1950 that the Standard & Poor's 500 Index has declined in January, it has preceded or extended a bear market, a flat market, or a 10 percent correction. If the Standard & Poor's 500 Index gains during the first five days of January, the market ends the year higher 86.5 percent of time.

Yale Hirsch, the *Stock Trader's Almanac*'s founder, created the January Barometer in 1972. Only six major errors have occurred since 1950. Why does the barometer work? It works because the Twentieth Amendment to the U.S. Constitution was passed in 1933, changing when defeated politicians left office. In January, the President of the United States delivers the State of the Union address and presents his annual budget, and this tends to motivate the market.

The January Effect is more narrowly focused than the January Barometer. The January Effect is one of the most widely traded events on Wall Street. The January Effect describes the strong performance of small-capitalization stocks during the first month of the year. In 1983, Donald Keim, a graduate student at the University of Chicago, discovered that small-capitalization stocks traded at the New York Stock Exchange and the American Stock Exchange outperform the stocks of larger companies. (For a long list of such stocks, see the iShares Russell 2000 Index Fund, an ETF.) Keim published his thesis, "Size Related Anomalies and Stock Return Seasonality: Further Empirical Evidence," in the *Journal of Financial Economics* in 1983. Because he found that a large portion of the return occurs in the first five trading days, the January Effect trade begins well in advance. Sometimes, investors begin buying small-capitalization stocks, or even ETFs that track those stocks, in the middle of November. This is another example of how the stock market discounts the future, and acts in anticipation of events.

The January Effect is so powerful that it worked after the Great Crash of 1929 and during the Great Depression: According to Jeremy Siegel, University of Pennsylvania Finance Professor:

> From August 1929 to the summer of 1932, when small-cap stocks lost 90 percent of their value, small stocks rose each January, posting monthly returns of 13 percent, 21 percent and 10 percent in 1930 and 1931 and 1932. It is testimony to the power of the January Effect that investors could have increased their wealth by 50 percent during the greatest stock crash in history by buying small stocks at the end of December in those three years and selling them at the end of the following month, putting their money in cash for the rest of the year.[2]

From 1925 through 2006, Siegel says, the average return of the Standard & Poor's 500 Index was 1.57 percent, compared to 6.07 percent for small-capitalization stocks.

February is typically a quiet month. After so much action in January, the Dow Jones Industrial Average tends to drift lower, almost as if investors have worn themselves out in the previous month. By February, stock market strategists, who maintain performance targets for the Standard & Poor's 500 Index, and analysts, who follow individual stocks, have typically already issued their best ideas in January, or perhaps December. Thus February is often spent calibrating predictions against realities and visiting clients to expand upon what was already said—and hopefully generating trading revenues for their banks.

The Dow Jones Industrial Average has declined in February by 0.12 percent for the past 100 years, 0.03 percent for the past 50 years, and 0.10 percent for the past 20 years, according to the Bespoke Investment Group. This muted performance is likely a reflection of market inflows. So much money pours into the stock market in January that there is little left to propel stocks higher in February. In the absence of new sources of money, stock prices stall, or in the parlance of Wall Street, move sideways.

March often sees modest gains. This is the last month of the first quarter and the start of pre-earnings season positioning as investors prepare for corporations to release earnings reports. In March, analysts update their earnings models. They also release research reports that identify companies expected to deliver better than expected earnings per share, and those that aren't. Major investors are often in close contact with analysts who share their thinking with their best clients before the research is made public. This inevitably incites investors to get ahead of the actual earnings reports, effectively trying to buy low that which is expected to trade higher. The market is often pushed higher as the natural position of investors is long, which is to say that they buy stocks rather than sell them. The Dow Jones Industrial Average's rise for March has been 0.65 percent for the past 100 years, 1.09 percent for the past 50 years, and 1.12 percent for the past 20 years, according to Bespoke Investment Group.

April is usually one of the best months of the year. The Dow Jones Industrial Average has risen 1.36 percent in April over the last 100 years, 2.02 percent over the last 50 years, and 2.65 percent over the last 20 years. The bulk of corporate America releases first quarter earnings reports during April. Investors calibrate stocks against earnings estimates and stock strategists prognostications. If stocks fall short of expectations, earnings guidance from corporate executives can prove powerful enough to persuade investors to look past a quarter of less than stellar results. The market always looks forward. And there is not as much risk giving companies the benefit of the doubt at the start of the year, as toward the end.

April's stock market can be volatile because of the April 15 tax deadline. This sometimes causes, or is blamed for causing, market declines due to people selling stocks to pay tax bills.

April is an important piece of the sentiment puzzle. If stock prices decline, or earnings are not as good as expected, a warning signal is issued. Market conditions may get rocky. If the stock market moves in the opposite direction of what was predicted by market pundits earlier in the year, it is dangerous to ignore the diversion.

May is often an in-between month that is neither bullish, nor bearish. It is the second month of the second quarter and investors are often waiting for another batch of earnings reports and reacting and responding to events and economic data. In May, the Dow Jones Industrial Average has risen 0.02 percent for the past 100 years, it has declined 0.09 percent for the past 50 years, and it has been up 0.99 percent for the past 20 years, according to Bespoke Investment Group. May also anchors the end of one of the stock market's most profitable six-month trends: Sell in May and go away. The old saw, according to the *Stock Trader's Almanac*, advocates selling all of your stocks in May, and investing in bonds. The results are powerful, though it is not clear the trend is actually traded by many portfolio managers, even though $10,000 invested from November to April from 1950 to 2009 grew to $527,388. What happened to the same $10,000 invested in stocks from May to October? It declined by $474. Why? Summer and fall are often punctuated by sheer boredom—or terror.

The sell in May saying is widely known all over Wall Street. Yet, almost no one does anything about it in a large-scale, meaningful way. What if the stock market surges from May to October? Try explaining that to investors if you are a portfolio manager who is paid to invest other people's money.

June coalesces hope and reality. This is when investors start focusing on second-quarter earnings reports. Stock analysts start checking with the companies that they follow in anticipation of earnings reports. Investors call analysts for insights so that they can calibrate positions or trading strategies. The end of the month also marks the end of the first half of the trading year. It is a time of reflection and action for money managers if their fund is trailing benchmark indexes, such as the Standard &

Poor's 500 or Russell 2000 indexes. In June, the Dow Jones Industrial Average has risen 0.38 percent for the past 100 years; it has had a decline of 0.63 percent for the past 50 years, and it has been flat for the past 20 years, according to the Bespoke Investment Group.

Meanwhile, schools are getting out all over the United States, and the focus of many people on Wall Street and Main Street turns toward thoughts of summer vacations, three-day weekends, and keeping kids busy.

July is a data-heavy month. Many corporations release second-quarter earnings reports, and investors now have data on half of the trading year. The *Stock Trader's Almanac* says July is the best month of the third quarter.

The Dow Jones Industrial Average's July gain has been 1.4 percent for the past 100 years, 0.87 percent for the past 50 years, and 1.47 percent for the past 20 years, according to Bespoke Investment Group.

August is supposed to be the quietest month of the trading year. Every August, so the conventional narrative goes, senior traders and portfolio managers leave for their vacations, as do many Europeans. The stock and option markets are left in the hands of junior traders or fund managers with instructions not to do anything stupid.

Statistics show August is a slow month. The Dow rose in August 0.97 percent for the past 100 years and 0.15 percent for the past 50 years, and it declined 0.65 percent for the past 20 years, according to Bespoke Investment Group. Since 1987, the *Stock Trader's Almanac* says that August has been the second worst month for the Dow Jones Industrial Average and Standard & Poor's 500 Index.

The summer of 2010 and 2011 are notable exceptions to the slow August expectation. Then, the European Union was rumored to be in danger of collapse, if Greece and Italy defaulted on their debts. The markets reacted with great volatility. Many senior fund managers and traders left their weekend homes to man the turrets.

September is often the most volatile month of the trading year. All of the stock market's historic crashes have happened in October. So the collective mass of humanity that forms the stock market—and which has the emotional depth of a 13-year-old kid experiencing puberty—spends September worrying about what will happen in October. September also marks the 2008 bankruptcy of Lehman Brothers. The bank's demise is always mentioned each September and it has an ask-not-for-whom-the-bell-tolls psychological effect on many investors since major U.S. investment banks do not typically go bankrupt.

In September, the Dow Jones Industrial Average has fallen an average 0.83 for the last 100 years, 0.79 percent for the past 50 years, and 0.60 percent for the past 20 years, according to Bespoke Investment Group. The month also coincides with one of Wall Street's most important events: annual bonuses. This is a very big deal. Wall Street operates on OPM—other people's money—until bonus time. September is when everyone is evaluated on how much money they made handling OPM. If they performed well, they get big bonuses. If they performed poorly, they do not get a big bonus, and maybe they get a pink slip, or no bonus at all. Investors who are ahead of performance benchmarks for the year often start reducing their market risk and taking profits in September so they don't jeopardize their annual bonuses. Investors and traders trailing benchmark indexes, such as the Standard & Poor's or Russell 2000 indexes, often take on more risk because they want their bonuses.

"Fear often outstrips greed in September or October," says Steve Sosnick, a senior trader with Timberhill, one of the world's largest trading firms. "This coincides with people locking in a good year, and sometimes you get a sell off because people panic and want to get out."[3]

October is surprisingly not as fierce as its reputation. At least that is what the statistics show. The Dow Jones Industrial Average has gained in October an average of 0.05 percent over the last 100 years, 0.51 percent in the past 50 years, and 1.36 percent in the past 20, according to Bespoke Investment Group. But when October is bad, it is really bad. The major crashes occurred in October in 1929 and 1987. The global financial crisis—GFC, to insiders—also started in October. Yet, October is often a great time to buy stocks. Why? The six-month bull streak that ends in May begins in November. Anyone who buys in October gets in early. Besides, as all contrarian investors know, it is often smart to buy when everyone else is afraid.

October also marks the start of the fourth quarter. Since 1928, the Standard & Poor's 500 Index has gained an average of 2.31 percent in the fourth quarter, with positive returns 71.6 percent of the time, according to the Bespoke Investment Group. The previous three quarters seem to influence the last quarter. When the Standard & Poor's 500 Index rises in the first three quarters of the year, the index has averaged a fourth-quarter gain of 4.19 percent, with positive returns 82.7 percent of the time, according to Bespoke. When the Standard & Poor's 500 Index has declined in the first three quarters, it has averaged a fourth-quarter decline of 1.06 percent.

October also marks a major mutual fund industry event. October 30 marks the fiscal year-end for many mutual funds. This is when funds declare capital gains and losses. The event is so well known that it even has a name: window dressing.

Fund managers do not want to include the names of loser stocks on year-end reports that are published and sent to shareholders. Therefore, they sell loser stocks to cover up the fact that they made poor decisions. This can push stocks, and even the entire market, up or down. Many stocks trading near their 52-week lows often drop even further. This is a trading event. Investment bank trading strategists compile and circulate lists of the top holdings of various mutual funds. Some hedge funds do the research on their own. Institutional investors, for instance, hedge funds, short "window dressing" stocks in anticipation of the forced selling, and then position for them to advance when the forced selling subsides. Big banks even create baskets of window-dressing stocks and sell them to big investors who trade them as customized ETFs.

November is often a good month. This is probably due to the onset of major U.S. holidays, including Thanksgiving and Christmas. The trading year is almost over. In November, the Dow Jones Industrial Average gain for the past 100 years was 0.72 percent, 1.22 percent for the past 50 years, and 1.70 percent for the past 20 years, according to Bespoke Investment Group. This month marks the start of the *Stock Trader's Almanac's* best six months strategy of buying in November and selling in May.

December belongs to Santa. The country has the yuletide spirit, as does most of the world, and people spend. This makes retail sales a powerful indicator of the stock market and the economy. Because consumer spending drives the U.S. economy, accounting for a full two-thirds of the Gross Domestic Product (GDP), retail sales are embedded with meaning far more profound than just getting junior a Tickle-Me-Elmo doll.

Robust holiday sales indicate that Americans are economically confident and willing to spend money, which means that they feel good about the stability of their jobs and their ability to pay bills—if not in full, at least in monthly installments sent to credit card companies. Ripples move through the economy, all the way to factories and other manufacturers who make the stuff that people buy.

Bad holiday sales are a disturbing omen. If people are not spending money, it means people are worried about their jobs and the economy, and their lack of spending could send shock waves through the economy. This is so disturbing to Wall Street that it merits its own trading adage: If Santa Claus should fail to call, bears may come to Broad and Wall. This fearsome jingle was coined by Yale Hirsch, the founder of the *Stock Trader's Almanac*. If the yuletide spirit is absent, it can get very grim inside the New York Stock Exchange at the intersection of Wall and Broad streets in Lower Manhattan. Mostly, though, Santa delivers, and the stock market rallies in the last five days of the year, and the first two in January, the *Stock Trader's Almanac* notes.

The Dow's average December gain in the past 100 years is 1.39 percent, 1.51 percent for the last 50 years, and 1.80 percent for the last 20 years.

Mysterious Repetitions

The curious fact about seasonal stock market patterns is that it is a systematic effect without a definitive cause. No one really knows why the market does certain things in certain months. Even Donald Keim, who discovered the January Effect in 1983, ended his research paper without a definitive explanation for the phenomenon.

The most plausible reasons for seasonality appear to be psychological and structural. Because everyone is conditioned to expect the patterns, some say they continually occur. Structural events—like the end of mutual fund fiscal years—clearly play a role. Those events cause widespread stock trading, anticipated by other investors who position accordingly. The reaction to the event helps solidify the perception that the seasonal effect exists. This is even evident at certain times of the month. Many traders look for short-term opportunities at the beginning and ends of months on the theory that the market can lift higher because many people are investing in mutual funds or retirement accounts.

Repetition creates psychological realities. Media and technology play supporting roles. Not a month passes without some journalist, blogger, trader, or market strategist, talking about seasonal patterns. The *Stock Trader's Almanac* is largely responsible for establishing seasonality as a major market force. Published since 1966, the *Stock Trader's Almanac* is Wall Street's equivalent of Benjamin Franklin's *Poor Richard's Almanac*: a compendium of facts, insights, and observations about seasons and patterns. The Almanac is widely distributed on Wall Street. Traders use it as a reference book. Banks give it to clients as holiday gifts. *Stock Trader's Almanac* aficionados can even register to receive e-mail alerts of seasonal trading opportunities. Many Wall Street stock market strategists also notify clients in daily stock market reports about seasonal influences.

In totality, media reports, strategy notes, and alerts arguably create flash mobs in the market. A flash mob describes groups of people wired together via e-mail, mobile phone texts, and other electronic messaging, who may or may not know each other, and unite around an objective for a short period of time. The computerized trading programs, or algorithms, that are increasingly used to trade stocks and options, likely exacerbate the mob's impact.

Flash Mobs

Bill Wasik, now an editor at *Wired* magazine, is often credited with organizing the first flash mob. In June 2003, he sent an e-mail that ultimately reached about 200 people. Everyone was invited to meet in the rug department at Macy's in New York City. When asked by the salesmen if they needed assistance, they each said that they lived on a commune and were looking for a love rug. Another time Wasik got 500 people to meet by a giant animatronic T-Rex dinosaur at the Toys "R" Us in Times Square, New York City. At an agreed upon time, in unison, the mob rushed the T-Rex, fell to their knees, and began screaming and waving their hands.[4]

Does something similar happen in the stock market? Absolutely. Swap out rugs and dinosaurs for stocks or indexes or rumors or seasonal trends and you have focus for a financial flash mob. The mob is the crowd on Wall Street. Can the crowd move the market or stocks? Absolutely. Is the mob powerful enough to move the Dow Jones Industrial Average or the Standard & Poor's 500 Index higher for an entire month? Maybe.

Flash mobs are powered by social networks. And Wall Street, in its own way, is filled with social networks linked together by instant messaging networks, and e-mail DLs—or distribution lists. These networks are used by banks, strategists, and others to send research and strategy notes to like-minded investors, who in turn often forward the notes to clients or colleagues. The communiqués are often spread from one group to the next. Often, journalists are part of the network and that helps the idea reach the maximum number of people. After a while, it doesn't matter who sent the idea first or even if the stock market does what it was supposed to do. If investors are told to expect stocks to rise in January, they buy in anticipation of a rally, and the January Effect is authenticated if stocks rise. If stocks decline, the dialogue turns to learning why stock prices fell in violation of the seasonal trend.

The media telegraphs and reinforces the seasonal messages. The danger of the stock market social network, in its broadest definition, is that it also empowers individual investors who have no discriminating market knowledge, or experience. Soon, the least knowledgeable people in the stock market feel the most empowered by the information and they act because good things are supposed to happen. Often they do. Sometimes they don't. Sometimes the T-Rex wakes up and starts eating people. It just depends on the season.

History's Hiccups

Seasonal patterns are like navigational systems in cars. They provide a general sense of direction, but sometimes, they tell you to turn left and drive off a cliff. The same is true of technical analysis. Everyone looks

at charts to see what happened in the past so they can better understand the present and future. But no one bets it all on technical analysis
trading signals. Why? The past can be an unreliable market indicator.
There is a colorful saying among traders that all ships at the bottom
of the sea are filled with charts. It is also true that lots of ships without charts sank because they ran into stuff they didn't see. The important fact to remember about patterns and seasons is that they are tools
investors should use—but not be used by.

The Economy in Slow Motion

A lengthy discussion of seasonal patterns may encourage the idea of the
stock market as a giant monolith that makes its own reality in reaction
to, and anticipation of, the world around it. That is only partially correct. The U.S. economy heavily influences the U.S. stock market. So
do other economies because various U.S. companies derive significant
revenue from foreign nations. This is a key reason why December retail
sales reports are important to the stock market. Retail sales reflect economic activity. If people are buying toys and computers and all kinds of
presents, factories are busy and people are employed.

The economy is the ground under the stock market's feet. The
economy shifts and ripples in response to monthly data assessing
its health. Those movements are reflected by the stock market as
different stocks and sectors perform better or worse during different phases. Most investors would quickly find little time to analyze stocks if he tried tracking the slew of economic indicators to
determine what, if anything, the Baltic Dry Index's latest reading
means for the Consumer Price Index and what that might portend
for U.S. GDP.

To make things simpler, and because most seasoned investors are
always trying to apply the KISS principle to information and investment decisions, investors focus on a critical economic report that is
released on the first day of every month by the Institute for Supply
Management. The Institute's Report on Business, known simply as
ISM, is widely used by stock investors to measure the business cycle's
growth and contraction.

ISM's reports have a powerful influence on the stock market. A good ISM report could make a good month even better. A bad report could overpower seasonal tendencies and prompt sophisticated investors to reallocate their stock portfolios. Stocks that have rallied higher—and which are like catnip to retail investors who often buy stocks with rising prices and motion and lots of media talk—could soon decline as the business cycle shifts, because not all stocks advance during different phases of the economic cycle. To be sure, not all portfolio managers immediately adjust their investments when ISM data are released, but strategists at top banks say ISM often drives client conversations and portfolio analysis.

ISM's beauty is its simplicity, its age, and its provenance. The data are expressed as a single number that immediately indicates if the economy is growing or contracting. If ISM is above 50, the economy is growing. If ISM is below 50, the economy is shrinking. Since the 2007 credit crisis, ISM has increased in popularity as the stock market has increasingly been influenced by macroeconomic factors.

ISM data have been produced since 1923. This is important to investors because it provides almost 100 years of data to provide context for analyzing ISM's movements.

Perhaps best of all, the data come from corporate America, and it is thus viewed as particularly authentic. The U.S. federal government releases most economic data. The U.S. Department of Labor's Bureau of Labor Statistics produces the Consumer Price Index that measures monthly changes in the prices urban consumers pay for goods and services. The U.S. Department of Commerce's Bureau of Economic Analysis produces GDP data. All of these reports are important parts of the investment puzzle. But at times investors have questioned the integrity of government data. This occurred during the 2007 credit crisis when reports were less dour than expected. Some thought politicians manipulated data to win votes or influence perceptions that the economy was not as bad as feared. There is no evidence the reports were manipulated, but the skepticism is a hangover effect from a period in the market that will define the next few generations of investors just as the Great Crash of 1929, and the economic depression of the 1930s, altered investor outlooks, of another generation.

The Guts of ISM

The ISM report has two really critical parts: new orders and PMI. When investors refer to ISM, they mean PMI. The acronym once stood for purchasing manager's index; it was abbreviated to avoid diluting ISM's brand.

The new orders data are considered "the guts of ISM." New orders data show if the economy is slowing, or accelerating, because they show if corporations are ordering more or less than before. Sometimes, new orders will slip below 50 before PMI dips lower. This is why many seasoned investors view new orders as a leading indicator of PMI.

PMI measures five pieces of ISM's monthly-data: new orders, production, employment, supplier deliveries, and inventories. Each sector accounts for 20 percent of PMI's total value. When PMI is above 50, it indicates economic expansion. Below 50, it indicates economic contraction.

Some investors criticize ISM data because consumer spending—not manufacturing—drives the U.S. economy. That is an important caveat, but not fatal. PMI data explains about 60 percent of the annual variation in GDP, according to the Institute for Supply Management, with a margin of error of 0.48 percent, up or down. A 60 percent coverage rate might seem weak, but almost all major investment banks produce various economic indicators that function like ISM data. That is how important ISM is on Wall Street. Many investors track global PMI data to gauge economic activity in the United Kingdom, China, and Europe. PMI has become Wall Street's common measure of economic cycles. Goldman Sachs maintains a Global Leading Indicator. The GLI is based on 12 economic indicators and was built to lead other economic reports. J.P. Morgan has the Global Manufacturing Report PMI that gathers data from more than 7,000 purchasing executives in almost 30 countries. The report is estimated to cover 86 percent of global manufacturing, and to provide an early indicator of global economic and business conditions. The report is released on the first day of the month, like ISM, but one hour later. The report is often available on ISM's website.

Numerical Nuances

Simple is almost always best, but understanding nuance is not far behind. The key to interpreting ISM—and some would say this is true of all economic data—is focusing on rates of change from one month to the next. This provides another early warning signal. Say PMI was at 58, and then it dropped to 54 and then 53, or that it rose from one month to the next by three points and then four points and then it stalled. All of those data points indicate some degree of economic expansion because PMI is above 50. But that is not the real message. If PMI was increasing at a rate of 4 percent month-to-month, and suddenly dropped to 2 percent—even though the absolute number was above 50—it is a sign that the economic expansion is stalling and could be preparing to contract. Portfolio managers would respond by thinking about readjusting portfolio allocations, because some stocks do better at different stages of the economic cycle.

Says Who? Says Goldman Sachs

Timing is everything in investing. Success is often determined not only by what you own, but when you own it. You can buy a stock for all the right reasons and still lose money because you were out of synch with the economic cycle, which can be more profound than seasonal patterns. This is critical because certain stock market sectors work best at different ISM stages. Cyclical sectors—energy, materials, and industrials—usually do best when the economy is growing. Defensive sectors—healthcare, staples, and utilities—often outperform when the economy is shrinking. All the other sectors are somewhere in between.

ISM has four phases. Each phase favors a particular sector. Stock sector memberships are easy to determine. Yahoo! Finance lists stock sector membership under the Profile tab that appears on the left-hand side of each stock summary page. This is market sensitive information. ISM's business cycle measurement is an important part of how stock market portfolio strategists, including Goldman Sachs, view the Standard & Poor's 500 Index, and each sector.

The four parts of the U.S. business cycle, as measured by ISM, and according to Goldman Sachs research, are:

1. **Early contraction:** When ISM drops below 50 and troughs, or hits bottom, healthcare, utilities, consumer staples, and telecommunications services perform best. This cycle's median length is nine months. (Median means that half of the cycles lasted longer than nine months, and half lasted less.)
2. **Late contraction:** When ISM moves from trough to 50, materials, information technology, consumer discretionary, and financial stocks perform best. This cycle's median length is seven months.
3. **Early expansion:** When ISM moves from 50 to peak, energy, materials, industrials, and information technology sectors perform best. This cycle's median length is 11 months.
4. **Late expansion:** When ISM moves from peak to 50, financials, utilities, telecommunications services, and consumer staples sectors perform best. This cycle's median length is 11 months.

In total, the median economic cycle lasts 38 months. During this time, the economy expands and contracts. Half of the economic cycles last longer, and half are shorter. This is important. It touches upon the importance of five-year windows in the market. Remember, every five years tends to witness the birth of a bull market, its death, and its rebirth. During those cycles, the economy also shifts gears, and the average investor scrambles after rallies and frequently buys high and sells low as economic and market cycles roil stock prices. Understanding ISM, and how its movements influence stock sectors and stock selection, provides another level of defense against buying or selling the wrong stock or ETF at the wrong time. Understanding ISM's cycles also improves investment returns because it provides a map of what performs best during each cycle.

Because ISM phases can last for seven months or more, they heavily impact the stock market. Portfolio managers are compensated based on annual performance. Many reallocate their portfolios to benefit from sectors, or groups, that work best during certain phases of the economic cycle. This is not trading. It is still investing. In fact, it is very disciplined investing, and another indication that no one really practices buy-and-hold investing as it is explained to Main Street. Only Main Street blindly buys-and-holds stocks. The median annualized returns of the 10 sectors of the Standard & Poor's 500 Index react differently as ISM advances and declines above and below 50, as demonstrated by the absolute annualized median returns since 1973, according to Goldman Sachs data.

When ISM rises from 50 toward its peak, the Standard & Poor's 500 Index gained 13.7 percent; Energy, 16.9 percent, Materials, 20.2 percent; Industrials, 18 percent; Discretionary, 11.9 percent; Staples, 10 percent; Health Care, 3.3 percent; Financials, 7.2 percent; Technology, 20.8 percent; Telecommunications, 1.7 percent; and Utilities, 1.7 percent. These numbers tell a story. When the economy is expanding, it creates demand and earnings power for the energy, materials, and industrial sectors as the manufacturing sector increases production to meet consumer demand. The technology sector does well, too, as semiconductor chips are now used to power everything from automobiles to computers to household appliances. The sector performance will influence stock and ETF selection in the stock market. Investors will want to buy that which is rising, and avoid that which is not.

When ISM falls from its peak to 50, the performance of the 10 sectors changes again. The Standard & Poor's 500 Index gained 13.6 percent; Energy, 23.8 percent; Materials, 7.9 percent; Industrials, 9.9 percent; Discretionary, 9.5 percent; Staples, 13.9 percent; Health Care, 18.3 percent; Financials, 23.8 percent; Technology, 7.9 percent; Telecommunications, 17.9 percent; and Utilities, 23 percent.

When ISM falls below 50 and hits its trough, or bottom, the sector performance changes once more. The Standard & Poor's 500 Index gained 7.5 percent; Energy, 13.8 percent; Materials, 4.3 percent; Industrials, 3.8 percent; Discretionary, 7.1 percent; Staples, 15.3 percent; Health Care, 22.3 percent; Financials, 6.5 percent; Technology, 6.5 percent; Telecommunications, 13.5 percent; and Utilities, 14.5 percent.

When ISM troughs, and moves back to 50, the market ripples with even more changes. The Standard & Poor's 500 Index gained 25.9 percent; Energy, 10.8 percent; Materials, 51.9 percent; Industrials, 28.8 percent;

Discretionary, 42.3 percent; Staples, 19.8 percent; Health Care, 14.9 percent; Financials, 24.8 percent; Technology, 17.6 percent; Telecommunications, 1.7 percent; and Utilities, 1.7 percent.

The numbers tell a simple story. The stock market is like an engine with 10 cylinders. Each cylinder rises and falls in reaction to different parts of the economic journey. Energy is needed to power a growing economy, while the financial sector gets busy providing financing needed to buy things or finance construction, while utility and telecommunication companies benefit from increased activity.

People feel confident when the economy is growing and they consume more (consumer staples) and spend money on information technology, such as computers and iPads and iPhones. They buy cars and washing machines. Commodities like copper often increase in value, too. Industrial commodities that help make things rise in prices because of demand. People visit health care providers and take care of themselves. That may seem strange, but ask your dentist during your next visit how the economy influences his practice. During good times, people take care of their teeth. In rough times, they may have teeth pulled because it is less expensive than a crown.

A lot of effort is exerted trying to time the stock market's twists and turns, and the economy perhaps even more. If you are attracted to this pursuit, try to focus on the tops and bottoms of economic cycles. That is what most impacts stock market sector rotation of major investors. The rotation at various stages of ISM's movements is right about 70 to 80 percent of the time. Outliers always occur. During the credit crisis, for example, the out-of-favor technology sector was actually in favor because companies like Apple and Microsoft had clean balance sheets and tens of billions of dollars in cash. The key is getting the core right, smoothing the inevitable rough edges, and always monitoring risk.

ISM below 50 does not necessarily mean the economy is in a recession. For that to happen, the National Bureau of Economic Research (NBER) must declare a recession. The popular definition of a recession is two consecutive quarters of declining GDP data—though NBER has its own methods—and its own distinct sense of time.

GDP measures an economy's total economic output. In the United States, consumer spending dominates GDP. In 2004, when the U.S. GDP totaled $11.7 trillion, consumer spending represented 70 percent of the GDP. The rest was comprised of government spending at 19 percent and capital spending at 16 percent. (GDP equals 100 percent after subtracting 5 percent for net imports.) By 2010, U.S. GDP was $14.9 trillion. Many investors believe 3 percent annual GDP growth is reasonable, and that anything slower is not. From 1991 to 2010, U.S. GDP has increased at an average annual rate of about 2.5 percent.

To stay ahead of economists, whose pronouncements seem to often occur after the fact, many investors consider copper, high-yield bonds, and small-capitalization stocks as sensitive economic indicators.

Copper, an industrial metal, is used in a broad range of consumer and capital goods and in construction. Copper is the ultimate harbinger of trends in goods-producing industries, according to Randall Forsyth, a *Barron's* columnist and editor. "So acute is the red metal's sensitivity to business trends that it has been dubbed Dr. Copper, in recognition that it is the commodity with a PhD in economics," Forsyth says. "That's a misnomer since copper can call economic turning points better than most academics, many of whom prefer to dissect the past rather than try to figure out the present, let alone where we're headed."[5] High-yield bonds are so named because they pay higher yields to buyers to compensate them for the risk of loaning money to companies and business ventures that typically have weaker balance sheets than, say, a blue-chip company such as Coca-Cola or General Electric. If investors think the economy is deteriorating, high-yield bonds typically reflect those concerns. Why? Small companies, or risky ventures, tend to issue high-yield debt. High-yield debt is expensive to issue because companies have to pay investors much higher debt payments than, for example, a proven blue-chip stock. If the economy sours, it typically means those companies will have trouble servicing their debts. Why? Small-companies typically have high-fixed costs and small financial resources to withstand an economic crisis. Major investors know this and are quick to adjust high-yield debt prices.

By definition, a company that issues high-yield debt may lack the classic "margin of safety" that many wise investors consider the most important words in investing. If the economy turns down, the companies tend to have more debt to service. The companies also tend to have lots of financial and operating leverage. Operating leverage means that earnings are highly variable. Consider airlines. They have high fixed costs and flying a plane 50 percent full or 100 percent still costs the same.

Those leveraged conditions often exist at companies that issue high-yields bonds, which is why they are a working investor's economic indicator. The same is true of the iShares Russell 2000 Index Fund (IWM). This ETF is made of 2,000 small companies. Many hedge funds view IWM as a proxy of the U.S. economy. They buy IWM when the economy is growing, and bet on its decline when the economy is shrinking.

Investors also focus on consumer spending, which is a key indicator of corporate profits and is critical to the stock market because a slowdown in earnings usually means stock prices will fall. But consumer spending is more difficult for most people to follow than ISM data that is pushed into the market and widely remarked upon by investment strategists. Consumer spending data are released by the U.S. Department of Labor's Bureau of Labor Statistics, but they are not as easy to understand as ISM data. The U.S. federal government's economists call consumer spending personal consumer expenditures (PCE). There is even a glossary of terms comprising it.

Joseph Ellis, a former Goldman Sachs analyst who was consistently ranked as the top retail analyst on Wall Street, believes consumer spending is a good indicator of stock market advances and declines. He says in his book, *Ahead of the Curve*, that this relationship is not well recognized by most investors and economists. "In other words, consumer spending is dominant in the economy as a whole to such an extent that it is, by itself, the sector that cyclically determines the direction of the overall economy. This being the case, carefully monitoring overall consumer spending—or, even more significantly, forecasting the direction of consumer demand—is the key that unlocks effective forecasting for most other developments and sectors in the economy."[6]

Because consumer spending drives the U.S. economy, Ellis sees it as a powerful indicator. He focuses on real consumer spending. In economics, "real" means that the dollars were converted to units to remove the impact of inflation. John Paulson, the hedge fund manager, used a similar method when he studied U.S. housing prices to see if they had ever before declined when he famously decided to bet that they would. Ellis feels so strongly about the importance of using consumer spending to forecast the stock market and the economy that he has created a website, www.aheadofthecurve-thebook.com, that lets investors create and maintain charts that will help them track rates of change in consumer spending.

Action

Entire books have been written about seasonal patterns, technical analysis, business cycles, and the reams of indicators that supposedly telegraph signals of this or that before it happens. They are all useful for anyone who likes following them or takes comfort in models. But they likely provide more information than anyone will ever use and who simply hopes to buy and sell stocks at propitious times. That is why ISM and seasonality are a type of practitioner's shorthand for the primary cycles that influence stock trading. They are both powerful reminders that the stock market is influenced by forces beyond its control. Those forces can turn bull markets into bear markets and vice versa.

Let ISM data be a reminder of the importance of thinking in terms of three- to five-year investment and economic cycles. If you buy good stocks that pay dividends and make real products, and hold them for three to five years, or longer, and you are always evaluating them against market and economic realities, even better. That analytical exercise should help insulate most stock portfolios from the worst of the stock market's woes, and provide comfort in the inevitably difficult stretches of the economy and stock market.

The key point with indicators and cycles is that they provide context to the stock market. The stock market is not static. It changes. The principles of motion and change are intuitively understood by

most people in their nonfinancial lives, yet they often have great difficulty comprehending the same truth in the financial markets. They
so want the stock market, and especially their own stocks, to rise in
value, that they forget stocks, like trees, do not grow to the sky, but
instead rise and fall like waves on the ocean.

Chapter 8

Behavior

Everyone thinks there are only two parties to every trade: a buyer and a seller. That is not true. There are actually three: you, whoever buys or sells in response to you, and your own distinctive psychology that permeates the transaction.

Until recently, practitioners and scholars viewed the psychology of investing with some derision. They viewed the markets through mathematical models; soft sciences were not of much import. And then in 2002, Daniel Kahneman became the first psychologist to be awarded the Nobel Prize for Economics. A Nobel Prize apparently does wonders for helping an idea gain acceptance, especially at tradition-bound business schools whose professors can be resistant to new ideas. Ever since, the study of how emotion and psychology influence investment decision-making has steadily entered the financial mainstream. Many of the pioneers of behavioral finance, including Kahneman, are still alive. They include Terrence Odean, Richard Thaler, and Colin Camerer. Some may win Nobel prizes in the future.

It is arguably easier to analyze stocks than the human mind. To wade through the ideas of psychologists and behavioral economists is to journey into regions that seem to have no end. But in investing, one must think with probabilities, make decisions, and act, and it is clear that some major psychological pitfalls hurt most investors most of the time.

Most investors believe they know more than they do. They think that their experiences enable them to make better decisions. They are *overconfident* in their abilities and never realize it. They engage in *fast-thinking*. They put *halos* on people and things; they see what they want, not what is. They *anchor* on certain facts, or think that what just happened is indicative of a pattern. The behaviorists call that the *recency effect*.

These biases—and that is a word that psychologists use for pitfalls that adversely influence rational thought—tend to emerge when making complex decisions with uncertain outcomes—like investing.

One Brain: Two Minds

In 2009, Daniel Kahneman was in Munich. He was speaking at a conference in the wake of the credit crisis of 2007. He was on a panel called "Reflection on a Crisis," with Nassim Taleb, the philosopher-trader who introduced the world to the idea of black swans. They were an odd couple. Taleb was animated with indignation and plans to fix the world. Kahneman was quiet. He softly smiled at Taleb, and spoke of how the mind works, and doesn't work.[1]

Kahneman said the mind has two systems. System One is intuitive. System Two is more calculated and reasoning. Sometimes, System One makes decisions that should be made by System Two, and that can create problems for investors. To illustrate the point, he asked everyone to imagine a medallion with two faces in profile, one facing right the other facing left. He was describing the famous coin of Janus, the Roman god of doors and beginnings. He said the images were often used in experiments to show how quickly people see patterns—even if patterns do not exist. The image with a single face is shown to people. They see the image many times. First right, then left, and so on. When people are presented for the first time with the total image of the two faces together, one staring right and other staring left—the first conflict—people think they saw the last image they had just seen, not the total image. He said the experiment shows that it is easy to make people see patterns even when they do not exist. He noticed a similar tendency when he lived in California. Sometimes years passed without rain. If three years passed, Kahneman said, people began believing that the climate had changed. Experiments with coins, and observations about the climate, seem far removed from the stock market, but they are not. According to Kahneman, who has since written a book, *Thinking Fast and Slow*, that elaborates on the mind's two systems, says it is clear that people easily develop ideas about new worlds or new regimes.

"It takes about three years for people to think they are in a new regime," Kahneman said. "This turns out to be very important when you are looking at mass phenomenon in the economy, the speed at which people will feel that things will go on forever. They may know it's a bubble; they may, but this is like System Two knowledge—it is not System One knowledge—and people do act a great deal on System One knowledge."[2]

Neither Kahneman, nor Taleb, who had once written a book about derivatives trading, elaborated on how the three-year phenomenon might impact investing. But it is likely more than coincidence that every five years marks one market cycle—which is to say that a bull market is born, dies, and is reborn—and that DALBAR data on stock ownership patterns shows people maintain stock investments for an average of 3.27 years, just a smidgeon longer than the time needed to develop ideas of a new regime, and far short of a full market cycle. This suggests many stock investors operate on intuition more often than generally understood. It also offers more insights into why so many investors are easily rattled when the stock market sharply declines. It suggests too many people invest money based on emotion and intuition—not analysis. Put another way: Many people seem to buy securities using System One, and sell on System Two. They buy stocks that have advanced for some time, and conclude the price may continue to rise. After all, the media and stock charts often present very compelling evidence that hot stocks will remain hot. Seasoned investors, however, may focus on different facts. They may look at how much money they have already made owning the hot stock, and decide to take profits. When major investors exit the stock, the stock price often declines, and that can kick-start System Two knowledge for investors who bought the stock without conducting much of their own research and analysis. Lost money is a cold, hard fact.

Maps and Models

The emotions of fear and greed are apparently more powerful than memory. Perhaps this is why most investors tend to forget the pain of investments gone bad. Perhaps it is because people are wired to believe in systems and models, something bigger than ourselves, to make sense of the chaos of the world, and of the financial market.

Kahneman told a story that illuminates those conditions. Once, a Hungarian army officer sent a troop of men into the Alps on a patrol. They were caught in a snowstorm. Three days passed. The officer thought they were dead. On the fourth day, the troop returned to base. The officer asked what happened. The soldiers said they had given up hope and were preparing to die when one of the men found a map in his pocket. The map rallied their spirits. They used it to discover where they were, and make their way back to base. The officer asked to look at the map. "This is a map of the Pyrenees," he said, "not the Alps!"

Kahneman says the story shows that people need things that contribute to their sense of well-being, and their confidence, and their ability to go on. It can be a useless number, or even a map of mountains in an entirely different country. It is important to be confident—but only up until a point in investing, lest one learn too late that all of the money one has spent has been predicated on an erroneous assumption based on a faulty map.

Few people have thought more about financial models than Emanuel Derman. He is one of the world's preeminent thinkers and practitioners on derivatives. He has headed risk management at Goldman Sachs, and now teaches at Columbia University, while also maintaining a partnership in a hedge fund. He is that rare financial engineer who communicates clearly with people who are not as mathematically gifted as he is. Derman has even written a book on models and man: *Models Behaving Badly: Why Confusing Illusion with Reality Can Lead to Disaster, on Wall Street and in Life*. Derman says that it is important to recognize that the models have limitations.

"The financial world is so confusing," Derman says, "that people have to put metrics on it to order things. I think models are mostly there to project a very multi-featured world onto a linear scale."[3]

Wall Street's banks and trading firms spend millions of dollars, and tens of thousands of hours, developing sophisticated trading models. Goldman Sachs has even sued programmers over taking information about codes to other firms. That is how important the models are on Wall Street. But even those models that are so critical to Wall Street's trading operations are not so reliable as to be operated without intense human oversight. Pat Neal, of Treepoint Capital Management, a global macroeconomic hedge fund, say models must be monitored to find out why they do not work because even the best systems will fail.[4]

But it is often difficult to recognize models are limited, especially for people who cannot construct models, or who skip along the surface of the financial world. Individual investors mostly perceive the financial market as a monolith expressed by indexes, and even those who know better about models are often slavishly devoted to their models because their compensation is tied to that worldview. After the credit crisis began in 2007, some derivatives traders were asked to review the models used by fixed-income mortgage traders to securitize subprime mortgages that were sold in bundles to other investors. One of those traders said he found variables—such as interest rates or default rates on loans—were actually fixed rates, which proved to be a costly mistake because interest rates change and some people stopped paying their mortgages and defaulted.

In finance, Derman says financial models are used to turn multidimensional problems into a unidimensional problem. By using a yield-to-maturity model for bonds, Derman says, it becomes possible to compare the value of many similar bonds, none of which are identical, by mapping their yields on a linear scale. The Black–Scholes model that is used to price options uses a known stock price and bond price to price a hybrid security—an option. Derman says the Black–Scholes process is like determining the value of a fruit salad from the price of the fruit in the salad.

Most people will never build financial models, but they order their decisions around well-known indexes, for example, the Dow Jones Industrial Average or the Chicago Board Options Exchange's Volatility Index. The challenge with models is that they are only used to estimate the future, and the market, Derman says, eventually outwits people.

"The greatest danger in financial modeling is the age-old sin of idolatry. Financial markets are alive, but a model is a limited, human work of art." Derman says. "Although a model may be entrancing, we will not be able to breathe life into it, no matter how hard we try. To confuse the model with the world is to embrace a future disaster driven by the belief that humans obey mathematical rules."[5]

This Is Your Brain Visualizing Money

Science is starting to prove that visual cues heavily influence investment decision-making. Everyone with kids worries that watching too much TV, or incessantly playing video games, will rot their brains. Well, it turns out investors have similar problems. Risk-based decisions, like buying stock, can be manipulated by visual cues that stimulate a region of the brain called the nucleus accumbens. The nucleus accumbens is part of the brain's reward circuitry. Although the nucleus accumbens—which is activated by drugs, alcohol and sex—has traditionally been studied by scientists to understand addiction, it is now at the center of emerging research into investing.

Brian Knutson, a Stanford University psychologist, stumbled upon this when searching for a control mechanism in a study of human emotion. He needed something that would cause everyone in his experiment to react the same way. He tried food. He tried pornography. Everyone reacted differently. "Money seemed to do the trick," Knutson said.[6] Everyone reacted the same. Everyone wanted money.

At his laboratory in Palo Alto, California, Knutson scanned people's brains with a functional Magnetic Resonance Imaging (fMRI) machine. The machine illuminates the flow of blood to let researchers obtain anatomical and functional views of the brain. Since the fMRI was developed in 1992, just two years after the online brokerage industry formed, the fMRI has been used to illuminate regions of the human body that had been mostly hidden. With this new view into the brain's inner workings, Knutson saw that money stimulated primordial tendencies in the brain's reward circuitry. Using cue cards, Knutson found he could prompt people into making risky financial decisions. Knutson flashed one of three cue cards. The cards had pictures of circles, triangles, or squares. Like the bell that scientist Ivan Pavlov rang in 1890 and caused his dogs to salivate in anticipation of food, Knutson's cue cards alerted people to what would come next. When he wanted people to gamble, he showed erotic pictures of couples. To encourage risk-adverse behavior, he used a cue card of snakes and spiders. Household appliances like washing machines were neutral cues. After flashing the cards, Knutson waited a moment to let the anticipation increase, and then he presented them with a choice: gamble $1 or 10 cents on a random outcome, like a coin toss, in which they had even chances of winning or losing. If they had wagered correctly, they kept what they earned. To make them care about the outcome, losses were deducted from their $20 hourly participation fee. By study's end, Knutson said he could predict people's decisions before they spoke.[7]

His insights into financial-decision making should delight bank marketing and advertising departments charged with attracting new clients, and give investors reason to ruminate and reevaluate. Knutson's findings suggest that one reason ordinary people have such trouble with the good investor rule—remember bad investors think of ways to make money; good investors think of ways not to lose money— is because they often make decisions in a visual stimulation funhouse. Everyone thinks they make calculated, cunning financial decisions based on cold facts, such as stock trading charts, news stories, corporate earnings reports, and stock analyst research reports. But those reports, even though they are facts, are clouded by initial perceptions.

Investors are initially cued to be bullish or bearish by media reports, or stock charts that show a company's share price rose or fell and could turn higher or lower. Those images prime investors for the big decision of buying or selling. An active nucleus accumbens is distracting, and even detrimental. That fact is well known to neurologists and also major pharmaceutical companies.

Compulsive Gambler

Medicines for Parkinson's disease, a degenerative disorder of the central nervous system, turned some patients into compulsive gamblers or sex addicts. The medicine floods the nucleus accumbens with dopamine, a neurotransmitter that the central nervous system needs to properly function. The dopamine deluge sometimes creates uncontrollable urges to gamble, or have sex. In 2005, Boehringer-Ingelheim Pharmaceuticals, maker of Mirapex, a Parkinson's drug, listed compulsive gambling as a potential drug side effect.

Knutson, who is interested in human emotion, not finance, has since received more than $400,000 from the FINRA Investor Education Foundation. (The Financial Industry Regulatory Authority (FINRA) regulates most of Wall Street's activities.) Since the 2007 financial crisis, the group is increasingly interested in understanding how people make financial decisions, because many of those decisions produce unexpected results.

B. F. Skinner Goes to Wall Street

The idea that simple cues can induce people to gamble, or assume financial risk without understanding the issues, is powerful in the financial world. The parallels between the stock market—especially the parts that appear on broadcast financial news—and casinos are undeniable. "If you go to the gambling casinos," Knutson says, "people are wearing skimpy costumes, they're giving you free alcohol, there are bells and lights and things like that, which don't necessarily seem related to the odds of gambling. But these are cues that might activate brain regions that encourage risk taking and get people to gamble more."[8]

Las Vegas style cues are increasingly used to describe and frame investing. The stock market is regularly portrayed as a quasi-casino by major broadcast media whose television studios are filled with flashing lights and beautiful women and handsome men who enthusiastically and confidently comment on the passing scene. Big winners are widely praised and sometimes appear on camera to talk about their victories or offer their views. The most powerful cues are rising stock prices. They are unsubtle, incredibly seductive, and accompanied by such a celebratory cacophony that if Lazarus arose from the dead he would rush to trade stocks.

Rising stock prices arguably cause individual investors to behave like the rats behavioral psychologist B. F. Skinner manipulated to test his conditioning theories. In his now famous experiments, Skinner put a rat in a cage. He dropped food into a metal bowl. It landed with a thud. The thud caused the rat to scurry to the bowl. How does that differ from the investor who rushes to buy stocks after hearing someone talk (or shout) on financial TV shows? Eventually, Skinner changed the rates at which various behaviors were repeated to earn a reward. Soon, he concluded he had found gambling's primary mechanism. Why do people spend hours in front of a slot machine, pulling the arm again and again? Skinner says it is because of "variable-ratio reinforcement schedule."

"It is familiar in gambling devices and systems which can arrange occasional but unpredictable payoffs. The required number of responses can be easily stretched, and in a gambling enterprise such as a casino the average rate must be such that the gambler loses in the long run if the casino is to make a profit," Skinner wrote.[9] His description sounds a lot like the plight of many investors.

The similarities between Sin City and Wall Street are ingrained in the market's culture.

"What's the difference between Las Vegas and Wall Street?" goes an old stock market joke.

"In Vegas, they buy the losers drinks."

The Casino Culture

The stock market's casino culture blossomed in the 1990s when technology stretched Wall Street across America, turning every computer screen, in any house, into a trading monitor. Anyone could effortlessly trade stocks and mutual funds as if they were pulling the arm of a slot machine at a Las Vegas casino. No special training was needed—just a few thousand dollars. The days of phoning stockbrokers to buy stocks were over.

Public discussions of similarities between gambling and investing bother most Wall Street executives. Many exchange executives, and even trading strategists, take issue with journalists using the term "betting" in articles to describe a particular trade, the motivations behind a strategy, or any element of the market. Even though the definition of "bet" refers to something laid, placed, or staked on an outcome, "bet" is a dirty word on Wall Street. The preferred word for what happens on Wall Street is "investment" which at once sounds respectable, as the history of the word shows. "Invest" entered the English language around 1387, borrowed from the Latin *investire*. The word historically described furnishing kings with power and authority.[10] "Bet" entered the English language around 1590 from the argot of petty criminals. The word comes from German and though it now connotes risking money on an unknown outcome, it is thought to have been formed by dropping the *a* in abet, as in aiding and abetting criminals.[11]

If a picture is truly worth a thousand words, betting, not investing, is the daily image on financial TV. All day long, stock prices crawl across the bottom of the television screen. Stocks are going up. Stocks are going down. Anchors and guests are emotional. This flows through a massive global distribution network wired into computers and televisions and handhelds. Print and Internet media often amplify these cues by covering the stock market like a sporting match, which makes it easy for investors to forget that something more than momentum animates stock prices. At the major banks, TVs are almost always turned to CNBC. Many major trading floors hang TVs from pillars so everyone can watch. Some investment bank traders have altered their trading monitors so they can watch CNBC on their computer screens. The broadcast volume is usually turned off. But the images are still there and so are the headlines.

So far, no academic researcher has determined the role ubiquitous financial TV plays in market booms or busts, but serious people are concerned financial TV misleads many people who don't know any better—and even some who do. "During the late-1990s bubble, it struck me that the discourse on CNBC was remarkably similar to the sort of discourse that I had read from news archives preceding the 1929 crash," says John Hussman, an influential money manager. "As I wrote at the time, what was surprising was the extent to which investment professionals, who ought to have known better, were fully endorsing valuations that were clearly inconsistent (at the time, and certainly in hindsight) with prospective cash flows—even if one assumed that economic activity, earnings, and dividends would achieve and sustain the highest growth rates ever observed in history."[12]

It is easy to pick on CNBC. But the cable channel has been successful, and the fastest way to lose viewers, or readers, is delving into the minutiae that actually propel investing and trading. Therein lies a fundamental problem: Investors are conditioned by primary sources of financial information to focus on what the market produces—profits—rather than on processes and risks that lead to profits. The good investor, the Indomitable Investor, who advances, and rarely loses money, is obsessed with process. The bad investor chases returns like one of Skinner's rats.

Hussman adds:

To analyze a company or the market, you have to think carefully about the long-term stream of cash flows that investors actually stand to receive, and how they should be discounted to arrive at an appropriate price. Instead, the only question today is whether earnings and economic reports are delivering "surprises" versus what "the Street" estimated the day before the data were released. The quality of earnings, the cyclicality of profit margins, dilution from option and stock grants, the implied total return reflected in the stock price, the return on retained earnings, cost of entry, competitive structure, market saturation, the potential for organic growth from reinvested capital—all of those things *matter* over the long run. But to watch a half hour of CNBC today is like watching an old episode of *Gomer Pyle*—"Well, surprise, surprise, surprise!"[13]

Of course, it is difficult to get people to pay attention to anything financial, even for someone like Jim Cramer, one of CNBC's top personalities. "I'm a guy trying to do an entertainment show about business for people to watch," confessed Cramer, host of CNBC's *Mad Money*.[14]

Your Own Private Stock Market

Larry Summers, a former U.S. Treasury secretary and past president of Harvard University, believes technology misleads investors. "It is like when you build better highways," he says, "people tend to drive faster. And actually more people end up dying in auto accidents on these new highways because they make a mistake in estimating how fast they can drive, and they end up driving much faster than they should."[15]

Couple technology with low interest rates, which historically precede major financial crises because almost anyone can borrow money, and you have the recipe to create "market morons." Leon Cooperman, one of Wall Street's elder statesmen, and chairman of hedge fund Omega Advisors, knows just what happens to market morons. Cooperman says:

> In the last five years the guy who normally takes his savings and buys Treasury bills to make sure he never lost any income has gone out and bought the bonds instead. And the guy who would normally buy bonds, because he was ready to take a little more risk to get a little more return, has gone out and bought emerging-market bonds from places like Russia or Brazil, and the guy who would normally buy emerging-market bonds is now out buying emerging-market stocks. What has to happen—and it will happen—is that some people who have moved up this risk ladder will lose a lot of their money and they will move back.[16]

If recent history is a reliable guide, the move back to safer parts of the risk ladder is temporary. No one wants to miss the chance to make money, or recoup losses. Besides, as dealers say in the stock and options market, losers always come back to Las Vegas.

Often Wrong; Never in Doubt

Overconfident investors tend to engage in anchoring. They focus on one fact that they think is important, rather than doing fuller research. This, also, is a side effect of information overload. Because too much information exists, people often focus on easy facts. This can happen by dismissing negative news, or positive news that contradicts an avowed position. Such rigidity in viewpoint is dangerous, and a hallmark of ineffective investing. Some people think it is noble to take a position, and take a stand, but the market is not static. It changes. Remember the Hapsburgs. They ruled the Holy Roman Empire from 1400 to 1806. Henry Kissinger, the former U.S. Secretary of State, said the Hapsburgs' enemies benefited from the dynasty's inability to understand emerging trends, or tactical necessities of power. "The Habsburg rulers were men of principle," Kissinger said. "They never compromised their convictions except in defeat."[17]

The absorption of financial information is not something many people think about. This is perhaps why so many investors are often wrong, but never in doubt, which is one of the most puzzling aspects of the stock market. Why do so many people make the same mistakes again and again and never learn from their experiences?

In a 1977 landmark study on confidence, *Knowing with Certainty: The Appropriateness of Extreme Confidence*, scholars, Baruch Fischhoff, Paul Slovic, and Sarah Lichtenstein, set out to answer a simple question: how often are people wrong when they are certain they are right?

It turns out more often than not. People are most overconfident when accuracy is near 50/50 levels. When accuracy of their decision exceeds 80 percent, they found people are no longer confident.

Illusion of Memory

Memory distorts confidence. People view memories as exact copies of the original experience. Yet, memory, psychologists conclude, is cobbled together from fragments of information similar to how paleontologists decipher the appearance of a dinosaur from pieces of bone.[18]

If people are unaware of the reconstructive nature of memory and perception and cannot distinguish between assertions and inferences, they will not critically evaluate their inferred knowledge. In general, any process that changes the contents of memory unbeknownst to people will keep them from asking relevant validity questions and may lead to overconfidence.[19]

Memory is clearly influenced by news media. In one experiment, scholars asked people to determine the most frequent cause of death in the United States. Lethal events ranged from smallpox to syphilis to car accidents, heart disease and cancer, fire, and all other manner of woes. They found that many people chose deaths that were caused by "dramatic, well-publicized events" and underestimated "quiet killers."[20] Academic research convincingly demonstrates that people who think they know something about investing are the most susceptible to failure. They fall for scams because they think they know more than they actually do.

A NASD Investor Education Foundation study conducted in 2006 found that investment fraud victims were more likely than others to rely on their own experience and knowledge to make financial decisions. The study concluded that self-reliance could isolate people, and cause them to rely on their own judgment when seeking advice from others might be more appropriate.

A 2009 report on the psychology of scams that was prepared for England's consumer protection agency, the Office of Fair Trading, found that the more people knew about an issue, the more likely they were to fall for a scam. Because they felt competent in the subject, they overestimated their abilities to make good decisions.[21]

This confidence in their ability appears to lead people to find information that confirms their point of view. The scientific name of this phenomenon is *confirmatory information search*, and it causes people to overestimate the quality of information that supports their preferred standpoint. Few mediums make it easier to confirm one's opinion than the Internet. This is likely exacerbated by the ease at which one can metabolize Internet information and absorb it as one's own.

The U.K. scam study found:

> As a consequence, it is likely that people will have a higher tendency to respond to a scam which falls into their area of background knowledge than to one that does not: they are over-confident in their preliminary preferences (that is, to respond to the scam) and thus neglect inconsistent (warning) information that would help them to recognize the scammer's intention.[22]

The most common tactics used in frauds: claiming to be from legitimate business, dangling the prospect of wealth, and showing examples of other people who have invested. By now, most people are likely thinking to themselves that they would never fall for a scam. Let's see. Some scams are subtle, and have all the hallmarks of a legitimate business.

Safe Havens in the Age of Madoff

In April 2011, the SEC investigated a Florida Ponzi scheme that defrauded more than 100 investors.[23] Many of the people scammed were Florida teachers or retirees. The remarkable fact about the scheme was not that the fund told investors that it earned annual investment returns of 14 to 124 percent, but that the alleged scam occurred in the shadows of Bernard Madoff's Ponzi scheme that had long dominated national and international news—especially in Florida where Madoff bamboozled so many people.

The SEC alleged that James Davis Risher used Safe Harbor Private Equity Fund, Managed Capital Fund, and Preservation of Principal Fund as part of a Ponzi scheme. The fund names likely appealed to people as the worst financial crisis since the 1929 stock market crash had people everywhere worried about safeguarding their money. Risher distributed materials that portrayed Risher as someone with substantial experience in trading stocks and providing wealth and asset management services.

"In reality, Risher had no such experience but rather a lengthy criminal history, spending 11 of the last 21 years in jail instead of growing a thriving retail brokerage business as he claimed," the SEC stated in an August 2011 press release announcing charges.

But Risher knew how to treat clients. He held golf tournaments and promotional events for investors. At a March 2010 event at an Orlando resort, attendees heard a rousing speech with universal appeal. They were told investing in the fund could change their lives.

According to federal court documents filed by the SEC against Risher in U.S. District Court of Middle Florida, Risher's pitchman told his audience:

> [Y]ou invest in this fund and all of a sudden you start making more money than you've ever made in your life with your investors. And then all of a sudden you start making enough money where you don't have to work . . . [a]t Safe Harbor, you could retire today, like right now. And I'm telling you, you get rid of the struggle.[24]

At the same event, SEC said Risher told investors that it was his job to keep the funds "market neutral," so that they had the ability to profit when the market rose or fell. Many sophisticated hedge funds are able to do what Risher described. The SEC said the speech was recorded and included with investor testimonials and offering materials distributed to existing and prospective investors.

This had to be appealing. The stock market was still in the midst of one of the most destructive financial crises in U.S. history. On phone calls and in meetings with some investors, several investors were told they would never lose their principal investments. Some investors even received written guarantees from a company called Safehaven Inc., that said all money deposited into the fund was, according to the SEC, "guaranteed against loss, and that Safehaven would reimburse any loss." According to the guarantee, a stop loss was held on all active trades placed in the fund, and the fund was required to maintain a certain cash reserve at all times. All of those facts are reasonable, and not uncommon among legitimate business.

All of the statements and representations must have seemed incredibly realistic to investors who received account statements that showed impressive quarterly returns of 2.28 to 5.64 percent. SEC investigators alleged that an associate had entered percentage returns provided by Risher into a computer software program that was used to generate account statements. The quarterly statements displayed account and percent returns, but SEC noted, contained no information about specific trades, securities held in the account, and it never showed losses.

Illusions

Many people think they know something, when they really don't. The behaviorists call this *hindsight bias*. When people are presented with new information, they think that they knew it all along. A 2008 study of bankers in London and Frankfurt found that this condition causes people—even professionals—to inaccurately estimate asset returns, which leads to bad trades and portfolio performance, and to even underestimate volatility, which leads to ineffective use of risk reduction strategies.[25]

Hindsight bias is a serious problem when combined with overconfidence, particularly for well-educated, successful professionals. Bruno Biais and Martin Weber decided to test a group of 85 bankers in London and Frankfurt to see how they were impacted by hindsight bias. They found that bankers who made the most money had the lowest bias. This reinforces the idea that hindsight bias is a trait that influences people's behavior and prevents them from rationally processing information and learning from the past.

Biais and Weber, of Toulouse University and the University Mannheim, respectively, wrote in a study of hindsight bias:

> In financial markets the inability to be surprised, to learn from the past and to reject hypotheses can be very damaging. Hindsight biased traders will fail to recognize that their view of the market was wrong. Hence they will fail to cut their losses when it is optimal to do so. Hindsight biased investors will inaccurately take into account the informational content

of new signals, such as earnings announcement or macro-news. This will lead them to form sub–optimal portfolios.[26]

What they found when interviewing bankers is that those with the lowest hindsight bias are most likely to be top earners, while bankers with medium bias are most likely to earn somewhere in the middle, and those with the highest bias earn the least amount of money.

"Agents who exhibit this bias fail to remember how ignorant they were before observing outcomes and answers. We show that this hinders learning, and, in particular, lead[s] agents to underestimate volatility. This results in inefficient portfolio choice, loss-making trades and poor risk management," they concluded.[27]

The curious fact about the hindsight and overconfidence biases are that people are often incredibly confident that they have no biases. In fact, they are often highly confident of those facts. Whitney Tilson, a hedge fund manager, sees overconfidence in all walks of life:

- 19 percent of people think they belong to the richest 1 percent of U.S. households.
- 82 percent of people say they are in the top 30 percent of safe drivers.
- 80 percent of students expect to graduate in the top half of their class.
- When asked to make a prediction at the 98 percent confidence level, people are right only 60 to 70 percent of the time.
- 68 percent of lawyers in civil cases believe they will win.
- Doctors consistently overestimate their ability to detect certain diseases.
- 81 percent of new business owners think they have at least a 70 percent chance of success, but only 39 percent think any business like theirs would be likely to succeed.
- Graduate students were asked to estimate the time it would take to finish their thesis under three scenarios: best case, expected, and worst case. The average guesses were 27.4 days, 33.9 days, and 48.6 days, respectively. The actual average turned out to be 55.5 days.

- Mutual fund managers, analysts, and business executives at a conference were asked to write down how much money they would have at retirement, and how much the average person in the room would have. The average figures were $5 million and $2.6 million, respectively. The professor who asked the question said that, regardless of the audience, the ratio is always approximately 2:1.[28]

What happens when investors are overconfident? Tilson says they make decisions beyond their competence and use excessive leverage. The credit crisis, in which investors all over the world bought mortgage derivatives that they did not understand, with money they really didn't have, but could borrow due to the magic of leverage, is a fine example of how overconfidence humbles the high and the low.

Victor

Honore de Balzac, the great French writer, once remarked that it was a shame people had to live with novelists—and not their novels. The same is true of many of Wall Street's most successful investors. Victor Niederhoffer is an exception. He also unfortunately happens to personify, like a modern Greek tragedy, what Mr. Market does to the overconfident. After attending Harvard University on a scholarship, this son of a New York City cop earned a doctorate in finance at the University of Chicago. He was a champion squash player. He grew up to collect art and live in a house with 15,000 books. He also, legend has it, likes to trade in his socks.

He was once a partner of hedge fund grandee, George Soros. He also was, at varying times, widely regarded as one of the world's best traders. He went on to lose enormous sums of money trading Thai stocks and U.S. options. His fund blew up in 1997 when he bet wrong on Thai stocks and some options positions moved against him. He came back only to crater again in 2007, during the worst of the credit crisis, showing that intelligence and bad timing are a lethal combination.

"Unfortunately I was so successful for so many years in that particular field that I began to believe in my own success. I thought that because my method worked in markets that I knew about and had quantified, I could apply the same methods to something I didn't know about," said Niederhoffer, who still manages some money, and operates a blog, dailyspeculations.com, which shows the breadth and majesty of the man's mind.[29]

An Antidote for Overconfidence

If investors are often wrong, but never in doubt, the natural question becomes: Is there a way to circumvent the process? Some simple tactics may prove helpful.

In 2007, a few years before Lehman Brothers filed for bankruptcy, Dick Fuld was one of the most influential and respected men in the global financial market. He ran the fourth-largest U.S. investment bank, which he had largely built. He sat on the board of the New York Federal Reserve, essentially the federal government's eyes and ears on Wall Street. He had access to everyone, and everything. Yet, when asked what kept him awake at night, he had a humble answer: "What I don't know."[30]

Sandy Frucher, vice chairman of NASDAQ OMX, which runs the NASDAQ stock market, is one of Wall Street's shrewdest executives. He has a simple definition of intelligence. He defines smart as knowing what you don't know.[31]

This type of basic intellectual questioning characterizes the very best investors. Good investors are highly skeptical. They believe almost nothing they hear, and double-check, at minimum, what they read. Remember what Blackstone's Stephen Schwarzman does when he, or his firm, makes a mistake? He finds out why, so it doesn't happen again.

The most famous example from the credit crisis is how John Paulson, the hedge fund manager, decided to see for himself if it was really true that U.S. housing prices had never before declined. Well, we know how that ended.

Tilson, the hedge fund manager, keeps a written checklist to battle overconfidence.[32] He asks himself:

- Is this within my circle of competence?
- Is it a good business?

- Do I like management?
- Is the stock incredibly cheap?
- Am I trembling with greed?

Tison seeks out contrary opinions to rebut—rather than confirm—his hypothesis. Sometimes he gets someone to take the opposing position, or he invites a bearish analyst to give a presentation.

Slowing down is another tactic. A side effect of overconfidence is rushed thought. The psychologists call it fast thinking. Because most people perceive the stock market through the prism of real-time news—CNBC, the Internet, blogs, websites—rather than through trading patterns and formulas, there is always this sense of urgency to act now or miss out. This compulsion to act is exacerbated by the concept of induced scarcity—act immediately because product X will not be available or the price will change. Studies have shown induced scarcity is a tactic scammers use to compel people to buy now.

Fast thinking is connected to the "recency effect."

According to J.P. Morgan Asset Management research, people often overemphasize recent stock returns when making decisions, which can influence individual stock prices, and also the entire stock market.

All of these forces conspire together and cause emotions—not the mind—to start making decisions. The mind should function like a brake in a car, it should slow down this process, but instead the mind accelerates much like a car racing down the highway at 80 miles per hour, because it picks up fragments of ideas, or facts, and glosses over them, or creates patterns and models that perhaps do not really exist.

When Kahneman spoke in Munich he said that there is a mismatch between the time scales of individuals and society. He said people are very present oriented. They are focused on the now. Everyone knows the saying, carpe diem—seize the day, for time is fleeing, which is not particularly sound advice in matters of finance, and risk.

Kahneman says that people are so present oriented that their system of expectations intuitively allows them to begin to feel safe after a short period of time. This tendency creates other financial difficulties. People are living longer, and not saving enough for retirement.

Economists estimate that people within 15 years of retirement are saving two-thirds less than needed to maintain their pre-retirement life style.[33]

Hal Hershfield, a New York University business professor, says savings rates may be influenced by an inability of people to relate to themselves in 50 years. Research shows that people care more about the present outcomes than the future, a condition psychologists call *temporal discounting*. Savings, which requires giving up today something for tomorrow, is an intertemporal choice.[34]

Hershfield has developed a software program that shows people what they might look like in the future. He is working with Allianz, a major global financial company, about rolling out his software. In experiments with college students, Hershfield found that savings rates doubled when people saw their aged image.

"Our hunch is that exposure to one's future self is creating somewhat of an empathic response," similar to the feelings of protectiveness one might feel when seeing an aged parent, Hershfield said.[35]

Go Slow to Go Fast

Fast thinking is dangerous to your financial health. If you are an expert, and each data point that washes over your brain is backed my experience and study, fast thinking could be expeditious. But many people who come to the market are not trained investors. They just want to make money. They often fail to think about risk, especially when the tom-tom drums of the bull market are being pounded by TV commentators. In such instances, fast thinking is not thinking at all but visceral knee jerk reactions. It is easy to lose money. It is hard to make money. That is a fact. If you know it to be a fact then it should serve as a brake on your rush to invest. When you rush to buy a stock, you are not investing—you are not even trading. You are a lemming running in a herd.

You need systems checks like a jet pilot. The old American Stock Exchange, when it occupied 86 Trinity Street and had not yet been bought by the New York Stock Exchange, had a trading firm named

TANSTAAFL. The firm's name was an abbreviation of There Ain't No Such Thing As A Free Lunch. TANSTAAFL is a good antidote for fast thinking. When you think you have to rush, say TANSTAAFL.

Think Week

Bill Gates, Microsoft's founder, who helped create information overload, has his own strategy for coping. When he ran Microsoft, he always scheduled "Think Week." Twice a year, for seven days, he spent time alone in a secluded cabin in the Pacific Northwest. "Staying focused is one issue: that's the problem of information overload. The other problem is information underload. Being flooded with information doesn't mean we have the right information or that we're in touch with the right people," Gates said.[36]

Gates had to cut himself off from technology to think about the future of technology. It was in his cabin, perhaps in his study there with a portrait of Victor Hugo, a refrigerator filled with Diet Orange Crush and Diet Coke, and a bookshelf lined with classic literature, that Gates wrote in 1995 *The Internet Tidal Wave*, which led to the creation of Microsoft's Internet browser, which crushed Netscape's browser.[37]

Since he left the company to work fulltime at the Bill and Melinda Gates Foundation, he no longer needs "Think Week," because he has more time for reading and research.[38] Anyone can see what he is reading and doing, and where he is traveling on his personal website, www.thegatesnotes.com/personal. But "Think Week" still lives on at Microsoft. Gates says the company's top 50 "engineering thinkers" have participated in "Think Week" for several years.

Halos and Angels

Huey Long, the late governor and senator of Louisiana, liked to say every man is a king, but no one wears a crown. Had he spent much time on Wall Street, he would have learned that many of its denizens wear halos. This is not to suggest angels work on Wall Street, but rather that the mind can bestow celestial qualities on people and even things: stockbrokers and successful investors, stocks, and mutual funds.

In many ways, the halo effect is similar to how people view investing or the market. They see the end results, but not the process, and thus make decisions or reach conclusions based on price, not value. Price is a seemingly concrete fact flashed in the stock market. Value is a measurement of price determined in the privacy of one's mind.

Yet many heads are crowned with halos by people who see things as they wish them to be. Emily Pronin, a Princeton University professor who investigated the halo effect for the FINRA Investor Education Foundation, says the classic example of the halo effect is judging people you like as being more attractive and smarter than others.

Consider stockbrokers. Pronin conducted an experiment using a stockbroker who presented himself as an Ivy League graduate. He wore a suit and tie. She wanted to see if he would be judged as being especially competent and trustworthy. People were told the stockbroker graduated from Cornell University. The same "stockbroker" was also presented wearing an oxford shirt, but no jacket. People were told he was educated at Elmira College in upstate New York.

The stockbroker in the business suit with the elite college education was deemed more competent, and less in need of a background check than the other stockbroker with the less fancy clothing and college degree. Pronin said people wanted to invest more of their money with the supposedly well-dressed stockbroker—without conducting a background check.

"The particular problem of the halo effect is that it leads people to judge others positively on dimensions for which they do not know if the other person is deserving of such positive judgment," Pronin says.[39] The halo effect also exists for stocks. And fund managers. And chief executives. And almost anything in your life that you judge positively—and support with your investment dollars—without taking the time to determine what lies beneath the surface.

Big Brother Is Studying You

If there is a criticism to be made of behavioral economics, it is that while there is clearly some truth to the matter, it remains a decidedly soft discipline in the rough and tumble world of investing. A behavioral economist will likely never run a major bank or honcho a trading desk. Those jobs will always be held by bankers and traders. But people who understand the psychology of investing, and who can talk with investors are increasingly likely to be hired by a major bank. Put another way: Even if you decide to ignore behavioral economics, the banks are not, and they are using it to learn more about you, and other investors. Ignore behavioral finance at your own peril.

Since 2006, Barclay's Capital, one of the world's largest banks, has employed a behavioral economist to help clients understand why and how they make decisions. Since then, other banks have adapted a similar focus, including Bank of America, Merrill Lynch, J.P. Morgan, and Allianz Global Investors. And more will join the fray.

It is easy to imagine that the banks will use the data they collect on clients to more effectively market investment products. It is also easy to imagine that clients can be taught to be better investors if they are taught to make better decisions. Investors are likely to lose less money if they avoid the standard psychological pitfalls that trap most investors.

Greg Davies heads Barclays' Behavioral and Quantitative Investment Philosophy Group. He oversees four behaviorists spread around the globe. One works in Singapore, two in London, and one in New York. Davies has developed a Financial Personality Assessment that bank clients are asked to complete using multiple-choice questions to determine their financial personality. The questionnaire measures six dimensions: risk tolerance, composure, market engagement, perceived financial expertise, delegation, and belief in skill. So far, Barclay's has data on more than 13,000 clients and prospects all over the world. Some of the data was even collected during the financial crisis. Davies says people commonly fall into four groups based on the six dimensions:

1. High on first four, high on last two
2. High on first four, low on last two

3. Low on first four, high on last two

4. Low on first four, low on last two.

The exercise is useful because Davies says it helps investors be honest with themselves, which is usually quite difficult. Some people think they are composed risk takers, but not everyone is. When people invest in ways that are incompatible with their financial personality, they often lose money. Consider the most basic construct of portfolio management: diversification. Most investors are told to diversify their portfolios to reduce risk and maximize reward. But that strategy often fails to take into account what happens in the short term when the stock market swings sharply lower. The standard advice does little to keep an investor from selling in a panic, or instructing their broker to do the same.

Davies believes that prevailing economic theory abdicated its responsibility to investors by failing to address what he calls "the problem of Ulysses and the Sirens."

In the *Odyssey*, Ulysses is on his ship trying to make his way back to Ithaca. In his journey, his ship passes by the Sirens, who try to charm sailors with beautiful song. Everyone who hears their song throw themselves into the sea where they drown. Ulysses, having been warned by the goddess Circe, protects himself and his men from the deadly songs. He tells his men to tie him to the ship's mast and to stuff their own ears with wax. As the great classicist Thomas Bulfinch recounts:

> As they approached the Sirens' island, the sea was calm, and over the waters came the notes of music so ravishing and attractive that Ulysses struggled to get loose, and by cries and signs to his people, begged to be released; but they, obedient to his previous orders, sprang forward and bound him still faster. They held on their course, and the music grew fainter till it ceased to be heard, when with joy Ulysses gave his companions the signal to unseal their ears, and they relieved him from his bonds.[40]

In a financial context, investors meet with their advisors in the calm of an office. Everyone goes over plans and allocations, and sips coffee or tea and has a nice quiet time. When they leave the office, they are left to confront the temptations of Mr. Market who sings pretty songs as prices rise, attracting more and more people, who inevitably will cast themselves into the sea when Mr. Market howls and the stock market tumbles. There is often no structure that exists to strap investors to the mast.

The key thought, Davies says, is to think about blending the long-term investment goals of classical finance with the insights of behavioral finance. "How does the long-term self purchase cooperation of the short-term self?" Davies asks. Perhaps by sacrificing some long-term upside for short-term emotional comfort. This is another way of looking at the ideas in Chapter 5 of this book, "Chaos," and the use of investments like the PIMCO Global Multi-Asset Fund that uses options and other hedges to protect assets against losing more than 15 percent of their value.

Davies encourages people to look at their investing portfolios as journeys, not as end goals. Most portfolio theory is about balancing risk and return for the long term. Investors can sacrifice some of the long-term gains in return for insurance.

"Why give up 1 percent of annual return for something rational that classical finance says you do not need? But you are only rational if you are an automaton. The rest of us need to buy comfort," Davies says.[41]

"It all goes back to System One and System Two. You are trying to do something that follows a set of rules that possibly you don't understand, but you have been told this is the right thing to do," Davies added. "You sign up in calm times, but what you failed to do—like in the Ulysses example—is recognize that there are things you need to keep going through the journey. But the decision was made at another time when the market was going well and you didn't need to tie yourself to the mast."

Big Bank Is Watching You

J.P. Morgan, which emerged from the credit crisis as one of the world's most powerful banks, has long used behavioral finance. The bank has a family of mutual funds that invest according to behavioral principles, including overconfidence and anchoring. They even use information to market to clients. In 1999, the bank hired Larry Samuels, a cultural anthropologist, to study the rich. He came up with personality types that tend to be dominant among wealthy people: Wellville, Legacy, The Good Life, Unplugged, and Artisan. J.P. Morgan called those types "wealth signs." The research was pushed out to J.P. Morgan's brokers who asked clients questions to determine their sign. The keywords were connected to "passion points." The bank gave brokers "cheat sheets" to collect other core client passions by asking questions—or observation.

"The contention was that investment decision-making followed the 80-20 rules: 80 percent emotion and 20 percent fact," observed Malcolm Baker, a Harvard Business School professor in a case study he wrote in 2007 on J.P. Morgan's adaption of behavioral finance.

The wealth signs were important parts of J.P. Morgan's relationship with clients. Baker said the bank had even identified the "key service requirement" for each wealth sign. A broker with a "good life" client needed to make them feel important, pay attention to details, and keep them current on trends. It was also important to let good life clients talk about their accomplishments. An "artisan" client required a different approach. Brokers treated them less formally, talked about investments in visual ways, and took time to explain new concepts.

"J.P. Morgan held that if advisors understood their clients' investing biases, it would lead to better relationships with clients and, as a result, to improved client acquisition, retention, and referrals," Baker said.[42]

Ancient Lessons

Most people do not think of themselves as part of the great untidy mass of humanity. They see themselves as rational, smart, discriminating, and more attractive than others. When events prove them wrong, they often do not engage in any meaningful introspection to see why an error was made.

Instead, they blame other people, or blame institutions and say the stock market is rigged. In many ways the market is stacked against outsiders, but the game is not so complicated that it cannot be understood. To say that investing is like war seems melodramatic, but Sun Tzu's *Art of War* naturally expresses something all successful investors know, and all failed investors ignore.

> If you know the enemy and know yourself, you need not fear the result of a hundred battles. If you know yourself but not the enemy, for every victory gained you will also suffer a great defeat. If you know neither the enemy nor yourself, you will succumb in every battle.[43]

There must be something to this. Sun Tzu wrote those words more than 2,500 years ago and still they hold true.

If you prefer a more peaceful perspective consider this story about a Western theologian who was an expert in Buddhism. After waiting many years, the theologian was invited to meet a great Buddhist monk at the Drepung Loseling Monastery in Tibet. He traveled from the United States to the hills of Lhasa, where the monastery had been founded in 1416. He was ushered into the great monk's rooms. He was excited. He could not stop talking. The old monk softly interrupted. He asked his visitor if he would like tea. The visitor said yes, and the monk poured, and the visitor kept talking, and soon the tea spilled over the side of the cup.

"The tea is overflowing," the visitor said.

"Yes," replied the monk, "and when you have emptied your cup, come back again."

The monk then walked out of his room. The Western theologian, expert in Buddhism, was stunned. He did not know what to say.

When you come to the market, make sure have you emptied your cup. Bring your investment discipline. Bring your analytical powers. Bring humility.

Chapter 9

Watchman, What of the Night?

I n 1953, John Kenneth Galbraith was finishing his history of the 1929 stock market. He needed a title for the final chapter of his book, *The Great Crash*. Somehow he came across verse 11 of Chapter 21 in Isaiah: "Watchman, what of the night?" It was a fitting title.

In less than eight pages, Galbraith described how new laws, including the Securities Act of 1933 and the Securities Exchange Act of 1934, would better regulate Wall Street. But the chapter, which mostly detailed how politics and other realities would insure those rules fell short of their promise, and their spirit.

Galbraith likely never imagined just how far short those rules would fall. Those depression-era laws, forged when Franklin Delano Roosevelt was President, now loom like monuments immune to the technological and financial innovations that have changed the fundamental nature of markets and Wall Street. The stock market of 1929 bears no resemblance to the stock market of 2012, which will not resemble the stock market of 2112.

In 2011, in the shadow of a financial crisis that rivals the Great Crash in scope and destruction, but lacks a suitable poetic sobriquet, the federal government once more enacted laws to rid the market of self-destructive behaviors that nearly led to its destruction. The watchman has seen this before. His answer to the eternal question, as contained in verse 12, Chapter 21 of Isaiah, offers as little solace as Galbraith's conclusion: "Morning is coming, the watchman replies, but also the night."

The market will, of course, recover from its excesses, and it will, of course, fail again. The birth of every bull market will always occur in every bear market. Laws will always be passed. And those laws will fail to prevent another crash while burdening businesses with the expense of complying with massive regulatory requirements destined to be circumvented, if not outdated, shortly after they are passed. The laws will do little to improve the lot of the individual investor. The primary beneficiaries of the new laws will be law firms and management consultants. Who will reap huge profits helping corporate America implement, interpret—and likely step around—more than 2,000 pages of new laws passed after the credit crisis. By 2011, Debevoise & Plimpton, one of Manhattan's top law firms, was charging $100,000 to write a 17-page letter that explained the meaning of bank-owned hedge fund.[1] Davis Polk & Wardwell, another top law firm, that hired top SEC market regulators before and after the crisis, charged clients a $7,500 monthly online subscription fee to track the Dodd-Frank amendment progress. The amount of money expected to be spent on technology to comply with new rules is simply stunning. From 2011 to 2013, the Tower Group, a technology consulting and research firm, estimated firms would spend more than $3.8 billion.

This dim view is of Washington's regulatory response more than cynicism. It is warranted by history. The Sarbanes-Oxley Act of 2002, passed in reaction to corporate accounting frauds at companies—including Enron, Tyco, and WorldCom—failed to prevent or anticipate the subprime credit crisis. The Dodd-Frank Wall Street Reform and Consumer Protection Act, signed into law in July 2010, will similarly be humbled, and perhaps even embarrassed, by the extent of its own shortcomings, despite the bombastic vow in the act's 16-page executive summary to "Create a Sound Economic Foundation to Grow Jobs, Protect Consumers, Rein in Wall Street and Big Bonuses, End Bailouts and Too Big to Fail, Prevent Another Financial Crisis."

Wall Street's banks are skilled at dealing with Washington, and blunting new, and old, regulations. They deploy an army of lobbyists, strategically donate to political campaigns, and most importantly reallocate every available dime and dollar that financed once unregulated financial activities that are now regulated into areas that are not yet regulated. Somewhere, even now, someone is figuring out how to create something out of nothing, how to turn a penny into a $1, even if it means creating something that has never before existed. Each crisis shows that the regulatory regime is permeated with gaps. "Money is like water; it will find its way to those holes," says Pippa Malmgren.[2] She knows of which she speaks. She was President George W. Bush's special assistant on economic policy. Her London-based firm, the Canonbury Group, advises financial firms about how political policies impact the markets.

The Next Crash

Perhaps the next financial crisis will occur in the foreign exchange market that is increasingly trying to lure investors with promises of quick riches. Maybe the next crisis occurs in the futures market where some brokerage firms are trying to persuade investors to invest in gold and silver futures to diversify into different asset classes. Maybe the next crisis occurs in the municipal bond market or in the fast growing exchange-traded fund industry. Perhaps the next crisis occurs in some area of the financial market that has yet to be invented by Wall Street's financial engineers. All that is certain is that another crisis will occur. It will occur someplace unexpected. It will hurt many people, many of whom can ill-afford to be hurt again by another financial crisis. Those people will be hurt the worst. They will be lured to buy just before the game ends. They will hold on throughout the worst of decline, hoping for the stock market to bounce higher so they can at least break even. But that will not happen when they most want it, or need it. This will panic them and they will sell right at the bottom just as the stock market readies to advance. That sad dance is well documented. Still, it persists.

Before the next crisis redistributes much of the nation's wealth to the few, Washington needs to use its mighty bully pulpit to start a conversation with the country about investing that people can understand—rather than speaking at people through securities laws that are too complex to follow for anyone without specialized knowledge, or access to a securities lawyer. In an ideal world, Wall Street begins the conversation, but the world is not ideal, and there is little money to be made teaching Dumb Money to be Smart Money. Increasing financial literacy is an endeavor worthy of the federal government.

Misperceptions and Illusions

It is not even clear that the Securities and Exchange Commission fully comprehends how disconnected it appears, and thus the financial market, from investors. In 1937, William O. Douglas, who served as SEC chairman before joining the U.S. Supreme Court, said the SEC was the investor's advocate. If only that oft-quoted quote rang true. It seems the SEC is increasingly losing the ability to keep pace with change, and missing opportunities to fix major issues because it is so focused on minor issues.

This gives SEC's pronouncements, at least as they relate to individual investors, a theatrical irony. The SEC says on its own website that the purpose of regulation is to insure companies selling stocks and bonds tell the truth about their businesses, the securities they are selling, and the risks involved in investing, and that people who sell and trade securities—brokers, dealers, and exchanges—treat investors fairly and honestly by putting their interests first. Yet, it is hard to find anyone short of a corporate lawyer, securities regulator, or Wall Street executive who thinks anything close to that ever occurs.

Gib McEachran, of HMC Partners, a wealth-management firm in Greensboro, North Carolina, says many people feel the financial system is rigged. "Individual investors feel the system is so complicated that only Goldman Sachs and J.P. Morgan and others of their ilk know how to make money." Therein lies the problem—and an indication of the solution. Individual investors are mostly absent from the dialogue to reform U.S. securities regulations. They may glean some benefit, and get some regulatory protection, but mostly they are lesser concerns in the power play between Wall Street and Washington. Washington spends too much effort trying to regulate Wall Street, and too little effort effectively protecting Main Street.

Revolving Doors

Government attacks corporations and banks by passing laws that limit their operations. Corporate America uses lobbyists and strategic campaign contributions to weaken those laws. The most helpful congressmen and senators are richly rewarded. Consider Phil Gramm, the former Texas senator. He led efforts to deregulate the banking industry. He was instrumental in abolishing the 1933 law that prohibited commercial banks from owning investment banks, which helped create the "too big to fail" syndrome that now defines Wall Street and hangs over the global market. Gramm opposed efforts to regulate derivatives that figured so prominently in the 2007 credit crisis. When Gramm left Washington, he joined UBS, a major Swiss bank formed in 1998 by the merger of Union Bank of Switzerland and Swiss Bank Corporation.

Steve Bartlett, a former Texas congressman who helped deregulate Wall Street in the 1980s, is the head of the Financial Services Roundtable. The group represents 100 of the nation's largest financial institutions, including Blackrock, Charles Schwab, Fidelity Investments, Ford Motor Credit Company, General Electric, and NASDAQ OMX, the exchange company. Bartlett reportedly earns about $2 million annually, far more than the approximately $174,000 salary of the average congressmen, to lead a group that often fights against regulation.

Few people fare as well as politicians who were germane to Wall Street. The less-exalted citizenry is left in the same position after the crisis as before. It is forced to deal with an increasingly volatile market that they must somehow try to conquer should they ever want to retire. Of course, timing is everything.

The 2007 credit crisis disrupted the retirement plans of many people on the edge of leaving the work force. Some were forced to keep working and delay retirement. Others scaled back retirement plans. The future remains murky in 2012 even though the stock market has recovered from the worst of the crisis. Social Security, which is more important to retirement incomes than recognized, may prove inadequate to meet the rising demand of retiring Baby Boomers. This will force more people into the stock market. Many people will find that they do not have enough money to retire. They will have difficulty making ends meet. This will make them more susceptible to the get-rich-quick sales tactics. They will want to believe the stock market will make them rich. Somehow, someone, or something, will prompt all of these people to invest. All the new money will push stock prices higher. Many people will desperately chase the stock market, afraid to miss a great opportunity to make money. History will repeat. If Social Security runs out of money, or begins to experience real financial difficulty, many people will suffer even more.

Investor Laureate

If we know the past, and have a sense of the future—and we do—it will be a great travesty if nothing meaningful is done to address the nation's financial literacy crisis before the next financial crisis. If people can be taught how to think and frame financial and investment issues they have a better chance of productively navigating the financial market. They have a better chance of not falling for investment scams. They have a better chance of making risk-based financial decisions that will protect them from the inevitable booms and busts.

To protect investors, Washington and Wall Street must work together to develop a nationwide program that talks to people—not

at them—about the principles and processes of sound investing that
are almost always absent from the mass-media driven dialogue about
the stock market. Some critics will say that such an approach inter-
feres with the natural function of the market, or that many institutions
and banks already have investor education programs, but those are nar-
row views. Besides, many of those programs are ineffective. Surely,
the financial health of investors is as important as advising them of
their caloric intakes, and dietary guidelines, as the U.S. Department
of Agriculture does with its food pyramid. If financial literacy is
increased, Big Brother can spend less energy protecting investors. This
is the principle of teaching a man to fish so he will eat for his life,
rather than giving him a fish that he will eat in one day.

A Fox in the Henhouse

To foster financial education, the U.S. President or the Secretary of
the Treasury, should appoint an investor laureate to serve the nation.
This person would serve a multiyear term, and be charged with issu-
ing a minimum of four quarterly reports each year that detailed his or
her view of the markets based on research and conversations with various firms and other investors. The laureates would be investors' investors. John Bogle, the semi-retired founder of the Vanguard Investment
Group, would be great in this role. So would Warren Buffett. The
list is long. The principle is old. When President Roosevelt appointed
Joseph P. Kennedy, father of President Kennedy, to serve as the first
chairman of the SEC, he was asked why he chose someone who had
made so much money doing many of the things the new SEC would
be charged with regulating and preventing. President Roosevelt reportedly quipped that it took a crook to catch a crook. Naturally, Kennedy,
whose sons served this nation as President, Attorney General, and
Senator, was very successful at the SEC. He understood the markets
in ways that only someone who knew enough to sell before the Great
Crash could know. He did a lot to help investors. Under his leadership,
corporations were required to file financial disclosure documents with
the SEC so everyone could determine a company's financial health,

and weigh management's words against financial facts. But Kennedy fell short in one important measure—investor education. Subsequent SEC chairmen have not done much better. They all talk about investor education, just as Kennedy did in his first major speech as SEC chairman; a speech that was delivered to the Boston Chamber of Commerce on November 15, 1934, when the Great Crash was a fresh memory, and the Great Depression was a stark reality. Kennedy's speech was broadcast on the radio.

The Tremendous Task

Each and every one of you is a prospective or actual member of a 'sucker' list, and when the stranger calls you on the phone to interest you in the purchase of securities, beware. Unless you have confidence in the integrity of the sponsors you ought to take special precautions before you sign on the dotted line or surrender your cash or the securities you now own. Over the country from time to time springs up the promoter with a worthless issue, a tipster sheet to lure you, and a battery of telephone salesmen to close the deal, to your misfortune. Be on your guard. The Commission cannot in the very nature of things police every transaction in America. Where it has evidence, rest assured it will strike. We have the tremendous task of educating the American public to protect itself against high-pressure salesmanship. No law has ever been devised or administered which successfully eradicated crookedness. The federal government, however, hopes to fill a much needed want, hopes to be a vigorous factor in the relentless war on stock frauds.

—Address of Hon. Joseph P. Kennedy, Chairman
of the Securities and Exchange Commission, at Meeting of the
Boston Chamber of Commerce, Nov. 15, 1934, U.S.
Government Printing Office, Washington, 1934

It is debatable if Kennedy's enunciated goal has ever been satisfied. Arthur Levitt, who led the SEC from 1993 to 2001, tried harder than most to protect the rights of individual investors. Even today, his speeches on investor education, financial literacy, and financial advertising, resound with passion and truth. But the scope of future crises suggests Levitt was arguably no more successful than Kennedy in increasing financial literacy. Had Levitt been successful, perhaps fewer people would have been ensnared in the financial calamities that seem to be occurring with greater regularity, and greater intensity. Since Kennedy was appointed in 1934, the American public has increasingly become reliant on the market to fund their lifestyles. This has been encouraged by Congress, which has passed laws that encourage stock investing. Wall Street has become very sophisticated in marketing investments. Main Street has yet to make corresponding strides in financial literacy. Part of the problem is that technology has vastly increased the amount of available information without people making any corresponding strides in filtering useful information from "noise," to once again borrow that market phrase that describes financial information with no value. The investor laureate can lead and structure the financial literacy dialogue in ways an SEC chairman cannot.

Sane Money, Not Mad Money

Appointing an investor laureate appeals to basic human psychology that animates investing. Anyone who is very rich, or has made other people very rich, is universally admired and studied. Just look at the adulation that surrounds Warren Buffett, and the excitement to attend annual meetings of his Berkshire Hathaway company.

Appointing an accomplished investor to the national role of educating, if not safeguarding, Main Street could be a very effective mechanism to reach people. We know people buy stocks simply because they hear self-proclaimed gurus on TV or at investment seminars, say they should, so it makes good sense harness that very power to teach investors how to think about investing, and how to think of risk before reward. The investor laureate's pronouncements would attract media coverage and over time this could have a significant impact on the public dialogue about the markets, and how people think about investing. The dialogue need not be dry, clinical, and overly complex. A simple chart—similar to the U.S. Department of Agriculture's iconic food pyramid—can help investors focus on healthy market conditions and risk-based investing. Howard Marks, who would be a leading candidate for investor laureate, has already developed a good chart that he calls the "Poor Man's Guide to Market Assessment."[3] See Table 9.1.

Table 9.1 Poor Man's Guide to Market Assessment

Economy:	Vibrant	Sluggish
Outlook:	Positive	Negative
Lenders:	Eager	Reticent
Capital Markets:	Loose	Tight
Capital:	Plentiful	Scarce
Terms:	Easy	Restrictive
Interest Rates:	Low	High
Spreads:	Narrow	Wide
Investors:	Optimistic	Pessimistic
	Sanguine	Distressed
	Eager to buy	Uninterested in buying
Asset Owners:	Happy to hold	Rushing for the exits
Sellers:	Few	Many
Markets:	Crowded	Starved for attention
Funds:	Hard to gain entry	Open to anyone
	New ones daily	Only the best can raise money
	General partners hold all the cards	Limited partners have bargaining power
Recent Performance:	Strong	Weak
Asset Prices:	High	Low
Prospective Returns:	Low	High
Risk:	High	Low
Popular qualities:	Aggressiveness	Caution and discipline
	Broad reach	Selectivity

SOURCE: Howard Marks, *The Most Important Thing*, Columbia Business School Publishing, 2011, 131.

Investors should use the Marks' chart to take the market's temperature. The laureate's website could include the chart on the home page. Brokerage firms could be required to link to the chart.

Marks, whose Oaktree Capital Management manages about $80 billion, likes to invest when check marks line up on the right-hand column.

"Markets move cyclically, rising and falling," Marks says. "The pendulum oscillates, rarely pausing at the 'happy medium,' the midpoint of its arc. Is this a source of danger or of opportunity? And what are investors to do about it? My response is simple: try to figure out what's going on around us, and use that to guide our actions."[4]

Repetition and Velocity

To insure the investor laureate's reports are widely circulated, banks and brokerage firms could be required to mail the investor laureate's comments to all of their clients in a specially-designed envelope that indicates the material inside is more than just another prospectus or proxy or random regulatory disclosure document written by a lawyer.

The laureate could host a televised press conference each quarter to discuss the market. Repetition is important. Coupled with appearances in broadcast, print, and online media, this would help insure people hear the message. The more they hear the message the more they are likely to pay attention. A website detailing the sound principles of investing also would help. Naturally, Wall Street would decry this added regulatory burden. Critics might even complain that Wall Street is already one of the world's most heavily regulated businesses, and it's not fair to add another regulatory burden. The response to those complaints is simple: A lot of good the regulation does. Let Wall Street sponsor one less golf tournament, put one less bank's name on one less stadium, and instead fund a serious investor education campaign that becomes a model for other nations that face similar financial struggles.

The boom and bust cycle of the economy and market will never be eliminated, but success can be measured one investor at a time, and perhaps, over time, fewer people will fall into the chasm that separates Main Street and Wall Street.

More Education

In an ideal world, banks and brokerage firms would be required to allocate a certain percentage, perhaps 10 percent of the amount of their advertising budgets, to fund industry-wide educational programs. Another funding source would be levying a small fee of a penny or less on all securities and futures transactions, which is the approach used to fund the SEC. The options industry has a good model. The exchanges pay an annual fee, based on market share, to support the operations of an educational marketing group that teaches investors how to use puts and calls.

The key is teaching people how to properly think about investing in a language that they can understand, and in ways that are impactful. It is critical, too, to address the effects that people's financial decisions have on their overall well-being. This is not altruistic. Not everyone deserves to be a winner, live in a big house, and take fancy vacations. But everyone deserves to have a fair chance. Narrowing the information gap between Wall Street and Main Street is an important principle.

Plain Speaking

Washington needs to address the language of disclosure. Wall Street will not do it. Too many companies are too skillful at speaking and writing in a language and format that defies comprehension. How many people know that it is usually best to first read the footnotes on corporate filings? How many people know corporations can improve financial results by depreciating assets? Issues of timing are also pertinent. Should corporations be allowed to post negative news that will hurt the stock price after the stock market has closed on Friday and everyone is gone for the weekend? Corporations use this tactic because they hope no one will pay attention. Perhaps, corporations should be required to state, clearly and simply, in plain language what happened to impact quarterly earnings. Companies that comply with those consumer-friendly reporting metrics could be awarded some version of the Good Housekeeping Seal of Approval by the investor laureate. Any company found to be investor friendly would likely be rewarded by attracting investors.

Clearly, some people will always behave like idiots. The greater fool theory will always be a defining characteristic of markets. But at least let people make bad decisions using good information. People have a right to have the facts—not just the people who control the market. There is good business sense in truly democratizing and simplifying financial information. Just look at the cost of cleaning up the credit crisis and the huge deficits subsequently assumed by national governments. Who pays for the deficits? We do. And our kids. And their kids.

If fundamental strides are not made in teaching people about the principles of sound investing, we run the risk of larding up government with even larger deficits, which means higher taxes for you and me, and potentially dour futures for our children and grandchildren.

The Cause of Failure

One key lesson of the credit crisis is that moral hazard is a distinct, and pervasive, part of Wall Street's culture. Perhaps, the systemic risk regulator created after the credit crash will help control risk taking, but it is hard to forget that the U.S. Federal Reserve and the SEC dispatched staffers to banks to monitor operations during the worst of the credit crisis. It is not clear that anything productive emerged—other than allowing bank executives to claim that everything was copacetic because of the prudential supervision.

It's ironic, but moral hazard first entered the financial lexicon through fire insurance. According to *Black's Law Dictionary*, moral hazard's definition is:

The risk or danger of the destruction of the insured property by fire, as measured by the character and interest of the insurance owner, his habits as a prudent and careful man or the reverse, his known integrity or his bad reputation, and the amount of loss he would suffer by the destruction of the property or the gain he would make by suffering it to burn and collecting the insurance.

The definition seems to broadly apply to much of Wall Street's behavior prior to the credit crisis. It is not clear— though it is not very likely—if the behavior has fundamentally changed since the last crisis ended. The financial market and all of Wall Street is a distinct culture with its own rules, and social mores. There is a ruthlessness, and way of doing business, that is distinctly Wall Street, and some observers might argue, even satisfies the American Psychiatric Association's *Diagnostic and Statistical Manual of Mental Disorders* definition of antisocial personality disorder. The diagnostic check list, of which three or more of the following criteria apply, include a pervasive pattern of disregard for other people, a violation of the rights of others, deceitfulness, as indicated by repeated lying, and conning others for personal profit or pleasure; irritability and aggressiveness; reckless disregard for safety of self or others; consistent irresponsibility, as indicated by repeated failure to sustain consistent work behavior or honor financial obligations; lack of remorse, as indicated by being indifferent to or rationalizing having hurt, mistreated, or stolen from another.

Virtue

Wall Street has hardly cornered the market on immorality or virtue. But few industries massively impact as many people as Wall Street, and that is why it is incumbent on Congress to overcome petty turf wars to modernize the regulatory system and align it with the realities of the modern market. The regulatory system is the balance between the market and government. So far, the market is firmly in control. Wall Street's fire hazard insurer is the federal government, here and abroad. Main

Street pays the policy's premium. The credit crisis institutionalized the concept of moral hazard, which is now almost automatically assumed by national governments. At the onset of the twenty-first century, failure is not an option because the consequences are catastrophic. Letting Lehman Brothers file for bankruptcy is often cited as the reason why a financial crisis that began in the subprime mortgage market spread like fire through the world's financial system. The future will be difficult and the gap between the haves and have nots will widen even more than it is today. Increasingly, the gap will be measured not just by material possessions, but by knowledge. The financial industry must better educate their customers.

Ladders

Remember the risk ladder mentioned earlier in the book? As people climb that risk ladder, forgoing conservative investments that pay less for riskier investments that pay more, they need to be reminded of their actions, and the consequences. Too often, people forget they are climbing a risk ladder. All they focus on is the chance to make more money. Put another way: Everyone would be well served to remember the dictum that the higher a monkey climbs the more we see of his behind. If Las Vegas bookmakers can post odds for football matches, and casinos know the odds of all its games, something similar should be developed for stocks. Using a Sharpe ratio and standard deviation measurements are fine for those trained in their use, but the tools need to be translated for nonfinancial people who are increasingly active in the stock market. They need to understand basic concepts like how much of a stock's future return is based on risk, and how likely a stock is to move up or down. If we can create actuarial tables that predict when people will die, and even send people to the moon, we can surely come up with simple, intuitive tools to help people think properly about the risks—as well as rewards—about stocks and investing.

When New York City's Mayor Michael Bloomberg made it a law that restaurants post calories, a Stanford University study found that

Starbucks customers made healthier choices. A credit card debt survey found that people paid off their balances faster after the passage of a law that credit card companies must show on people's monthly bills how long it would take to pay off their debts only paying the minimum amount. This isn't about creating a nanny state. It is about making sure people have access to the proper context to consider information and make decisions. Perspective is key.

In the future, if people still struggle to make effective financial decisions, and all sins are passed to government, we likely all will pay higher taxes. Of course, perhaps someone will invent some new technology, or magic gizmo that enhances efficiencies, makes the U.S. economy grow at a rate much faster than its historical annual growth rate of 2 to 3 percent, that would let us earn our way out of a future of higher taxes, and an escalating cost of goods and services. The only downside to this is a not-yet-invented device that makes economies and incomes grow so much faster that we can pay off the debts of the last financial crisis that inevitably will incite a massive stock rally. Sooner or later stock prices will become unhinged from the economic realties, and well, everyone knows how that story plays out. The ever-looming question in the stock market, in all fields of human endeavor, is can one person's future be different than the past? The answer is yes, unequivocally yes, and forever yes. In the market, one must always remember what Anselm Rothschild knew to be true in 1831, words that have grown truer yet during the almost 200 years that have passed since he first put his pen to paper. "There is some money to be made," Anselm wrote to one of his brothers. "We must take things as they are, and profit off the folly of the world."[5] Of course, it is important to be able to recognize folly.

A Systematic Change

Good regulators, like good investors, must be able to identify folly. Ideally, both identify folly before the foolishness disrupts the market's equilibrium. The structure of the current regulatory regime makes that more difficult than is needed for regulators who are typically overworked, outgunned, and ill-equipped for the important task of effectively dealing with banks and exchanges, and monitoring the market. Part of the problem is how regulatory agencies are organized. The SEC regulates stocks and options markets. The Commodity Futures Trading Commission (CFTC) regulates the futures market. This harms investors by diluting the regulators' reach and power, and ultimately benefits politicians and banks.

All of Wall Street, and much of Washington, knows that futures trading influences, and often determines, the price of stocks. Yet, the SEC has a limited view of what takes place in the stock and options markets because Congress has divided regulatory functions along product lines—rather than the actual structure of the modern market. Merging SEC and CFTC—and harmonizing the rules that each agency uses to regulate the market—is an important first step toward modernizing securities regulations passed more than some 80 years ago when few people invested in stocks, corporations still provided for employee retirement programs with generous pension funds, mutual funds barely existed, and most people saved money in passbook savings accounts at their local bank.

In their current form, CFTC and SEC are remnants of simpler times when the markets, and investors, could be divided among product lines. When the Commodity Exchange Act was passed in 1936, the futures markets primarily dealt with agricultural products. In the 1970s, the futures markets began to list futures on financial products, which now dominate trading futures exchange volumes. Yet, the SEC has no authority to regulate futures even though futures trading often drives stock trading to the point of actually determining the price of stocks. Lanny Schwartz, a top regulatory lawyer, says the division between the agencies means that no one has a 360-degree of what is happening in the markets minute by minute, hour by hour.

"Everyone has a limited view, because there are so many different markets—and there are distinctions between futures and securities markets," says Schwartz, a partner at Davis Polk & Wardwell.[6]

Flash Crash

If you think these regulatory issues are too obscure to concern individual investors think back to the so-called *flash crash* of May 6, 2010. This one-day event seems innocuous compared to the more destructive credit crisis, or Europe's economic problems, but the flash crash personifies the realities of the modern market and shows how challenging it is for regulators to address that which occurs right under their noses.

On May 6, at 2:32 P.M., with one hour and 28 minutes left before the stock market closed, the Dow Jones Industrial Average began to plummet. In about 20 minutes, the Dow fell some 1,000 points, losing 9 percent of its value. Over 20,000 trades, in more than 300 securities, were executed at prices more than 60 percent away from the price they had traded before the crash. Some people bought and sold stocks for a penny or less or as high as $100,000. Procter & Gamble's stock fell to $39.37 from $60 in about three-and-a-half minutes. 3M fell to $68 from $82 in about two minutes. As the market declined, no one knew what caused the decline. Not the New York Stock Exchange. Not the NASDAQ stock market. Not the SEC. The stock market closed that day down 347.87 points. Six months after the crash, reasons emerged. A trader at Waddell & Reed, a mutual fund company, entered an order at the Chicago Mercantile Exchange to sell 75,000 e-mini Standard & Poor's 500 Index futures contracts. The trade was worth $4.1 billion. The selling immediately cascaded into the stock market. This sparked a computerized chain reaction. This leveled the stock market quicker than at any time in history. The futures sale caused computerized trading firms that use secret trading formulas to sell stocks and futures. When they finished, they stopped trading, and this caused prices to fall even further, and even faster, because buyers essentially walked away from the market. This series of actions, all in reaction to something that happened in the futures market, crushed stock market prices.

That a trade that took place in a Chicago futures market could crush U.S. stock prices shows how interconnected stocks and derivatives are, how stocks are actually traded—and how the futures market determines stock prices. Every time someone sells futures on the Standard & Poor's 500 Index it inevitably causes someone else to sell

the 500 stocks that comprise the index. The same is true when someone buys the futures contract. This back and forth trading between
futures and stocks, with inevitable stops in the options market, cali-
brates stock prices. SEC is not equipped to regulate this type of
trading—and apparently neither is anyone else.

The flash crash stunned many seasoned investors and exchange
executives. No one could figure out what happened. No one had
ever before seen anything like it. The post-flash crash bickering
among the futures and stock exchanges over who was responsible was
so rancorous that the head of the SEC told them to behave and work
together to investigate the cause of the crash. Ultimately, the SEC
and CFTC had to join forces to figure out what happened. They
issued a report describing the event, and not much has since happened even though the flash crash makes it painfully apparent that no
mechanism exists to monitor the effect of one market on another—
nor is there a way to untangle the technology that compresses different assets into complicated trading algorithms that mysteriously pace
daily market tempos.

Soft Spots

The flash crash should be a rallying cry for regulatory reform. That it
remains a footnote in the market's history book is an ominous warning. The lack of transparency in the stock market raises the specter of
extreme market volatility that few investors are able to anticipate, and
no one can effectively regulate. The flash crash was mostly over in a
day. What happens if the next flash crash takes longer to digest? No
one really knows. Merging the SEC and CFTC might reduce market
volatility by uniformly regulating substantially similar financial products, and insuring someone has a full view of what takes place in the
markets.

The futures and stock and options markets are actually the same.
This fact has been known—and ignored—for decades. The presi-
dential study of the 1987 stock market crash, the Brady Report,
concluded that the market for stocks, options, and futures were

actually one market and should be regulated by a single agency. Mary Schapiro, a former CFTC head whom President Obama appointed to head the SEC, has said it is a "basic fact of market dynamics" that much of the price discovery for the stock market occurs in the futures markets. Yet, the SEC and CFTC have different rules, sometimes contradictory, that encourage sophisticated investors to practice "regulatory arbitrage" by playing CFTC and SEC against each other. The lack of a unified regulatory view is the market's Achilles' heel. It is widely thought on Wall Street that the markets have become too big, and too complex, to regulate. Where you sit depends on where you stand on that issue. Clearly, some trading firms and banks are quite happy with the current schism.

Combining CFTC and SEC is an important first step toward insuring that the U.S. regulatory structure catches up with the evolution of the financial market. Everyone knows it. Months before the 2007 credit crisis, a U.S. Treasury Department paper prophetically concluded that U.S. market regulators faced increasing difficulties preventing and anticipating financial crises. Little did the Treasury staffers know that in less than six months they would be embroiled in an epic struggle to save the U.S. financial system, and thus the world, from collapse. Interestingly, Treasury's regulatory blueprint was sparked not by a desire to make markets safer for investors but by concerns to insure America's competitiveness with other nations. Sadly, the participants in Treasury's regulatory panel concluded the regulatory system was functioning a few months before the worst financial crisis since the Great Crash of 1929 demonstrated that the U.S. regulatory regime has more holes than a brick of Swiss cheese.

Since the credit crisis of 2007, much of Washington's regulatory efforts have focused on preventing a repeat of the credit crisis. That is a proper, and reasonable response. But history shows Washington treats the symptoms of financial diseases—not the underlying cause of the illness. Politicians and regulators react to events. They do not anticipate. That keeps them at a perpetual disadvantage with Wall Street. On Wall Street, investors are rewarded for anticipating and taking risk. The disconnect between reality and post-crisis laws may even contribute to a more destructive crisis in the future.

Arthur Levitt, the former SEC chairman, says merging CFTC and SEC regulatory agencies is "so basic to any kind of regulatory reform, that to neglect that is really outrageous."[7]

Regulators are ill equipped to effectively regulate the financial market. Various reports commissioned by Congress show the SEC is underfunded, understaffed, and outgunned by Wall Street's banks. One side effect of this is that the SEC is criticized for approving new trading systems that it cannot effectively regulate, and allowing banks to create and trade potentially disruptive financial products that SEC has no way to monitor, much less regulate, even though those products can upset the delicate market equilibrium. This poses a great threat to the market's future ability to function. "The gap between regulators' ability to surveil the market and the markets' ability to stay ahead of the surveillance has become a chasm," says Levitt. The chasm must be closed, or Levitt fears investors will flee the market.[8]

Washington

Reasonable people will wonder why something as important as merging CFTC and SEC is so difficult to implement. The reason for the inaction is simple. The Congressional committees that oversee the futures industry do not want to lose power. The politicians who sit on those committees, and need money to get re-elected, do not want to forgo campaign contributions from Wall Street, futures exchanges, and trading firms.

Merging CFTC and SEC would change Congress' power structure. CFTC is regulated by the House and Senate agricultural committees. SEC is regulated by the Senate Banking Committee and House Financial Services Committee. The agricultural committee members would lose a valuable source of campaign contributions if they lost oversight of futures exchanges and commodity trading firms. Meanwhile, membership on the banking and financial services committees is a source of almost unlimited campaign contributions.

Wall Street is not bothered by this lack of action. Wall Street loves gridlock in Congress, and among regulators, because it means the banks can do whatever they want while Washington fiddles and argues. In truth, many Wall Street firms and exchanges like the existing regulatory schism. CFTC is thought to be easier to deal with, and more pro-business than the SEC. Because financial products are increasingly alike, if the SEC says no, CFTC often says yes. But it is time for Washington to better balance the protection of investors with need for flexibility wanted by Wall Street firms.

The differences between the CFTC and the SEC even impact the most basic elements of market soundness, such as how much borrowed money can be used to trade stocks and futures. CFTC and the SEC have different margin rules. CFTC and the SEC bickering often gets in the way. In the summer of 2007, CFTC and the SEC clashed in court over the Sentinel Management hedge fund fraud. The judge overseeing the case asked: "Why doesn't this agency of government go over and talk to this (other) agency of the government and get your act together, for crying out loud?"[9] Apparently, the judge was not wise to the ways of Wall Street and Washington.

The two major U.S. financial crises since the start of the twenty-first century—the Internet bubble bursting in 2000 and the credit crisis of 2007—are strong evidence that the bureaucratic infighting needs to go away. If left unchanged, the U.S. market will lose ground to foreign markets.

A Global Problem

In the summer of 2011, months before Jean-Claude Trichet was preparing to retire as the head of the European Central Bank, he spoke at an economics conference in Aix-en-Provence, France. At the time, the European sovereign debt crisis was in full bloom. Greece and Portugal and Italy were feared to be near some state of economic collapse. Yet, Trichet said that what was needed were serious advances in the way systemically important institutions, including nonbanking institutions, are regulated. "The major revelation of the last four years was the fragility of the global economy," Trichet said. "Strengthening resilience is absolutely essential given the fragility exhibited by the global economy."[10]

Indeed, it remains unclear how, if at all, the global economy has been strengthened since the credit crisis. It is unclear how, if at all, the existing regulatory regimes in the United States and around the world are equipped to deal with a global market. This is a potentially dangerous issue that should be addressed by national governments convening a summit to discuss how to deal with global companies operating in a business environment defined by different regulatory regimes and even accounting standards. The gaps in the U.S. regulatory system are likely miniscule compared to what can be accomplished on the world stage. Perhaps nations need to consider forming an international regulatory body to monitor companies that are so large, and so diverse, as to endanger the stability of the global economy. Naturally, such an organization would repulse some people—and that is good—because opposition would balance the need to regulate systemically important institutions with the need for the markets to be flexible enough to innovate and evolve. This is a delicate issue and it is worthy of study as the rise of for-profit exchanges—the New York Stock Exchange and the NASDAQ stock market are now owned by shareholders—could ultimately push corporate exchange profits ahead of more nuanced issues of market safety, and soundness. What was once a market issue now becomes a business model issue. Again, the flash crash is instructive.

The Chicago Mercantile Exchange, which is where the flash crash began, defended itself after the SEC and CFTC issued a joint report on the flash crash. CME Chairman Emeritus Leo Melamed even criticized the report. "Our market performed exemplary," he said. "The report I think is skewed wrong because it talks too much about that [trade], but if you read it, you see our market worked."[11]

In other words, CME's market worked—but everyone else's market failed. If anyone had any doubts about the CME's market, the exchange issued an official statement on October 1, 2010. "Throughout the day on May 6, CME Group markets functioned properly," the CME statement said. "Our automated credit controls, order quantity limitations, stop and market order price protection points, price banding procedures, and stop logic functionality operated as designed and were effective in responding to challenging market conditions."

The CME, which is a for-profit company whose stock trades on the NASDAQ stock market, casts an interesting light on the rise of for-profit exchanges and the regulations of the market. Historically, exchanges were non-profit institutions that were owned by the members. Since 2000, exchanges, including the New York Stock Exchange and the NASDAQ stock market, became for-profit companies. They hired investment bankers and sold stock to investors in initial public offerings. Now, investors can buy and sell stock on the NYSE and NASDAQ and every other important exchange. Many investors consider exchanges to be legalized monopolies because the government grants exchanges licenses to operate. One of the draws of exchange stocks is that they tend to have very high profit margins. As time passes, and the companies become even more deeply involved in dealing with demanding institutional investors who could pressure management to raise profit margins, it is not improbable to think that the management teams may become more concerned with making money than anything else. This thought came to mind at a 2010 meeting of exchanges to discuss lessons learned during the crisis. All anyone wanted to discuss was how their particular exchange had the best plan to provide trading facilities for all of the exotic, over-the-counter trading products that they hoped would soon be traded in the listed markets in the wake of the credit crisis. Regulating markets costs money. Exchanges make money on trading volumes. The more trading volume that occurs on an exchange, the more money the exchange makes. This is not an issue when markets are not in crisis. It may be an issue, however, in anticipating and preventing crisis with effective exchange-level regulations.

Present at the Creation

Thomas Peterffy, one of the architects of the modern securities market, is concerned that exchanges and regulators have little control over the marketplace.

"Technology, market structure and new products have evolved more quickly than our capacity to understand or control them," he said in a 2010 speech in Paris at a meeting of the World Federation of Exchanges. For him to tell the world's top exchange executives of such concerns is like Steve Jobs or Bill Gates fretting that technology destroys people's attention spans and turns people into instant gratification junkies.[12]

Peterffy was one of the first traders to use technology to trade stocks and options. His firm, Timber Hill, is one of the world's most influential trading firms. Peterffy eventually founded an online, discount brokerage firm, Interactive Brokers, to offer investors professional level trading tools. Since the flash crash, Peterffy changed his business model.

Peterffy instructed his Timber Hill market makers to stop making markets in 50 exchange-traded funds. He now closely watches market conditions to determine if his firm should widen prices, and reduce the size of trading commitment. Many other trading firms base their prices and liquidity—the amount of securities they are willing to buy or sell—off Timber Hill's markets. If Timber Hill steps away from the market, other firms are likely to follow, and investors may find that prices for stocks, commodities, options, and futures are worse than merited by market conditions.

The Illusion of Regulation

The quiet action of Peterffy starkly contrasts with Washington's histrionics. Congress' post-crisis rule-making typically morphs into a form of propaganda. Society demands that someone pays a price after so many people lost so much money. The mob of public opinion, which was fixated on market riches, and shattered by the crisis, quickly congeals once more, and mobilizes, behind opportunistic politicians who lead the hunt to find someone to blame. Lehman Brothers' Dick Fuld was a scapegoat, circa 2009, and so were subprime mortgages. Goldman Sachs with its perhaps too perfect sense of timing and market insight is another. Yet, Bernard Madoff, who existed and succeeded with the permission of other people, is not a scapegoat. He is simply a criminal, and a symbol of corrupt conditions, even though it was the greed of investors that allowed him to exist. The 1987 crash was blamed on portfolio insurance, a supposed curative that would keep stocks from declining. A few years before, Ivan Boesky and Michael Milken were arrested as part of an insider trading scandal. Milken invented high-yield junk bonds. Charles "Sunshine Charlie" Mitchell, former president of National City Bank, Citibank's predecessor, had been prosecuted after the Great Crash of 1929.

The congressional hearings, and selection of scapegoats, are modern iterations of the ancient rite of casting evil from the village. In Sir James George Frazer's book, *The Golden Bough*, a study of myth and superstition throughout history, scapegoating is shown to be an ancient rite of all cultures. Every culture develops some mechanism to symbolically rid themselves of undesirables. This was true of the Mandan Indian tribe in the American West, in Europe, Ancient Syria, Tibet, and Asia.

Frazer writes—and anyone who has lived thorough a financial crisis will recognize this to be true—"that this public and periodic expulsion of devils is commonly preceded by a period of general license, during which the ordinary restraints of society are thrown aside, and all offences, short of the gravest, are allowed to pass unpunished."[13]

The iconic image of the modern financial crises is for well-dressed, emotionless leaders of America's largest companies to stand before a Congressional committee and solemnly raise their hands as they swear an oath to tell the truth, which of course never seems to fully find its way out.

The recrimination phase is part of every financial crisis. But the downside to scapegoating is that it often further victimizes the victims. When investors scapegoat Wall Street it further legitimizes what everyone thinks they know, namely that Wall Street is corrupt, and the game is rigged. Parts of Wall Street are less than honorable, as is the case with all human endeavors, but black-and-white thinking that turns complexities into meaningless simplicities inevitably hurts investors who are still stuck dealing with stocks to provide for their financial future. The only real beneficiaries of these post-crisis mobs are grandstanding politicians who pocket some votes, get some national media attention, and maybe even campaign contributions from big banks. In 2010, eight House members were investigated by the Office of Congressional Ethics for holding fundraisers close to a major vote on Wall Street reform. Some of the prominent contributors whose names surfaced in the investigation, included Goldman Sachs and the Investment Company Institute, the mutual fund industry's trade group.

Congressional hearings that focus the nation's attention on the market invariably devolve into cheap political theater that diverts attention from information that is actually useful to investors. Rather than watching Congressmen whose campaign chests are often larded with Wall Street money huff-and-puff about things they often do not understand, investors would be much better served if the hearings focused on the mechanics and motivations of institutions that participated in the crisis du jour. This type of information surfaced in interviews the Financial Crisis Inquiry Commission conducted away from Congressional committee rooms. Instead, the hearings encourage investors to vent their anger, which is easier than trying to understand why they themselves failed. Besides, no one really cares why investors failed. The hearings demonstrate that investors are stuck between two powerful groups with their own agendas. Wall Street wants your money. Congress wants your vote. No one cares if you understand the process, or if you succeed or fail.

No one ever talks about it, at least not publicly, but the hearings are embarrassing moments for Congress. These elected officials have oversight responsibility for Wall Street, and its regulatory agencies. The Senate's Committee on Banking, Housing and Urban Affairs shares oversight of Wall Street with the House's Committee on Financial Services. The members of these committees are arguably accomplices to every financial crisis because they failed to do their jobs or understand the risks of that which they supposedly were monitoring. In the tug-of-war between two powerful groups—Congress and Wall Street—politicians use the hearings to reassert their dominance. Inevitably, a few well-placed campaign contributions helps Wall Street regain the upper hand the moment the stock market begins trending higher.

Power

Wall Street's power now rivals national government. Like government, Wall Street can even garner the support of taxpayers. If Wall Street fails, the federal government bails out Wall Street. Like government, Wall Street's banks carry on foreign policy. The banks can spend decades engaged in diplomatic efforts to establish operations in foreign nations. Sometimes, even U.S. diplomats complain that they spend too much time arranging meetings for U.S. businesses. Goldman Sachs spent more than a decade establishing ties in China. When Hank Paulson, the former Goldman chief executive was U.S. treasury secretary, and dealing with the financial crisis, he flew to Beijing to meet with China's Vice Premier. Paulson had first met Wang Qishan, a former mayor of Beijing, 15 years earlier when Paulson was a senior executive at Goldman Sachs. At any given time, Washington's highest offices are filled with Wall Street's executives. This protects Wall Street. Perhaps the most famous example of this paternalism is when Robert Rubin, a former Goldman Sachs CEO, joined forces with Alan Greenspan, the U.S. Federal Reserve chairman, to battle derivatives regulation. Parts of the unregulated derivatives industry exploded like a bomb in 2007, leading to the demise of Bear Stearns and Lehman Brothers and almost claimed Morgan Stanley and Goldman Sachs. Washington rescued Wall Street. After Treasury, Rubin joined Citigroup, the global investment bank, and Greenspan created a consulting firm and took on a few major banks as clients.

The Balance of Power

After a financial crisis, power shifts from Wall Street to Washington—but only temporarily. Wall Street is expert at clouding complicated, commercial issues in the banner of national interest. Regulate Wall Street, they say, and money will move to international markets where there is less regulation. This resonates in Washington where constituents need jobs, and corporations need access to capital. Besides, Washington can be bought cheap. Congressmen and Senators need money to get re-elected. Few industries have more money than Wall Street.

In 2008, as Washington focused on the mess created by the banks, Wall Street spent a record $95.3 million on lobbying firms, up from $88.2 million in 2007.[14] From the 1990 to 2012 election cycles, Wall Street contributed $829.4 million to political campaigns. In 2010, Wall Street's political contributions totaled $97.2 million. In 2008, when Washington was debating bail-out packages, Wall Street's campaign contributions totaled $167.1 million. Before the credit crisis of 2007, Wall Street doled out $80.4 million in the 2006 election cycle.[15]

Meanwhile, Wall Street is expert at delaying the implementation of rules that would impact the ability of banks to make money. Many of the provisions of the much-hyped credit crisis laws will take years to implement. Some of the new laws, like the much vaunted "Volcker rule" that is intended to ban banks from using their own money to fund proprietary trading desks, even require a study before rules are drafted. "Based on our experience of government's ability to execute these things effectively and in a timely way, we are almost uncovered now from any future financial risk for at least another 8 or 10 years, and that's a little scary," said Roy Smith, a finance professor at New York University and retired Goldman Sachs banker, in the summer of 2010.[16]

Regulation is the balance between the market and government. Over time, the market tends to win, which is why it is critically important to learn how to effectively navigate the market, to be self-reliant, to be skeptical, and to be resilient. In the United States, even the President of the United States serves no longer than eight years, but Wall Street reigns forever.

Acknowledgments

I had a simple goal when I came to Wall Street in 1995 to work for Dow Jones Newswires. I wanted to understand what it meant when the evening news said the Dow Jones Industrial Average rose or fell during the day. That simple question sent me on a journey through the financial markets that is reflected in these pages.

I am beyond fortunate to have met Michael Schwartz, one of Wall Street's wise men. He read this book in various drafts, and was my trusted sounding board throughout. His wisdom imbues these pages. His friendship and insight have made a difference in my life, and work.

This book could not have been written without Conrad C. Fink. We met when I was a 19-year-old student at the University of Georgia, and he was my professor at the Henry W. Grady College of Journalism. His counsel shaped this book, as he has shaped me, ever since we first met and he pointed me toward adventures and distant horizons that I could experience if I worked hard and true. I owe him more than words can express. He passed on January 14, 2012. I miss him.

Steven Sosnick, shrewd and wise, generously reviewed the manuscript and refined my thinking. His comments were invaluable.

At critical points in this book's evolution, Eugene Colter played the critical role. We met as students in Mr. Fink's classes. (Old friends the most.)

I have been extraordinarily lucky since I stepped off the subway at the World Trade Center, nervously wondering if I could find the exit, and get to my office at 200 Liberty Street. If not for Rick Stine, who hired me at Dow Jones, and gave me many opportunities, my journey that took me from newsrooms to the executive suites of exchanges, might never have begun. Thank you, Rick.

I have been extraordinarily fortunate to work with Ed Finn, the editor of *Barron's,* and to be part of that magnificent tradition and team. That I work closely with Randall Forsyth has been my blessing.

Many people helped with this project. Some helped during the book's preparation, others during its gestation. List making is dangerous as it risks leaving someone out, but thanks are due to Carolyn S. Arnold, Robert L. Sears, Anne and Jerry Tarlow, Lamartine G. Hardman IV, Hobby Outten, John Marshall, Bill Brodsky, Sandy Frucher, Pat Neal, Catherine Keary, Jim Hyde, Jim Strugger, Karl Rozak, Dunstan Prial, Chris Grimes, Jason Zweig, Mark Neuberger, Dale Carlson, Jake Seher, Lanny Schwartz, Norman Steisel, Carol Kennedy, Jeff Shaw, Dennis Davitt, Jon Werts, Jamie Farmer, Gib McEachran, John Hardy, Stuart Kaiser, Jon Najarian, Larry McMillan, Bernie Schaeffer, Stephen Solaka, Mark Veverka, Alex Jacobson, my readers, the gang on Twitter, and a long line of traders, strategists, and executives across Wall Street who wish to remain anonymous. Special thanks are due traders at the Chicago Board Options Exchange, the late Pacific Exchange, and the American Stock Exchange, circa 1996 to 2000, who first revealed to me the market's mysteries—and some tricks of the trade.

Special thanks to my agents, Paul Bresnick and Martha Kaplan, my sagacious editors Debra Englander, Tula Batanchiev, Kimberly Bernard, Donna Martone and the editorial team at John Wiley & Sons for understanding what I was doing, and believing in it.

Some cynics believe get-rich-quick books are the only financial books that sell, even though they know that those books never deliver what the covers promise. I tried something different. Time will soon tell if my approach, or those who think the public is too dumb to know what is right, will prevail.

None of this would have been possible if not for my father, Michael J. Sears. He helped me choose my career, and his encouragement and wisdom taught me how to navigate. My mother, Patricia Sears, showed me the meaning of dedication and hard work.

For my darling children, Eden, Chloe, and Hudson, may your lives be filled with adventure and knowledge, and may your journey to Ithaca be filled with wonder.

Kathy, my love, my wife, read this book so many times, and listened to me prattle on about it for so long, with such good humor, and constructive feedback, that she is co-author. Her fingerprints are on every page. She so deftly edited this book that I am sure the best parts are hers, as any errors and shortcomings are mine.

S.M.S.

Notes

Chapter 1

1. Conversation with the author.
2. Conversation with the author.
3. Charles Schwab, "May 1 Marks 30th Anniversary of Brokerage Commission Deregulation," press release, April 28, 2005.
4. "This Much I Know," *The Observer*, January 18, 2009.
5. Jack Healy, "Cautiously, Small Investors Edge Back into Stock," *New York Times*, September 11, 2009.
6. Arthur Levitt, "Financial Literacy and Role of the Media" (speech, April 26, 1999).
7. Benjamin Graham, *The Intelligent Investor*, rev. ed. (New York: HarperCollins, 2003), ix.
8. Bernard Baruch, *My Own Story* (Cutchogue, NY: Buccaneer Books, 1957. Reprinted by arrangement with Henry Holt & Co.), 327.

Chapter 2

1. *Trader: The Documentary*, documentary (PBS, 1987)

2. John Cassidy, "The World of Business, Mastering the Machine, How Ray Dalio Built the World's Richest and Strangest Hedge Fund," *The New Yorker*, July 25, 2011.

3. "Barron's Art of Successful Investing." Conference Interview, New York, October 22, 2011.

4. Davis Funds, Clipper Fund, Annual Report, December 31, 2010.

5. Rebecca Mead, "Alice's Wonderland: A Walmart Heiress Builds a Museum in the Ozarks," *The New Yorker*, June 27, 2011.

6. Ron Baron, "Barron's Art of Successful Investing," Conference Interview, October 2011.

7. Conversation with the author, March 14, 2011.

8. Alan C. Greenberg, *The Rise and Fall of Bear Stearns* (New York: Simon & Schuster, 2010), 33.

9. Mamis, conversation with the author, March 24, 2011.

10. Conversation with the author.

11. Conversation with the author.

12. Natalie Angier, "Brain Is a Co-Conspirator in a Vicious Stress Loop," *New York Times*, August 18, 2009.

13. Ibid.

14. Conversation with the author, March 28, 2011.

15. Conversation with the author, March 14, 2011.

16. Kurt Vonnegut, *Slaughterhouse Five* (New York: Dell Publishing, 1968).

17. Greenberg, *Rise and Fall of Bear Stearns*.

18. Bernard M. Baruch, *Baruch: My Own Story* (Cutchogue, NY: Buccaneer Books, 1957. Reprinted by arrangement with Henry Holt & Co.), 259.

19. Schwarzman's Worst Trade, CNBC Interview, October 21, 2010, 8:48 A.M. http://video.cnbc.com/gallery/?video=1620962907.

20. Stephen Schwarzman, guest lecturer in a Robert Shiller class at Yale University (lecture, April 11, 2008).

Chapter 3

1. Davis New York Venture Fund, Annual Review, 2010, 7, http://davisfunds .com/downloads/DNYPMComm4Q10.pdf

2. Ibid.

3. Jason Zweig, "The Intelligent Investor," *Wall Street Journal*, April 3–4, 2010, B7.

4. "Hedge Fund Gurus," *Dan's Hampton Style,* August 1, 2008, 49.

5. Humphrey B. Neill, *The Art of Contrary Thinking* (Caldwell, Ohio: Caxton Press, 2010), 42.

6. *The Charlie Rose Show,* October 1, 2008, http://charlierose.com/view/interview/9284.

7. Bernie Schaeffer, conversation with the author.

8. Kent Engelke, "Early Morning Commentary," e-mail to clients, July 13, 2010.

9. Edwin Lefèvre, *Reminiscences of a Stock Operator* (New York: John Wiley & Sons, 1993), 36.

10. Schaeffer, conversation with the author.

11. Charles Mackay, *Extraordinary Popular Delusions and the Madness of Crowds* (Wells, Vermont: L.C. Page & Co. by Fraser Publishing Company, 1967), xiii.

12. Ibid., 90.

13. Ibid., 95.

14. Ibid., xx.

15. Jack Ewing, "Shiller's List: How to Diagnose the Next Bubble," *New York Times*, January 27, 2010.

16. "The Death of Equities," *BusinessWeek*, August 13, 1979.

17. Ibid.

18. Ibid.

19. Art Cashin, *Market Commentary*, March 2, 2011.

20. Ibid.

21. Bernie Schaeffer, "The Eternal Contrarian," *Sentiment*, Summer 2010, 14.

22. Ibid.

23. Ibid.

24. Ibid.

25. Financial Crisis Inquiry Commission, FCIC Staff Audiotape of Interview with John Paulson & Co., October 28, 2010, http://fcic.law.stanford.edu/resource/interviews.

26. Ibid.

27. Ibid.

28. Ibid.

29. Ibid.

30. Davis New York Venture Fund, Winter 2010 Review, 5.

31. Ibid.

Chapter 4

1. U.S. Department of Defense News Briefing, February 12, 2002, http://defense.gov/transcripts/transcript.aspx?transcriptid=2636.

2. *The History of the Philadelphia Stock Exchange*, privately printed by the Exchange.

3. Steven M. Sears, "The Striking Price, Corralling Information in the Cyber Age on The Trading Floor," *Barron's*, April 21, 2008.

4. Steven M. Sears, "For Markets, How Tweet It Is," *Barron's*, Monday, June 22, 2009.

5. Ibid.

6. Federal Reserve Bank of New York, Sentiment Analysis and Social Media Monitoring Solution RFP, Request for Proposal (Event-6994), Sept. 16, 2011.

7. Conversation with the author.

8. J. Felix Meschke, W. P. Carey School of Business, Arizona State University, CEO Interviews on CNBC, June 2004, http://ssrn.com/abstract=302602.

9. McMillan Analysis Corp., *The Option Strategist* 19, no. 16, (August 27, 2010).

10. George Orwell, "Politics and the English Language" (essay), 1946.

11. Arthur Levitt, "A Word to Wall Street: 'Plain English' Please," *Wall Street Journal*, April 2, 2011.

12. C. Wright Mills, *The Power Elite* (New York: Oxford University Press, 1956), 5.

13. Steven M. Sears, "The Striking Price, Trust Options, Not Corporate America," *Barron's*, October 23, 2008.

14. Ibid.

15. Randall Stross, "Where Yahoo Leaves Google in the Dust," *New York Times*, August 22, 2009.

16. Humphrey B. Neill, *The Art of Contrary Thinking,* 6th enlarged ed. (Caldwell, Idaho: Caxton Press, 2010), 34.

17. Wayne A. Thorp, "Using Investment Sentiment as a Contrarian Indicator," http://aaii.com/files/sentimentCIfeature.pdf.

Chapter 5

1. William Manchester, *The Last Lion: Winston Spencer Churchill, Visions of Glory 1874–1932* (New York: Dell, 1983), 351.

2. Raghuram G. Rajan, "Has Financial Development Made the World Riskier?" NBER Working Paper No. 11728, November 2005. www.nber.org/papers/w11728

3. Steven M. Sears, "Seeking Safe Returns in a Perilous World," *Barron's*, October 5, 2009.

4. Ibid.

5. Ibid.

6. Dealbook, "Bankers Face Tough Questions at Crisis Hearings," *New York Times,* comment posted January 13, 2010, 1:10 P.M.

7. "Long-Term Capital Chief Acknowledges Flawed Tactics," *Wall Street Journal*, August 21, 2000, C1.

8. Kana Nishizawa, "Mobius Says Fresh Financial Crisis Around Corner Amid Volatile Derivatives," *Bloomberg*, May 30, 2011.

9. Ali Alichi, *Finance and Development*, June 2011, 11; see also Ronald Lee and Andrew Mason, "The Price of Maturity: Aging populations mean countries have to find new ways to support the elderly," *Finance and Development*, June 2011, 7–11.

10. Steven M. Sears, "Seeking Safe Returns in a Perilous World," *Barron's*, October 5, 2009.

11. Ibid.

Chapter 6

1. David F. Swensen, *Unconventional Success: A Fundamental Approach to Personal Investment* (New York: Free Press, 2005), Preface.

2. Vanguard's Investment Philosophy, We Believe #5: Minimizing cost is vital for long-term investment success, https://global.vanguard.com/international/web/pdfs/webelieve5_042006.pdf

3. Vanguard, The Truth About Costs, https://personal.vanguard.com/us/insights/investingtruths/investing-truth-about-cost

4. Russel Kinnel, Morningstar Advisor, How Expense Ratios and Star Ratings Predict Success, August 10, 2010. http://advisor.morningstar.com/articles/printfriendly.asp?s=&docId=20016&print=yes

5. Conversation with the author.

6. Personal files of the author.

7. Standard & Poor's Indices Versus Active Funds Scorecard, August 20, 2009.

8. Daisy Maxey and Jay Miller, "Massachusetts Ousts Pension Managers," *Wall Street Journal*, August 7, 2008.

9. Dennis Gartman, The Gartman Letter, August 8, 2008.

10. Maxey and Miller, "Massachusetts Ousts Pension Managers."

Chapter 7

1. Bespoke Investment Group's data on historical stock market movements was instrumental in the preparation of this chapter. The company's website, www.bespokeinvest.com, is an important investor resource.

2. Jeremy J. Siegel, *Stocks for the Long Run* (New York: McGraw-Hill), 2008, 308.

3. Conversation with the author.

4. Big Think Interview with Bill Wasik, June 3, 2009. http://bigthink.com/ideas/15381

5. Randall Forsyth, "Up and Down Wall Street," *Barron's*, September 29, 2011.

6. Joseph H. Ellis, *Ahead of the Curve* (Boston: Harvard Business School Press), 22.

Chapter 8

1. Reflection on A Crisis, DLD 2009. http://fora.tv/2009/01/27/Nassim_Taleb_and_Daniel_Kahneman_Reflection_on_a_Crisis.

2. Ibid.

3. E-mail message to the author.

4. Conversation with the author.

5. Emanuel Derman, "Global Financial Crisis," *Financial Analysts Journal*, 2009.

6. Knutson, conversation with the author and various research reports.

7. Camelia M. Kuhnen and Brian Knutson, "The Neural Basis of Financial Risk Taking," *Neuron*, 47 (2005):763–770. DOI 10.1016/j.neuron.2005.08.008

8. Conversation with the author.

9. B. F. Skinner, *A Brief Survey of Operant Behavior* (B.F. Skinner Foundation), www.bfskinner.org/BFSkinner/SurveyOperantBehavior.html.

10. Wolfram Alpha.

11. Wolfram Alpha.

12. John P. Hussman, "When the Rubber Hits the Road," *Weekly Market Comment*, March 8, 2010. http://hussman.net/wmc/wmc100308.htm.

13. Ibid.

14. *The Daily Show with John Stewart*, interview, part 3, March 12, 2009.

15. Thomas Friedman, *The Lexus and The Olive Tree* (New York: Farrar, Straus & Giroux, 1999), 104.

16. Ibid., 106.

17. Henry Kissinger, *Diplomacy* (New York: Simon & Schuster, 1994), 60.

18. Baruch Fischoff, Paul Slovic, and Sarah Lichtenstein, "Knowing with Certainty: The Appropriateness of Extreme Confidence," *Journal of Experimental Psychology: Human Perception and Performance* 3 (1977): 563.

19. Ibid.

20. Ibid.

21. Office of Fair Trade, "The Psychology of Scams: Provoking and committing errors of judgement," May 2009, prepared by the University of Exeter School of Psychology.

22. United States District Court, Middle District of Florida, Securities and Exchange Commission, Plaintiff, v. James Davis Risher and Daniel Joseph Sebastian, April 29, 2011.

23. Ibid.

24. Ibid.

25. Bruno Biais, Toulouse University, and Martin Weber, Mannheim University, "Hindsight Bias, Risk Perception and Investment Performance," June 2008.

26. Ibid.

27. Ibid.

28. Whitney Tilson, "Applying Behavioral Finance to Value Investing," T2 Partners LLC, November 2005.

29. Kathleen Schulz Slate, "Hoodoos, Hedge Funds, and Alibis: Victor Niederhoffer on Being Wrong," Slate, June 21, 2010. www.slate.com/blogs/thewrongstuff/2010/06/21/hoodoos_hedge_funds_and_alibis_victor_niederhoffer_on_being_wrong.html

30. Conversation with the author.

31. Conversation with the author.

32. Tilson, "Applying Behavioral Finance to Value Investing."

33. B. D. Bernheim, L. Forni, J. Gokhale, and L. J. Kotlikoff, "How Much Should Americans Be Saving for Retirement?" *American Economic Review*, 90, no. 2 (2000): 288–292.

34. Hal Hershfield, G. Elliot Wimmer, and Brian Knutson, "Saving for the Future Self: Neural Measures and Future Self-Continuity Predict Temporal Discounting" (Department of Pyschology, Stanford University, November 30, 2008).

35. Jennifer Saranow Schultz, "Looking Ahead to the Spend-Down Years" *New York Times*, September 15, 2010.

36. Bill Gates, "How I Work," *CNN Money*, April 7, 2007.

37. Robert A. Guth, "In Secret Hideaway, Bill Gates Ponders Microsoft's Future," *Wall Street Journal*, March 28, 2005.

38. E-mail with John Pinette, Bill Gates' spokesman.

39. Emily Pronin, *Overcoming Biases to Promote Wise Investing* (Princeton University, FINRA Investor Education Foundation, August 1, 2007).

40. Thomas Bulfinch, *The Age of Fable or Beauties of Mythology* (Greensboro, NC: Tudor Publishing, 1937), 303.

41. Conversation with the author.

42. Malcolm Baker, "Behavioral Finance at JP Morgan," Harvard Business School, Case Number 9-2007-084, February 28, 2007.

43. Sun Tzu, *The Art of War*, ed. James Clavell (New York: Dell Publishing, 1983).

Chapter 9

1. Eric Dash, Feasting on paperwork, *New York Times*, Sept. 8, 2011.

2. Speech at CBOE Risk Management Conference, 2010.

3. Howard Marks, *The Most Important Thing: Uncommon Sense for the Thoughtful Investor* (New York: Columbia University Press, 2011), 131.

4. Ibid., 132.

5. Niall Ferguson, *The House of Rothschild: Money's Prophets, 1798–1848* (New York: Viking, 1998), p. 131.

6. Ibid., 253.

7. Conversation with the author.

8. Steven M. Sears, "Black-Hole Physics on the Street," *Barron's*, May 15, 2010.

9. William J. Brodsky, "A Real Regulatory Redunacy" *Wall Street Journal*, October 19, 2007.

10. Gabriele Parussini and William Horbin, "Trichet Urges More Regulation," *Wall Street Journal*, July 20, 2011.

11. MarketBeat, "CME: Don't Blame Us For Flash Crash," *Wall Street Journal*, October 1, 2010.

12. Thomas Peterffy, Chairman and C.E.O., Interactive Brokers Group, Speech Before the 2010 General Assembly of the World Federation of Exchange, October 11, 2010.

13. Sir James Frazer, *The Golden Bough: A Study in Magic and Religion* (New York: The MacMillan Company, 1951), 666.

14. Opensecrets.org, Center for Responsive Politics, Opensecrets.org/lobby/background.php?id=F07&year=2011.

15. Opensecrets.org, Center for Responsive Politics, Securities & Investment: Long-Term Contribution Trends, www.opensecrets.org/industries/totals.php?cycle=2012&ind=F07.

16. Christine Harper, "Crash of 2015 Won't Wait for Regulators to Rein in Wall Street," *Bloomberg News*, August 8, 2010.

About the Author

Steven M. Sears is a senior editor and columnist with *Barron's* and Barrons.com. He previously reported for Dow Jones Newswires and the *Wall Street Journal*. He has reported on major modern financial events, including the Asian Contagion, the bursting of the Internet bubble, the credit crisis that began in 2007, and Europe's sovereign debt crisis. He also was part of exchange executive teams that modernized the U.S. options market, and introduced electronic trading. He is a member of the Economic Club of New York. Connect with him on Twitter at sm_sears, and at www.indomitableinvestor.com.

Index